Building Financial Resilience

"Microcredit for the poor wins praise, while payday loans are seen as exploitative, but is it really so simple? Jerry Buckland provides an even-handed and wide-ranging assessment of the financial products, policies, and programs that increasingly shape the lives of low-income families. He gives readers the evidence and framework needed to understand how finance today affects the most vulnerable—and, ultimately, how finance can be improved."

—Jonathan Morduch, *New York University, USA; co-author of The Financial Diaries: How American Families Cope in a World of Uncertainty*

"This valuable book comprehensively tackles the question of whether financial inclusion efforts help build the financial resilience of vulnerable people. The book finds that such efforts are double-edged swords, with the potential to help if appropriately created and deployed, and the potential to harm if not. Buckland convincingly argues that a consideration of the nuances of potential actions is crucial. Such a cautionary note is particularly welcome in the financial inclusion literature."

—Charles Klingman, *Expert and Moderator of the US-based Unbanked Listserv*

Jerry Buckland

Building Financial Resilience

Do Credit and Finance Schemes Serve or Impoverish Vulnerable People?

palgrave
macmillan

Jerry Buckland
International Development Studies
Menno Simons College, Canadian Mennonite University, & University of Winnipeg affiliate
Winnipeg, MB, Canada

ISBN 978-3-319-72418-8 ISBN 978-3-319-72419-5 (eBook)
https://doi.org/10.1007/978-3-319-72419-5

Library of Congress Control Number: 2017964428

Cover design by Emma J. Hardy

Printed on acid-free paper

This Palgrave Macmillan imprint is published by Springer Nature
The registered company is Springer International Publishing AG
The registered company address is: Gewerbestrasse 11, 6330 Cham, Switzerland

This book is dedicated to my wonderful colleagues, friends, family, and loved ones, past, present and future.

Foreword

Neoliberalism and financialization have had pervasive effects on social welfare policies and provision across the world. These effects have been felt by citizens in developed and less-developed countries alike, although their precise nature, speed of implementation, and consequences differ both between these two broad groupings of countries and within them.

Neoliberal political ideology and economic theory had its roots in the doctrines of Friedrich Hayek and, later, Milton Friedman and espouses less state control and regulation of the economy. Individual freedom and well-being, it is maintained, can only be guaranteed by free global markets. In the words of Harvey (2005) it is:

> *... a theory of political economic practices that proposes that human well-being can best be advanced by the liberating individual freedoms and skills within an institutional framework, characterised by strong property rights, free markets and free trade. The role of the state is to create and preserve an institutional framework appropriate to such practices.*

Its two most prominent proponents were Ronald Reagan and Margaret Thatcher, although the ideology has permeated governments across the world as well as key development organizations like the International Monetary Fund and World Bank. In developed countries it has led to widespread privatization of state-run services, including a market-based approach to social welfare. In many less-developed countries it formed the bedrock of the development of such services.

As such, neoliberalism provided the foundation for a process of financialization, defined as:

> ... *the increasing role of financial motives, financial markets, financial actors and financial institutions in the operation of the domestic and international economies.* (Epstein 2005)

While this took place at a number of levels, it is the *financialization of the everyday* (Martin 2002; Van der Zwan 2014) that is most directly relevant to the lives of ordinary citizens. This has seen financial services play an ever greater role as individuals take on responsibility for their own social welfare and that of their families. A corollary of this has been the shift in focus from individuals as citizen beneficiaries of state-provided welfare services to their role as consumers in the financial services marketplace.

This shift in policy and practice raises a number of questions:

- Have the markets responded with appropriate products and services that promote the financial resilience and financial well-being of all individuals and their families?
- Are individuals able to make appropriate decisions that promote financial resilience and financial well-being?
- Is consumer protection regulation fit for purpose?

And, consequently,

- Can a market-based approach ensure the financial resilience and financial well-being of all, including people who are poor or marginalized?

Taking the response of financial markets, first, individuals require access to a range of products and services in order to meet their own social welfare needs and those of their family. This includes credit, savings (and pensions), insurance, and transactional banking. And in all of these areas, there has been a rapid increase in the number and variety of products offered by mainstream financial services providers. Despite this, academic and other researchers have questioned whether access to financial services and products is both universal and appropriate to all sections of the population—that is whether or not there is full financial inclusion. Such studies have found a number of key market failures in developed economies that disproportionately affect poor and other marginalized people (see e.g., Buckland 2012; Kempson et al. 2000; Leyshon and Thrift 1996) and raise challenges for providers of banking services in less-developed countries where financial inclusion is not the norm (Kempson et al. 2004). These include restricted access by poor and marginalized people (through risk assessment, money laundering regulations, lack of physical access, and lack of marketing), inappropriate product or service design, including inappropriate terms and conditions, affordability, and psychological and cultural barriers including a lack of trust in mainstream providers. In other words, a combination of exclusion and self-exclusion.

This has resulted in the emergence of a range of alternative providers who seek to fill the gap. These include a range of not-for-profit microfinance organizations, especially in less-developed countries, offering credit and savings products in particular. They also include commercial companies offering credit products such as payday loans and banking in the form of check cashing (often referred to as "fringe banks" (Caskey 1994)) particularly in Anglophone-developed economies and mobile telephone banking, such as M-PESA in Kenya and bKash in Bangladesh, bringing simple transaction banking to large numbers of people without access to mainstream banking services in less-developed countries. As this book notes, some of these new services promote the financial well-being of poor and vulnerable people, some actually harm it, and many simply do no harm but with no demonstrable benefit either.

There have also been concerted efforts by both national governments and inter-state bodies to promote greater financial inclusion which have led to the creation of a worldwide network, the Alliance for Financial Inclusion. But, as the World Bank has noted:

> *...effective financial inclusion means responsible inclusion... Financial inclusion does not mean increasing access for the sake of access...* (World Bank 2014)

This brings us to the second question: *Are individuals able to make appropriate decisions that promote their own financial resilience and well-being and that of their families?* Neoliberal policies implemented through a process of financialization of the everyday lives of citizens have led to a rapid growth in the number and diversity of products offered by a variety of providers, spanning the mainstream, not-for-profit and alternative commercial providers. Consequently, citizens must operate in an increasingly complex financial marketplace to meet their own social protection needs and those of their household. This has raised concern about the extent to which they are equipped to do so.

The earliest manifestation of this concern was in studies of financial literacy, which assessed knowledge levels of particular populations or groups within them and interventions developed that sought to raise knowledge levels. This approach is in line with standard economic theory that well-informed individuals will act rationally, and when they fail to do so, it is because they either lack information or are unable to understand or use it (Garcia 2013).

In the mid-2000s, however, a discussion began in earnest about whether policymakers should focus more on what people do rather than what they know—giving rise to the concept of financial capability, led by the Financial Services Authority, the then UK regulator (Atkinson et al. 2006). This approach has proved to be very influential in the thinking of policymakers.

At much the same time, behavioral economists were raising similar concerns about the focus on knowledge, arguing that psychological factors are the main determinants of the behavior of individuals. These included traits such as present-bias, loss aversion, overconfidence, use of heuristics, confirmation bias and inertia, or status quo bias (World Bank 2015).

More recently still, researchers and policymakers have turned their attention to the outcomes of the decisions and actions of individuals as they seek to meet their social protection needs—giving rise to surveys of financial well-being, which encompass both current finances and resilience for the future. The most recent of these is investigating the relationships between financial well-being, financial capability, financial literacy, psychological traits, and socio-economic environmental factors. Early reports seem to show that financial well-being is primarily determined by a combination of behaviors (most notably spending restraint, borrowing restraint, and active saving) and environmental factors that are beyond the control of individuals. Knowledge does have an indirect effect, by influencing these behaviors, but it is a minor role compared with psychological factors (Finney 2016; Kempson et al. 2017).

As with financial inclusion, many national governments and regulators along with inter-state bodies have promoted strategies to raise levels of financial literacy and capability. Much of this work has been led by the Organisation for Economic Co-operation and Development (OECD) through their International Gateway for Financial Education network (known as IGFE) (OECD 2015).

With the greater use of a diversity of financial services by a wider range of citizens, including many who are potentially vulnerable, it is appropriate to ask whether consumer protection regulation is fit for purpose. The neoliberalist approach has tended to dominate much of the thinking with regard to regulation of financial services in recent years, with an emphasis on information and disclosure by providers, supplemented by financial education of "consumers". However, as noted above, the knowledge individuals have plays a fairly minor and indirect role in determining their financial well-being; personality traits are far more important. More importantly, early results of research on the determinants of financial well-being show that a focus on the individual alone will not ensure their financial resilience and well-being. Structural factors also matter and call for structural solutions. In other words, we need a shift from the current regulatory focus on the individual as consumer to one where the individual is seen as both citizen (with rights) and consumer (with responsibilities). Looked at from this perspective—of individuals as citizen-consumers—it is clear that a market-based approach to social welfare cannot ensure the financial resilience and well-being of all.

That is the conclusion of this book, which offers a *critical and constructive* overview of policy, practice, and academic research across all of the areas discussed above, with a focus on poor and other marginalized people and on their access to credit and transaction banking services in particular. In doing so *It critiques the changes associated with this process while at the same time not idealizing past development practices or socio-economic realities* and … *endeavours to cast particular light on the problematic consequences for poor and marginalised people.* It looks at the roles played by mainstream providers, NGOs, and other not-for profit institutions, as well as new commercial players such as payday loan companies in some developed economies (the Global North), microfinance providers mainly in less-developed economies (the Global South), and mobile phone-based services in less-developed ones across developed and developing countries. The book concludes with a review of the role that the state plays and needs to play to ensure that the financial resilience and financial well-being of vulnerable people are promoted and not undermined by the processes or financialization and marketization of social welfare. As such it is relevant to policymakers, providers of products and services for individual citizen consumers and researchers alike.

Emeritus Professor, School of Geographical Sciences, University of Bristol, Bristol, UK
December 2017

Elaine Kempson

Additional References

Atkinson, A., S. McKay, E. Kempson, and S. Collard. 2006. *Levels of Financial Capability in the UK: Results of a Baseline Survey*. London: Financial Services Authority.

Epstein, G. 2005. *Financialization and the World Economy*. Cheltenham: Edward Elgar Publishing.

Finney, A. 2016. *Components of Financial Capability: Defining, Measuring and Predicting Scores in the UK Population*. London: Money Advice Service.

Garcia, M. 2013. Financial Education and Behavioural Finance: New Insights into the Role of Information in Financial Decisions. *Journal of Economic Surveys* 27 (2): 297–315.

Harvey, D. 2005. *A Brief History of Neoliberalism*. Oxford: Oxford University Press.

Kempson, E., A. Atkinson, and O. Pilley. 2004. *Policy Level Response to Financial Exclusion in Developed Economies: Lessons for Developing Countries: A Report Commissioned by the Department for International Development*. Bristol: The Personal Finance Research Centre University of Bristol.

Kempson, E., A. Finney, and C. Poppe. 2017. *Financial Well-Being: A Conceptual Model and Preliminary Analysis*. Oslo: SIFO (Forbruksforskningsinstituttet—Consumption Research Norway), Høgskolen I Oslo and Aherhus (Oslo and Akershus University College of Applied Sciences). SIFO Project Note No. 3-2017.

Kempson, E., C. Whyley, J. Caskey, and S. Collard. 2000. *In or Out? Financial Exclusion: A Literature and Research Review*. London: Financial Services Authority.

Martin, R. 2002. *Financialization of Daily Life*. Philadelphia: Temple University Press.

OECD. 2015. *National Strategies for Financial Education: OECD/INFE Policy Handbook*. Paris: OECD.

World Bank. 2015. Household Finance. Chap. 6 in *Mind, Society, and Behavior: World Development Report 2015*. Washington, DC: World Bank.

Acknowledgments

For five years of my early working life, in the late 1980s, I lived in Bangladesh and worked with and studied the efforts of non-government development organizations. This included watching with great interest the continued rise of microcredit of the Grameen Bank and BRAC variety. During that time I worked with Mennonite Central Committee (MCC), a United States and Canada faith-based organization that worked in the field of agricultural development. I am grateful to colleagues that I worked with at that time at MCC, BRAC, Grameen Bank, and ASA, to name just a few. Through observation, research, and conversations with colleagues, I learned much about microcredit in a Global South country. I think especially of Derek DaSilva, Matiur Rahman, Mark Nord, Farida Akter, and Rodney Reynar (a colleague of mine at Canadian Mennonite University) and I am grateful for what they shared with me.

Fast forward to the early 2000s, based at Menno Simons College—another Mennonite institution, this one based at a public university, the University of Winnipeg, Canada—I learned about a local network, the Alternative Financial Services Coalition (AFSC) that was looking for academics to investigate the rise of pawnshops and fringe banks in Winnipeg's impoverished North End. The AFSC was a group of able community workers who initiated the research. I am particularly grateful for the support from group members including Louise Simbandumwe, Blair Hamilton, Gary Loewen, Cindy Coker, Andrew Douglas, and from other community-oriented activists such as Judy Wasylycia-Leis (Member of Parliament at the time) and Gloria Desorcy. Dr. Thibault Martin and I guided the research project, and I am grateful to Dr. Martin, who has since passed away, for his enthusiasm, commitment, and deep insights.

I am grateful for a series of grants that I received from various sources including the Social Sciences and Humanities Research Council, the Manitoba Research Alliance, the Winnipeg Inner-city Research Alliance, the Wa Ni Ska Tan Hydro Alliance, and the Canadian Mennonite University. I am very appreciative of John Loxley, Jim Silver, and Lynne Fernandez at the Manitoba Research Alliance and to Stephane McLachlan and Kelly Jantz at the Wa Ni Ska Tan Hydro Alliance.

I am deeply grateful to many Indigenous Peoples who I have worked with and learned from, particularly given that some of my work has been completed on Treaty One territory which is also the homeland of the Métis people in Manitoba, Canada. I especially thank Leslie Dysart, Norman Moose, Dion McKay, David Claudie, and Wab Kinew.

Since my time in Bangladesh, based in an International Development Studies Department, I have been able to keep up-to-date about micro-credit and other financial service programs in the Global South. I am grateful to my colleagues in my department and college, including Stephanie Stobbe, Jonathan Sears, Kirit Patel, Ruth Rempel, Ruth Taronno, and Neil Funk-Unrau, for helping me to maintain an awareness of important issues related to finance in the Global South. I am grateful to other colleagues at Canadian Mennonite University and the University of Winnipeg from whom I have learned a great deal, including Melanie O'Gorman, Alan Diduck, Craig Martin, George Fulford, and Mark Golden.

Since 2015 and with a year-long research leave, I was able to travel to a microcredit conference in France, visit a new and innovative finance-based NGO in South Africa, and talk with many people engaged in financial literacy and inclusion projects in Australia and New Zealand. I am most grateful to Georges Gloukoviezoff and Nicolas Rebière who organized the microcredit-focused conference at the University of Bordeaux, France. I am also grateful to the staff at the Centre for Financial Regulation and Inclusion, CENFRIs, i2i (Insight to Impact), Cape Town, for their work in this field. In Australia I am grateful to Vinita Godinho, Roslyn Russell, Bob Frazer, David Claudie, Carmen Daniels, and Aaron Davis for sharing their time and thoughts with me. I am also grateful to Miles Larbey at the Australian Securities and Investments Commission and to Melanie Turner at the New Zealand Commission for Financial Capability. I am very thankful to Elaine Kempson who has written the foreword for this book and shared with me many of her latest insights about financial well-being during a conference in Melbourne, Australia. A special thank-you to Tracey Seida who helped me craft an effective title for the book.

I am grateful to Maureen Epp who edited an early version of this manuscript and carefully constructed the index. I am indebted to the editorial staff at Palgrave Macmillan including Tula Weis, Allison Neuburger, and Sarah Lawrence. I am thankful for the ongoing assistance of Ms. Weis and particularly grateful for all the support that Allison Neuberger provided me: thank-you! I am very grateful to the careful editing support I recieved from the copy editors including Ms. Minu Mohanasundaram and Md Saif.

Contents

List of Figures

List of Tables

CHAPTER 1

Introduction

This book examines if credit and finance schemes that span the globe such as microcredit, payday lending, and financial literacy education build financial resilience of vulnerable people. By building financial resilience is meant improving and making more durable an individual's and community's income and assets. By vulnerable people is meant people who struggle with material and/or psycho-social poverty so that a temporary or permanent decline in their income and/or assets would have disastrous consequences.

Microcredit is a product (and possibly a movement) associated with development and non-profit agents largely based in the Global South. It has been highly praised in much of the literature and is popular among practitioners and in society more broadly. There are detractors among those who have carefully examined its impact, but they are in the minority. Payday lending, on the other hand, is a commercial product that is common in Anglo-American nations and increasingly in other parts of the world such as Eastern Europe and South Africa. It has been widely criticized, and yet where it operates it attracts a strong and loyal (some say this is based on creating a dependency) following. Financial literacy education, also more common in the Global North, comes in many forms and through many organizations and is premised on the idea that increasing consumers' knowledge will protect and empower them.

The stories associated with microcredit tend to play up the borrowers who use the loan in a way that boosts their resilience through higher and

J. Buckland, *Building Financial Resilience*,
https://doi.org/10.1007/978-3-319-72419-5_1

more durable income which then enables them to repay the loan, a kind of virtuous cycle. Muhammad Yunus's story of his first loan is an exemplar of this. As he was investigating the micro-economy of poor people in Chittagong District in Bangladesh, he met a basket weaver who had to take out a loan from a money lender at a very high interest rate, perhaps over 100%, in order to purchase the inputs to weave the baskets. He found that by providing her a lower interest rate loan she was able to increase her profits and improve her livelihood. But there are also the "bad news" microcredit stories in which borrowers are unable to make a good investment and end up being unable to repay their loan, sometimes needing to sell off assets to repay it.

However the bad news stories tend to be more commonly associated with payday lending. One payday loan client I recently met in a focus group discussion about payday lending noted that he regularly got into a debt cycle with payday loans. In his most extreme case he reported that he had ten payday loans simultaneously and was unable to pay them off. He eventually required his spouse to take out loans in order to pay his off. This family's finances are becoming less resilient and payday loans seem to be part of the reason why. Less commonly do we hear the "good stories" about payday loans. In the same focus group discussion another person used payday loans, just occasionally, and to pay for unexpected expenses, in order to *not* draw down her savings. The payday loan created the external discipline to pay it off without requiring her to reduce her savings. The other types of financial programs that will be discussed in this book—asset building, cash transfers, financial literacy—all have similar "good" and "bad" news stories but they tend to get less media interest. But these stories give a sense of the types of challenges and opportunities that financial products present people.

The book focuses its analysis on a set of common credit and finance schemes. Microfinance, mobile phone-based banking, and financial inclusion are examples of these in the Global South, and asset-building and financial literacy programs are examples from the Global North. It is assumed that underlying the expansion of these schemes is the process of financialization, often defined as the rising influence of financial motives and growth of financial services in society. Financialization is a deep and challenging process that affects many aspects of modern life and is closely tied to neoliberal policies that promote markets and new technologies to foster change that affects us all at a deep socio-cultural level. Financialization has become intertwined in complex ways with development actions. This book considers how these credit and finance schemes affect the poor and vulnerable—people who experience poverty in one or more of its complex manifestations, including material poverty (a gap between material needs and their being met) and psycho-social poverty (gaps in esteem and control).

A note on terminology: *financialization* refers to the increase of finances in daily life, through the expanding availability of financial products and the growing demand for them. *Financial exclusion* refers to the situation faced by persons who have insufficient access to mainstream—that is, banks—financial services. Sometimes this is broken down into categories of complete financial exclusion, being unbanked or being under-banked, having insufficient bank financial services. In either case—whether un- or under-banked—the consequence is that the person is reliant on alternative sources for financial services, such as informal providers or fringe banks. Informal providers include corner stores that might cash one's cheque or a family member who might loan one some cash. Fringe banks are semi-formal operations set up to provide financial services such as pawnshops and payday lenders. *Financial inclusion* is the process whereby financially excluded people become integrated into the mainstream banking system for all of their financial service needs.

General Approach

This book draws on and extends "popular finance" theory (Aitken 2007; van der Zwam 2014) and examines the literature, discussed below, and in the cases of payday lending and mobile banking draws on primary research, on a variety of credit and finance schemes from around the world to learn how they affect the financial resilience of vulnerable people. Since we rely heavily on academic and policy literature, rather than primary data, we depend on the indicators (e.g., of financial resilience) used in these studies. An ideal indicator, but one that is not always available, is whether and to what extent vulnerable people themselves value the change. Everyday financialization is an important lens to assess credit and finance schemes because it focuses on the vulnerabilities of ordinary people, people who only recently have been brought into the financial world. But this lens is inadequate to assess finance and credit schemes of vulnerable people because it does not provide a framework to assess the impact on human well-being. What is needed for this is a theory of human well-being, and for this purpose we draw on the work by Goulet (1995) and human capabilities of Sen (1999) and Nussbaum (2006). Financialization proponents might argue that more (money, credit, income, etc.) is better, but scholars of human well-being understand that financialization is only a means but that the end is human improvement. Credit and finance schemes need to be assessed within that lens.

This book argues that finance and credit schemes can help vulnerable people in a limited capacity if they are carefully constructed, but they can also *not* help and sometimes harm people. This is because, by definition, vulnerable people have limitations and weaknesses that finance and credit providers may be ignorant and/or disinterested in. Moreover, without a clear understanding of the relationship between finances and human well-being, these schemes may not achieve valued outcomes.

Primary research has been completed by the author and colleagues on microcredit, payday lending, and mobile banking over the past several years, and results are published elsewhere. The relevant literatures on credit and finance schemes are dispersed across different disciplines and approaches, including economics, geography, and sociology. This book brings together elements of these literatures, as each contains insights that are useful to understand the others, and by looking at the "forest", one can better understand the individual "trees".

The ethical approach taken in this book is that poverty and excessive inequality harm people who are poor and relatively marginalized and this harms wider society. Credit and finance schemes that reduce poverty and inequality add to the common good, while those that increase poverty and inequality undermine it. A critical assumption that guides this analysis is that finances need to be constructed to build financial resilience, not the other way around. Financial services and technologies do not necessarily foster financial resilience, and in fact they can counteract it. That is why the services and technologies need to be designed with the end user in mind, which includes poor people and communities.

This book presents a critical and constructive perspective regarding these credit and finance schemes. It critiques the changes associated with this process while at the same time not idealizing past development practices or socio-economic realities. As a critical analysis, it endeavors to cast particular light on the problematic consequences for poor and marginalized people. In addition, where possible, the analysis identifies and explores constructive responses to these problems.

In terms of political-economic theory, the book is rooted in a reform market approach. That is to say, given that markets are currently the most prominent way to organize the economy but often fail to deliver on important human outcomes, a strong state and civil society response is needed. State and social actors' roles are critical to ensure that adequate market regulations are in place and enforced and that community needs are identified and planned for.

Because credit and finance schemes directed at vulnerable people are now a global phenomenon, this book examines them from a global perspective. This process has become intertwined in complex ways with development actions in what is known as the Global South—a rich and varied grouping of relatively poorer and geographically more southern nations of Africa, Asia, Latin America, and the Middle East. Here these schemes are manifested through activities such as microfinance, mobile phone-based banking, and financial literacy education. The book also takes into account the Global North—a relatively smaller and richer set of nations in Europe, part of North America, Japan, Australia, New Zealand, and most recently a diversity of other countries (e.g., South Korea, Singapore, the Gulf States). Here, prominent schemes include asset-building programs and financial literacy programs. The grouping of countries into Global South and North offers some assistance in our understanding, but it also blurs important changes such as the meteoric rise of China and India, to name two particularly important nations, in economic and banking terms.

Even though there are important similarities between finance schemes in the Global South and North, the contexts vary substantially between and within the Global South and North, so that outcomes vary. The rise of microcredit and mobile banking in the Global South, as compared with the Global North, is partly explained by the relative lack of formal financial infrastructure, so that lower-cost institutions (like microfinancial institutions) and technologies (like mobile phones) are more rapidly embraced in the South as compared with the North. Microcredit is often upheld as a powerful development approach in the Global South, whereas payday loans are generally vilified in the Global North. These are very different products with respect to duration and fees but have enough similarities to make it surprising that popular perception is so different. The rise of payday lending presents a parallel situation (to microcredit's rise in the South) in the North, but its rise relates to infrastructure gaps for certain groups within countries rather than for an entire country. Payday lending and other fringe banks have met an infrastructure gap for poor people in the North, but they have done so by charging high fees.

Actors Engaged in Credit and Finance Schemes

This book is organized by the key actors involved in credit and finance schemes, starting with an introduction to financialization and financial inclusion (Chap. 2) and then examining the commercial banking sector (Chap. 3), the consumer and finances (Chap. 4), civil society and banking (Chap. 5), and the state and financial inclusion (Chap. 6). The interconnections between these topics are depicted in Fig. 1.1. Chapter 3 looks at the commercial sector's role in credit and finance schemes by considering its history and the range of actors and products commonly available to poor consumers. Of particular interest in this chapter is payday lending and mobile banking. Chapter 4 examines studies of consumer behavior with respect to finances. Chapter 5 focuses on social sector engagement with credit and finance schemes and considers microcredit, cash transfers, asset building, and non-formal financial education. Chapter 6 examines

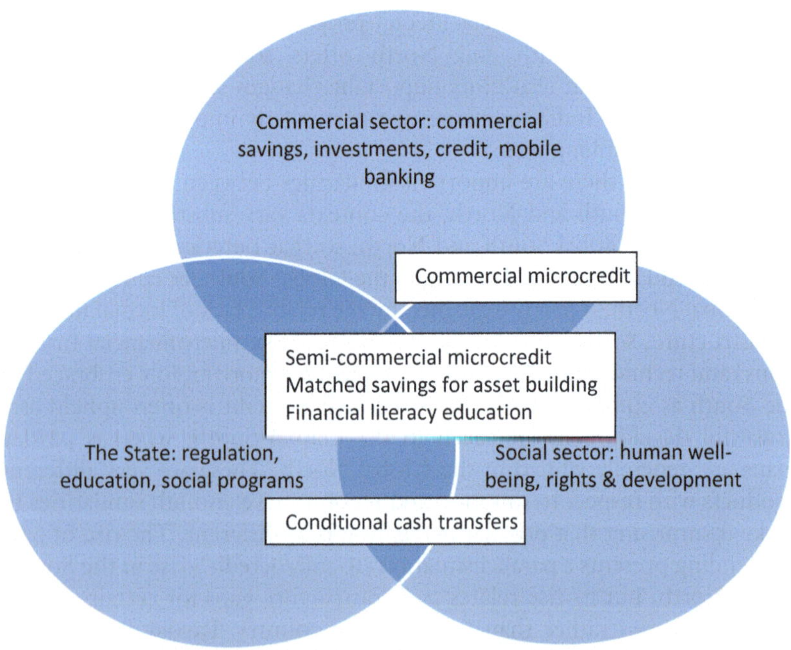

Fig. 1.1 Financialization flowing from different sectors

state programs and regulations that directly relate to financial inclusion, such as postal banking and formal financial education.

Some of these programs straddle more than one sector. For instance, commercialized microcredit flows from both the social and commercial sectors. Conditional cash transfers involve the state and the social sectors. Semi-commercial microcredit, asset building, and financial education straddle the state, the commercial, and the social sectors.

The credit and finance schemes considered in this book, by definition, draw vulnerable people into financial services. This is the process of financial inclusion. But financial inclusion is born out of the problem of financial exclusion, which is the situation in which a person is unable or unwilling to access financial services from a formal sector financial institution like a bank. The consequence is that person likely spends more on informal financial services that are often of lower quality than the formal sector alternative.

There are a variety of ways to think about financial exclusion. Buckland (2012) mapped different theories onto a two-dimensional space, with one axis representing competing assumptions about human rationality and the other axis representing competing assumptions about the role of institutions. Some theories (e.g., neoclassical economics) assume that humans are rational and operate within frictionless markets, so that institutions do not play a role in how society operates. Behavioral economics is silent about institutions—this point is discussed in Chap. 5—but assumes humans are bounded (limited) in their rationality. There are a number of more institutionally oriented theories (e.g., institutional theory of savings) that assume that institutions matter and that humans have bounded rationality. Finally there are theories that embrace human rationality but find that institutions also matter (e.g., post-Keynesian theory).

Responses to financial exclusion can be similarly mapped onto the human rationality–institution space by "activating" the variable and adding the adverb "more": that is, *more* rational humans, *more* effective structures, and so on (Fig. 1.2). Common types of responses to financial exclusion include more and/or different government regulation, government "nudging", corporate social responsibility, and citizen financial literacy. The first two—government regulation and "nudging"—are both a form of regulation but coming from different starting points. Traditional government regulation is premised on the idea that citizens are rational but not necessarily fully informed and/or markets are not frictionless. Placing a cap on chargeable interest rates or requiring lenders to use fair

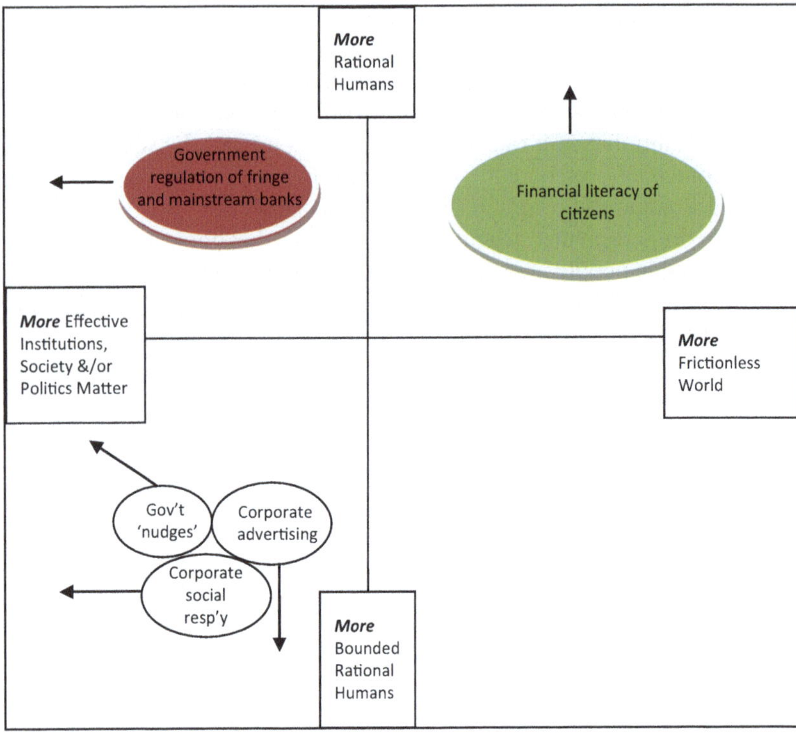

Fig. 1.2 Responding to financial exclusion

fee disclosure is a regulation flowing from this analysis. However, if people are bounded in their rationality, then interest rate caps and disclosure requirements may not be sufficient. Imperfectly competitive firms may not compete on price, and the cap may lead all remaining firms to raise their fees to the cap. Disclosure requirements such as the annual percentage rate (APR) may simply be ignored by customers. Thus work on behavioral economics, such as Thaler and Sunstein's (2008) *Nudge*, calls for the government to put in place programs that encourage people to make the best decision.

It is relatively easy to categorize different theories within the rationality–institution space but more difficult to synthesize a fully accurate theory. Each theory has its strengths and weaknesses. Neoclassical economics offers theoretical simplicity and elegance but this limits its ability to model the full complexity of the social world.[1] Behavioral economics opens up the simplifying human rationality assumption but fails to address the limiting assumptions in neoclassical theory regarding institutions. Institutionally based theories like institutional savings and post-Keynesian approaches offer insights about the impact of institutions but are sometimes so complex that it is difficult to determine recommendations for policy and practice.

Notes

1. Neoclassical economic theory was formed in the late nineteenth century by various people including Alfred Marshall, Stanley Jevons, and Léon Walras and rooted in the eighteenth-century work of classical political economists such as Adam Smith, David Ricardo, and Robert Thomas Malthus. One might argue that the classical political economy school was broader in scope than later neoclassical theory, perhaps the classical approach—to use a contemporary term—was almost interdisciplinary in nature. Classical political economy took a "broad-brush" theoretical approach and studied how countries grew economically (e.g., through economic specialization or international trade) and how they declined (e.g., through unregulated population growth). By contrast, the neoclassical school narrowed the scope of study to more particular issues, today referred to as the efficient allocation of scarce resources. Basically neoclassical thought shifted the focus to how markets could be structured so that buyers and sellers mutually benefit and that resources—land, labor, and capital—are used efficiently. The shift from classical to neoclassical thought moved the analysis from factors explaining the rise and fall of nations to examining the relationship between suppliers and buyers in markets. This also meant a methodological shift from broad analysis to a focused model-based analysis. The scope of neoclassical analysis is quite sharp, examining the allocation of resources such as labor, land, and capital. This is generally done by creating models of suppliers and demanders using mathematical equations, determining the equilibrium conditions, and then testing the model using relevant data via econometric analysis.

Bibliography

Aitken, Rob. 2007. *Performing Capital.* 1st ed. New York: Palgrave Macmillan.
Buckland, Jerry. 2012. *Hard Choices: Financial Exclusion, Fringe Banks, and Poverty in Urban Canada.* Toronto: University of Toronto Press.
Goulet, Denis. 1995. *Development Ethics.* 1st Publ. ed. New York: Apex Press.

Nussbaum, Martha C. 2006. *Frontiers of Justice: Disability, Nationality, Species Membership*. Boston: Harvard University Press.
Sen, Amartya. 1999. *Development as Freedom*. New York: Alfred A. Knopf Inc.
Thaler, Richard H., and Cass R. Sunstein. 2008. *Nudge: Improving Decisions about Health, Wealth, and Happiness*. New Haven and London: Yale University Press.
van der Zwan, Natascha. 2014. Making Sense of Financialization. *Socio-Economic Review* 12 (1): 99–129.

CHAPTER 2

Financial Inclusion and Building Financial Resilience

This chapter opens with a discussion of the 2007 subprime mortgage crisis, as an extreme example of financial change gone awry. This leads into a general discussion of financialization which was introduced in Chap. 1 and analyzed more fully in this chapter. The discussion then moves to the popular concept of financial inclusion which is followed by a discussion on the evidence for the expansion of financialization and financial inclusion. Since the book examines the impact of credit and finance schemes on vulnerable people, the chapter then moves into a discussion of the relationship between poverty and financial inclusion. Finally, anticipating Chap. 3's focus on commercial banking, the chapter presents a brief history of money and banking and identifies how major actors' roles have changed in the last century.

One of the most severe financial crises in recent times was the US-based subprime financial crisis of 2007 through 2010. In the period leading up to the crisis, financial markets in the United States and elsewhere had been deregulated and new financial products were being created. This process was encouraged by neoliberal policymakers, who believe that markets are largely self-governing and that markets and innovation are the root of economic growth. The crisis was linked with two types of financial devices: asset-based securities and subprime mortgages. These products were designed and primarily implemented in the United States; however, the asset-backed securities became popular with banks and governments across the Global North. Asset-backed securities were bundled assets sold to

J. Buckland, *Building Financial Resilience*,
https://doi.org/10.1007/978-3-319-72419-5_2

investors. The troublesome versions of these securities were bundled with subprime mortgages. Subprime mortgages were mortgages that were designed to bring into the mortgage market non-traditional home owners, but these mortgages had problematic features, such as "teaser" interest rates. These were starter rates that were close to the prime lending rate but would, after a short period of time, automatically rise. This would raise the cost of servicing one's debt, particularly problematic for many modest income Americans.

Problems occurred when housing prices stopped rising or started to decline and when the teaser interest rate period ended so that mortgage interest rates on the subprime mortgages jumped. This made servicing the mortgages by many mortgage holders unsustainable and might actually drop the value of the house so that it is lower than the value of the mortgage. Many subprime mortgage holders lost their homes. The value of the subprime mortgages in the securities dropped as did the value of the securities. So that security holders found that the value of their assets declined. In some extreme cases this led to bankruptcy. Security holders were found across the Global North so that indirect effect of the subprime mortgage crisis went global. Moreover, as an engine of the global economy, when the United States economy went into recession, this dampened its trade and investment with the rest of the world. The consequence of the crisis was a major global recession. Remarking on the outcome, George Soros noted:

> The human suffering caused by the housing crisis will be enormous. There is significant evidence that senior citizens are disproportionally defaulting on their mortgages. Communities of color are also disproportionately affected. Given that home ownership is a key factor in increasing wealth and opportunity in the United States. Upwardly mobile young professional of color will be particularly hard hit. (Soros 2009, p. 149)

This is an extreme case in which financial innovation did not build the common good and, in fact, did the opposite and caused considerable harm. And the global capitalist system is vulnerable to financial crises like the Great Depression of the 1930s.[1] Subprime mortgage holders, their neighbors, their communities, businesses, workers, and governments in the United States and around the world were harmed by the misapplication of these devices in relatively unregulated financial markets. This is not to say that financial innovation cannot improve the common good.

Financial devices are powerful and their relationship to human well-being or development is multifaceted. Undergirding the drivers of the subprime financial crisis is the process of financialization, introduced in Chap. 1, discussed further now.

Financialization

Views about Financialization and the Financialization of the Everyday

Academics and popular thinkers generally agree that economies of the Global North in particular as well as economies around the world are financializing. This means that finances are playing a larger role in virtually all walks of life, from banking through consumption to human motivation. A common definition of financialization, discussed in Chap. 1, is the growing integration of *financial motives* and the proliferation of *financial devices* in the socio-economy (Epstein 2005).[2] Measuring human motivation can be difficult, but there are many indicators regarding the rise of financial devices.

However, academic views about the causes and effects of financialization are mixed. Hudson (2015) provides a helpful rubric to understand the different views in the academy about the relationship between finances and development. He argues that there are four basic views about how finance effects economic development: neoliberal, liberal institutional, critical reformist, and radical (Hudson 2015, p. 49). The neoliberal view, advanced by people such as Milton Friedman and Paul Krueger, finds that money is a commodity that enables the economy to move to equilibrium, a metaphor for the economy finding a state of dynamic "health", in that market prices are set so that resources, including labor, are fully employed. The liberal institutionalists including Dani Rodrik and William Easterly argue essentially the same thing—that money and markets lead the economy to a healthy state, but this process requires institutions such as the legal system and a transparent and accountable state to ensure that this process happens, that is, markets are necessary but insufficient. Hudson considers the neoliberal and liberal institutional approaches are "orthodox", in the sense that they form the basis for policy making in the Global North and much of the Global South. The market is central and, at most, the state must support the market.

Heterodox approaches include the critical reform and radical approaches. Critical reformist such as Ha-Joon Chang and Robert Wade argue that the market does not on its own or with a few institutions automatically move to equilibrium. This is because uncertainty about markets, including financial markets, can lead them into disequilibrium which is associated with "unhealthy" outcomes associated with unemployed resources including high level of unemployment. Finally, radicalism, associated with Karl Marx and Andre Gunder Frank, is the view that markets and states in the rich countries and regions systematically exploit poor countries and regions and that finance is one means through which this exploitation takes place.

While Hudson (2015) identifies broad approaches taken with respect to the relationship between finances and development, Van der Zwan (2014) offers a synthesis on theories of financialization that leads her to identify three main types of financialization theories: financialization as a new regime for accumulation, financialization associated with the ascendancy of the shareholder value concept, and the financialization of the "everyday". The first approach, advanced by people such as Krippner (2005) and Lapavitsas (2009), argues that finances have become a new and important source of accumulation on the part of finance and non-finance corporations (Van der Zwan 2014). This is because the internationalization of production has led these firms to search for alternative means to accumulate surplus and thus a growing reliance on finance. The shareholder value approach to financialization, embraced by Boyer (2005), shares with the previous approach recognition of the growing reliance of the corporation on finances but it differs in that its focus is on how it affects the corporation internally, particularly focusing on shareholder benefits to managers and employees.

But the approach to financialization probably of greatest interest to this study of credit and finance schemes for vulnerable people is the financialization of the "everyday" (Van der Zwan 2014; Roy 2010). This approach focuses on the fact that financialization has made possible the extension of financial products to a large part of the population including modest and vulnerable people who were previously by-passed by the process. Roy (2010) argues that everyday-styled financialization, like that associated with Bangladesh-inspired microcredit, democratizes capital and, by extension, human well-being and development.

Theorists such as Aitken (2007) and Montgomerie (2006) argue that the consequences of the deeper reach of finance, including consumer credit, have both material consequences and consequences for the subjective understanding of financialization (Van der Zwan 2014). These analyses focus less on global elites and more on the non-elite everyday consumer of finances and find that they may lack the financial literacy to handle sophisticated and rising financialization (Van der Zwan 2014). Since this study seeks to explore the character and impact of credit and finance schemes on vulnerable people, this approach to financialization offers important insights.

Van der Zwan (2014) argues that the financialization of the everyday has facilitated the decline of the welfare state that previously provided "cradle to grave" services and has linked vulnerable people with capital markets in order to enable them to protect themselves from life's uncertainties (Van der Zwan 2014, p. 111). Financialization of the everyday scholars are concerned that this substitution involves risks for vulnerable people as commercial credit and debt are not a perfect substitute for a stream of income from the state.

Causes and Effects of Financialization

Lapavitsas and Powell (2013), drawing on the new regime of accumulation school, enlarge on the expansion of financial devices by identifying three tendencies associated with financialization: (1) the increased engagement by non-financial firms into finances, (2) increasing dependence of banks on lending to individuals and households, and (3) increasing dependence of individuals on financial service providers to make their basic needs, including pensions, housing, education, and health care. Innovation and extension of information technology have enabled finances to reach the "everyday" level (Van der Zwan 2014). Some additional indicators, correlates, and consequence of financialization noted in the literature include the following:

- increasing share of the financial sector of the economy
- rise in importance placed on shareholder value
- growth of public and private debt
- growth in income inequality, and
- increased instability of financial markets

The effect of financialization varies around the world and even within relatively homogeneous countries such as countries of the Global North.

One study found, based on a series of indicators, that the United States and United Kingdom have been more affected by financialization, Germany and Japan less affected, while France falls between these two groups (Lapavitsas and Powell 2013, pp. 375–76).

When there is a relative balance between the powers of actors involved in a market transaction then there is the scope for a mutually beneficial transaction, that is, synergies or win–win outcomes. This may be more the case when financial service companies are providing services for middle- and upper-income people. However, this book focuses on how certain manifestations of financialization, that is, credit and finance schemes, affects poor people. This is a particularly challenging dynamic because it brings together very large and powerful actors, such as banks, with poor people. This creates a classic development challenge associated with asymmetric power dynamics, in which one group is more powerful, wealthy, and organized than the other. The outcome of this type of relationship is likely to be tilted in the former group's favor.

What is driving financialization? There are a variety of factors driving financialization including the rise of select institutions such as banks, the liberalization/deregulation of markets, changing information and communications technology, and rising financial motivations on the part of consumers. Markets, financial markets included, have been liberalized through structural adjustment programs (SAPs) in poor countries and through general neoliberal ideology and reforms in rich countries. The subprime mortgage crisis might have halted deregulation for a moment, but the reforms have not led to a dramatic redirection.

Institutional changes relate to the expansion and deepening of financial markets like the markets for foreign exchange that have developed and deepened since the collapse of the Bretton Woods gold standard in the 1970s (Lapavitsas 2013, p. 3). The role and influence of banks, and more generally the service sector, in rich countries have risen as large segments of manufacturing have moved, at least its productive activities, to poor countries. Lapavitsas argues that the rise of banks relates to the establishment of the derivative, and he identifies the three decades following the 1970s as pivotal for increasing the role of finance on rich economies:

> The three decades that followed have witnessed unprecedented expansion of financial activities, rapid growth of financial profits, permeation of economy and society by financial relations and domination of economics policy by the

> concerns of the financial sector. At the same time, the productive sector in mature countries has experienced mediocre growth performance, profits rates have remained below the levels of the 1950s and 1960s, unemployment has generally risen and become persistent, and relative wages have shown no tendency to rise in a sustained manner. An asymmetry has emerged between the sphere of production and the ballooning sphere of circulation. (Lapavitsas 2013, p. 3)

Niall Ferguson's *The Ascent of Money* (2008) depicts the growing role that money has played in the Western world over the course of history. While this rise has been associated with financial bubbles that have burst, the overarching theme in the book is that money has taken on an every greater role in society. Expanding money's role has involved the creation and expanded use of cash money, the creation and expanded use of stock and money markets (e.g., money exchanges), and the creation and expanded use of information and communications technologies for the transmission of money. These changes are tied into the transformation of Western economies toward post-industrial service economies. As globalization has moved manufacturing from the Global North to Global South, the role of banks and financial companies—along with other service sector companies—increased.

Financialization and Human Motivations

Financialization raises the share of finance in the economy, leads to a proliferation of financial services and products, and ultimately affects human motivations. Diversifying financial services and expanding the role of finance in the economy may boost economic growth, but it is not clear if this is so, particularly in the medium and long term. And precisely how financialization affects human motives is complicated. Some argue that financialization forces people to be more careful with their finances and presents them with more options to use their finances to achieve their financial and life goals. This is the rationale behind the growth in financial education. Greater literacy will allow people to be better consumers, and if this literacy is used effectively, it will enable people to achieve their goals and become more fully human.

But a counter-argument is that the deepening financial motivations and expanding financial marketplace come at a cost, which is less attention to other motivations and goals. Major thinkers such as Mahatma Gandhi,

E. F. Schumacher, and Herman Daly, along with religious traditions and the contemporary voluntary simplicity movement, show the tension between well-being on the one hand and a focus on finances and/or consumption on the other. For instance, the UNDP (1998), drawing on Parthasarathi (1997), documents the views that world religions have with respect to the relationship between materialism and well-being. Western religions of Christianity and Islam have been critical of wealth as an end in itself. Among Eastern religions, the strongest critique of materialism comes from Taoism, which emphasizes that well-being is achieved not through finances and consumption but through frugality and voluntary simplicity (Parthasarathi 1997, p. 3).

Sandel argues that money motives crowd out other motives (Sandel 2012, p. 59), using several examples to make his case.[3] For instance, he discusses programs that pay people for certain types of "healthy" behavior: payments to lose weight, payments to quit smoking, or conditional cash transfers associated with sending kids to school. He argues that while the payments might succeed in getting participants to lose weight, quit smoking, or send their children to school, they do not affect either the participant's *motive* or *attitude* toward diet, smoking, or education and may possibly harm it. So the participant engages in the activity not through free will and the conviction that it is valuable but because it leads to some cash. Sandel opines that this could lead to weakening motivation and, in the medium to long run, when the payments run out, a return of the past practices. The payment is a kind of bribe and it is manipulative:

> Health bribes trick us into doing something we should be doing anyhow. They induce us to do the right thing for the wrong reason. Sometimes it helps to be tricked. It isn't easy to quit smoking or lose weight on our own. But eventually, we should rise above manipulation. Otherwise, the bribe may become habit forming. (Sandel 2012, p. 59)

Zelizer presents a more nuanced perspective, as compared to Sandel, on the question of whether money's role is expanding and eroding society. While she argues that money can and does do so, this is not universal and that sometimes this critique is rooted more in ideology than based on careful analysis (Zelizer 2011, p. 359). She argues that rather than an ideological anti-money view, what is needed is "[w]hen and why, we should ask, do certain economic arrangements produce injustice and which enhance welfare" (Zelizer 2011, p. 359). For instance, in her examination of the impact of markets on intimate relationships, she argues that the one does not necessarily diminish the other. She notes that intimate couples have long engaged in a variety of market transactions such as purchasing rings, childcare, give children allowances, and so on (Zelizer 2011, p. 177).

What is unclear is whether money incentives universally erode, expand, or have a neutral effect on attitudes. Moreover, given that people, particularly in the Global North, face so many money incentives and signals, it is not clear what the combined effect of these many influences might be. Is it possible that a well-tailored financial incentive that is well targeted and tapers off might expose a person to the benefits of healthy behavior, which would then change their motivations?

Financial Inclusion

While financial inclusion is related to financialization, the two processes should be differentiated. Financialization is a market-based process that is driven primarily by financial agents and supported by the state in terms of liberal regulation, with the purpose of improving financial returns which in turn, by supporting part of the state's interests, stimulate economic growth. Financial inclusion, on the other hand, is a reformist process driven primarily by the state and inter-state actors that seeks to bring vulnerable people into the formal banking system to foster their financial well-being and, again, to stimulate economic growth, enhance national security, and reduce the funding of criminal activity. Vulnerable populations include newcomers, Indigenous Peoples, income- and asset-poor people, rural and remote people, and unemployed people. Financial inclusion is primarily concerned with groups like these that have previously been excluded from formal banking. Financial inclusion is primarily concerned with groups that have previously been excluded from formal banking. It focuses on the extent and depth of a country's disadvantaged population's engagement with the formal or mainstream banking system. The principal goals of financial inclusion are to improve access to basic financial services such as bank accounts and basic credit and savings products for unbanked people; it is less concerned about sophisticated banking products such as mortgages and mutual funds. Financial inclusion has become an important goal for many states, for inter-state organizations like World Bank, and private donors such as the Gates Foundation, and has led to the creation of a major network in the field, the Alliance for Financial Inclusion. According to the latest estimates, 2.5 billion adults worldwide are unbanked, and generally speaking, the share of financial exclusion within a given country rises as income per capita declines. Many people and organizations place great hope in the potential of financial inclusion to promote development:

> Having greater access to financial services promotes entrepreneurship, lifts people out of poverty, and gives them greater hope for a brighter economic future. This is especially the case in regard to women and marginalized groups. In many places, these individuals lack access to financial services and therefore have little opportunity of advancing themselves beyond their current circumstances. (Villasenor and West 2015, p. 7)

In their analysis of financial inclusion, the World Bank notes that lack of financial access can lead to poverty traps, inequality, and poor people's inability to invest in education and limit poor people's occupational choices that in turn limit their future income (World Bank 2014, p. 15). They note that while differences in financial inclusion rates vary dramatically around the world, they are rising and that a significant amount of the variation relates to national income levels. Urban areas have higher financial inclusion rates, as do wealthier households, married, and employed people. A gender gap exists in financial inclusion such that 47% of women worldwide hold or co-hold an account as compared with 55% of men (World Bank 2014, p. 23). The gap relates to account holding, use of account, and access to other savings and credit products. This study found that women, in some cases, are more likely than men to rely on informal finances such as credit societies. Financial exclusion, for these women, acts as a barrier to self-employment and empowerment.

Most recently, efforts at financial inclusion in the Global South have been closely tied with digital financial services, which in turn are linked to the growth of mobile phone use around the world. It is estimated that there were 3.8 billion unique mobile phone subscribers in 2015 and this figure is expected to rise to 4.6 billion by 2020 (Villasenor and West 2015, p. 7). Since many people have more than one mobile device, the number of devices is much higher, at 7.1 billion in 2015, and is expected to reach 9.0 billion on 2020 (Villasenor and West 2015, p. 9).[4]

Common indicators of financial inclusion are the share of the adult population with a bank account and share of the population with a credit card. It is assumed that accessing a bank account and other bank products enables people to more effectively pursue their personal goals. Having a bank account has potential social benefits, providing one a sense of belonging, and economic benefits, such as reducing transaction service fees, and access to financial products that can enable financial improvement via savings and credit products. It is also assumed that financial inclusion is a voluntary and not mandatory process.

The Maya Declaration is a commitment agreed to by Global South states and international organizations to increase financial inclusion through goal setting and effective government policy (AFI undated). It is rooted in the Alliance for Financial Inclusion (AFI), a network of central banks and state regulatory agencies from over 90 Global South countries. As of 2015, 54 members have made particular commitments to expand financial inclusion, in line with the goals of the Maya Declaration.

Does financial inclusion always boost the interests of unbanked people? No, clearly it is not a "magic bullet"; it might not benefit some people and might harm others. Like other popular efforts such as microcredit, financial inclusion must be examined carefully to determine if poor people can and do benefit. Some limitations of financial inclusion are:

- State funding of financial inclusion might lead to fewer funds available for more effective poverty-reducing programs.
- Allocating funds to support financial inclusion can lead to non-productive displacement or reduced funding of more productive sectors: financial inclusion for business development may not foster economic growth but simply displace it from one group of producers to another. Displacement of economic activity is a noted challenge with microcredit, where the delivery of the product simply shifts production or processing from one group of unsupported producers to another group of newly included and supported producers. Bateman (2015) argues that capital directed at financial inclusion reduces capital available for small and medium-sized enterprises (SMEs), and it is the SME sector that is best placed to promote labor-intensive jobs. SMEs are also indigenous to the country and so create a more endogenous form of economic development.

- Financial inclusion might not be in the best interests of the individual. As noted in the figure below, financial inclusion must be a voluntary process, and efforts to coerce people to open accounts can lead to wasted resources if these services do not meet their felt needs. In some cases financial exclusion is due to poor accessibility, limited services, and poor staff training, but in other cases people choose to be unbanked. This choice may align with their principles and/or financial habits. For instance, a person may prefer a payday loan over owning a credit card because the former is more limiting with respect to credit availability and repayment timeframe as compared with a credit card. The payday loan provides some people parameters within which their credit use is limited. Note, however, that for many payday loans lead to a vicious cycle of debt and can aggravate their financial challenges. This is related to the lack of underwriting and credit scoring associated with payday loans. And this is a good example of the different consequences of financial products on different groups.

There are important barriers to financial inclusion. In the Global South low incomes make it difficult to establish bricks-and-mortar banks. In the Global North where one finds many bank branches it is often assumed that they are very accessible so that people who do not use them are freely choosing not to do so and that they could freely use them if they wanted. However, there is a long literature on the subject of barriers to modern institutions including banks (e.g., Caplovitz 1967). Buckland (2012) identified the following factors as creating barriers to using mainstream banks and/or opportunities to using fringe banks: physical proximity and operating hours, the structure of services and fees, and bank staff treatment of the customer. So in inner cities in Canada (and other Global North countries) fringe bank outlets are more numerous and open longer compared to mainstream banks in poor neighborhoods. While fringe bank services are more expensive than mainstream bank services, they tailor their products to meet the largely transactional demands of low-income people, for instance, through offering cheque-cashing services and providing them ways of ensuring their personal identification. Finally, evidence from Canada finds that mainstream banks do not place sufficient resources into training staff that respectfully support the financial needs of vulnerable people.

At a global level the World Bank reported some results. Based on its global database, it noted the following factors (and percentage of people responded this way) were reported as reasons for not having a bank account: not enough money (30%), family member already has account (25%), too expensive (23%), too far away (20%), lack of documentation (18%), lack of trust (13%), and religious reasons (5%) (World Bank 2014, p. 34).

Indicators of Financialization and Financial Inclusion

The increasing financialization of economies around the world and the expansion of financial inclusion can be measured through various indicators. These include the rising share of the financial sector in the economy, the rise in non-financial sector's share of income from financial services, and the rising profits for all financial services. The value of the financial sector in the United States represented 2.3% of gross domestic product (GDP) in 1947 and this increased to 7.7% in 2005 (Ferguson 2008, p. 5).[5] A study of the US economy, perhaps the most financialized, examined the latter two indicators (financial earnings of non-financial firms and profitability of financial firms) and found evidence that supported the financialization theory. These indicators demonstrated rising trends in financialization in the post–World War II period (Krippner 2005).

Another common indicator of financialization is the share of financial system deposits to GDP. Data for this indicator are widely available. The share of financial system deposits to GDP rose for all world regions from 1991 through 2011; for instance, for sub-Saharan Africa it rose from 13.7% in 1991 through 15.1% in 2001 to 26.5% in 2011 (Table 2.1).

Commercial bank density per 100,000 population has increased from 2005 to 2011 in all regions. This growth was most marked in East Asia and the Pacific and in South Asia and least marked in sub-Saharan Africa (Table 2.2). It has grown the most in the Middle East and North Africa (MENA), from 9% to 17%, and grown second most in developing regions in Europe and Central Asia, from 12% to 19%. The lowest base levels and the lowest growth occurred in sub-Saharan Africa and South Asia. Branch density slightly declined in high-income countries during this period but increased in all other economic regions. Branch density increased in all eight countries for which data are available and particularly fast for South Africa and Kenya.

Table 2.1 Indicators of financialization for world regions

Region	*GDP per capita*	*Financial system deposits to GDP (%)*		
	(Constant 2005 USD)	*1991*	*2001*	*2011*
East Asia and Pacific (developing only)	2673	29.7	33.6	44.7
Euro area	32,219	60.8	77.4	105.2
Europe and Central Asia (developing only)	4660	31.0	11.1	38.9
Latin America and Caribbean (developing only)	5481	21.0	30.9	37.5
Middle East and North Africa (developing only)[a]	1925	40.2	44.5	62.3
South Asia	989	21.7	34.4	54.1
Sub-Saharan Africa (developing only)	967	13.7	15.1	26.5
High income	30,595	54.3	66.7	79.5
Low income	403	11.4	13.9	24.6
Lower middle income	1189	20.1	22.3	32.0
Middle income	2623	23.0	26.6	38.6
Upper middle income	4117	34.5	34.5	46.7
World	7547	30.3	32.8	44.1

Source: Global Financial Development, last updated 11/12/2013

[a]GDP per capita value for Middle East and North Africa is for 2001

Automated teller machines are another basic infrastructure of banking and data are provided regarding their density in select regions and countries for 2005 and 2011 (Table 2.2). High-income countries, particularly Canada, have high levels of ATMs and there was a rapid growth in this indicator for middle-income countries and MENA and developing regions of Europe and Central Asia.

The expansion of financial inclusion is also demonstrated by various indicators, such as access to personal bank accounts and other banking services, and use of mobile banking. The share of the world adult population with a bank account increased from 51% in 2011 to 62% in 2014 (Kelly and Rhyne 2015). The banked share of the population conforms closely with the commercial bank density except that Middle East and North Africa have a low banked share—in fact the lowest and lower than sub-Saharan Africa—as compared with its commercial bank density (Table 2.3). In terms of regions grouped by income level, in the next

Table 2.2 Commercial bank branches per 100,000 adults by region, 2005 and 2011

Country or region	*Commercial bank branches (per 100,000 adults)*		*Automated teller machines (ATMs) (per 100,000 adults)*	
	2005	*2011*	*2005*	*2011*
East Asia and Pacific (developing only)	6.6	8.1	3.0	17.7
Euro area	34.6	38.5	85.1	90.5
Europe and Central Asia (developing only)	11.6	18.5	14.8	46.6
Latin America and Caribbean (developing only)	11.9	14.9	22.9	33.0
Middle East and North Africa (developing only)	9.0	17.2	3.4	21.9
South Asia	7.2	8.3	0.2	5.8
Sub-Saharan Africa (developing only)	2.0	3.4		4.5
High income	26.1	25.8	70.9	76.6
Low income	1.5	2.7		2.7
Lower middle income	6.4	8.5	3.5	17.1
Middle income	8.2	10.7	11.5	31.7
Upper middle income	12.2	16.0	22.9	45.8
World	10.4	13.5	22.8	37.6

Source: G20 Financial Inclusion Indicators, last updated: 10/15/2013

table, there is a clear correlation between average income and banked share. In the final table in this section a selection of countries from low-, middle-, and high-income levels is charted and once again the correlation between average income and banked share is strong, although average income per capita jumps faster between South Africa and Canada than does the banked share. In other words, while there is a large gap in average incomes between these two countries, the gap in the banking population is not as great. This might be explained by income distribution, banked depth, or both.

In terms of financial exclusion—having little or no access to mainstream banking—the largest absolute numbers of people in this situation are found in China and India, but it is projected that China's unbanked population will drop substantially by 2020 (Kelly and Rhyne 2015, pp. 15–16).

Table 2.3 The share of adults with an account at a formal bank, 2011

Country or region	*Account at a formal financial institution (% age 15+)*[a]
Sub-Saharan Africa (developing only)	17.5
South Asia	30.3
East Asia and Pacific (developing only)	26.8
Europe and Central Asia (developing only)	42.1
Latin America and Caribbean (developing only)	27.7
World	38.2
Euro area	95.3
Middle East and North Africa (developing only)	24.4
Low income	13.4
Lower middle income	21.4
Middle income	29.5
Upper middle income	43.1
High income	90.1

Source: Global Financial Development, last updated: 11/12/2013

[a]The percentage of respondents with an account (self or together with someone else) at a bank, credit union, another financial institution (e.g., cooperative, microfinance institution), or the post office (if applicable) including respondents who reported having a debit card (% age 15+)

An interesting phenomenon is that mobile banking is catching on more rapidly in some poor countries than in richer countries. For instance, mobile payment services were used by over 2.5% of respondents from low-income countries as compared with 1.6% of respondents from upper-middle-income countries (Fig. 2.1). Mobile banking has been embraced most dramatically in East Africa and particularly in Kenya. Globally, mobile banking has captured a small share of the banked market (Kelly and Rhyne 2015). The World Bank (2014, p. 52) noted the potential for mobile phones to address financial exclusion by noting the following:

- In 2011 there were 127 mobile phone subscriptions for every 100 inhabitants in South Africa whereas only 54% of the population had a bank account.
- In India 72% of people had a mobile phone while only 35% had a bank account.

Various indexes have been created to measure financial inclusion, such as the World Bank's formal financial service index (Table 2.4). It is made up of variables related to access of basic banking services such as bank branch and ATM density and utilization of various banking services such

Fig. 2.1 Percentage of respondents who report using a mobile phone to pay bills in the past 12 months (% age 15+)

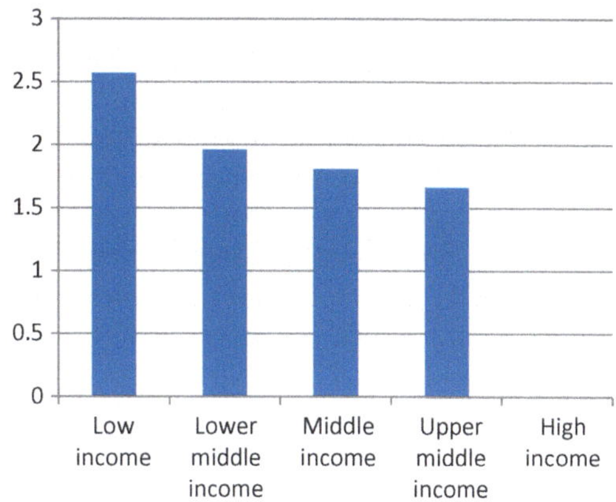

Table 2.4 Index of formal financial services

Country	*Formal financial services index (%)*[a]
Canada	89.7
United Kingdom	78.9
United States	63.9
Kenya	33.3
South Africa	23.8
China	22.0
Bangladesh	15.4
Tanzania	7.7
India	6.4

Source: Global Financial Development, last updated 11/12/2013

[a]The index was constructed by normalizing data for indicators and then calculating average for each country. Indicators were ATMs per 100,000 adults; account at a formal financial institution (% age 15+); bank branches per 100,000 adults; credit card (% age 15+); debit card (% age 15+); electronic payments used to make payments (% age 15+); loan from a financial institution in the past year (% age 15+); mobile phone used to pay bills (% age 15+); mobile phone used to send money (% age 15+); and saved at a financial institution in the past year (% age 15+)

as account and credit card and mobile banking. Two versions of the index were created: one that weights some features more (e.g., 3 for bank branch density) and one that weights some features less (e.g., 0.5 for mobile banking used to send money). The results vary only slightly and Global North nations demonstrate much higher levels of financial service access, with Canada at the top in both variations.

Another index, the Brookings Institute's Financial and Digital Inclusion Project (FDIP) index, involves variables from four different areas: country commitment, mobile capacity, regulatory environment, and adoption of traditional and digital financial services (Villasenor and West 2015, p. 12). Out of 21 countries from the Global South, Kenya, South Africa, and Brazil ranked first, second, and third, respectively.

This chapter has examined the concept of financialization, sought to understand its recent historical origin, and presented evidence of its rise. The indicators support the view that financialization is proceeding, this process is quite universal, but the rates of financialization vary around the world. Financialization is a controversial process as some see it as universally beneficial for human well-being and some see it as a flawed process that will harm development. The premise of this book is that financialization offers potential benefits and costs on vulnerable people and it is not universally beneficial.

Financial inclusion and financialization are, in part, financed by foreign capital. And the character of foreign capital flows has changed substantially over the last 20 years. While the size of government "official" aid has risen only slightly, the size of private flows has increased and it is much larger now than official flows. Private flows include direct and portfolio investment and much of it goes to the better off majority nations. While official development assistance was valued at US $135 billion/year in 2014, this was usurped by private flows which amounted, in the same year, to over US $400 million/year (Fig. 2.2).

Another interesting development in terms of foreign capital flows is the rise of the BRICS (the group of fast-growing middle-income countries including Brazil, Russia, India, China, and South Africa) and, in particular, China's establishment of the Asian Infrastructure Investment Bank (AIIB). While still small in comparison to the Bretton Woods Institutions, the AIIB has a capital base of US $50 billion as compared to the World Bank's capital base of US $223 billion (Economist 2015).

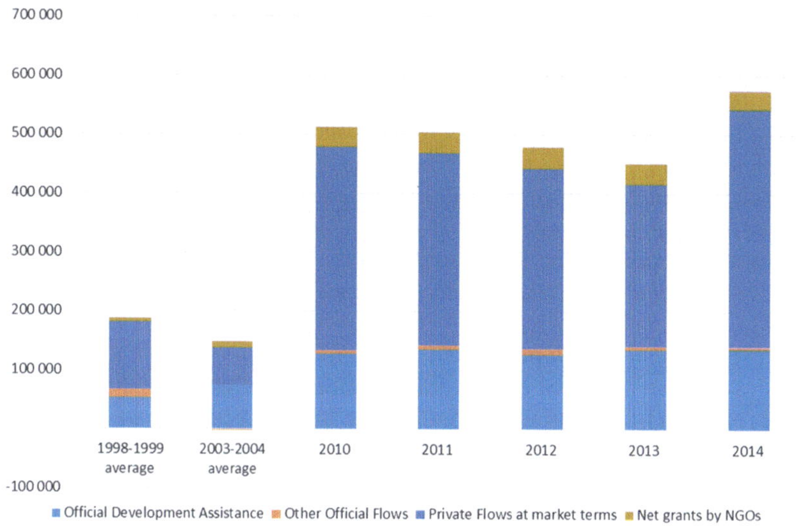

Fig. 2.2 Private and public flows from Global North to Global South, 1998–2014

Poverty, Capability, and Financial Resilience

References have been made to poverty, financial resilience, and human well-being. What are these concepts and how do they relate to finances? There is so much controversy about these concepts. They are elastic concepts that mean many different things to many different people. Poverty can refer to a material, a psycho-social, or a political deficit. It can be used in a constructive or a pejorative fashion. Financial resilience, discussed in Chap. 1, relates to the size and sustainability of an individual's or community's income and assets. Human well-being, sometimes referred to as development, could mean economic growth, rising social conditions, or greater community solidarity. A note on terminology: in this book the word vulnerable is used more often than poor as a descriptor for the people it seeks to understand. The reason for this is that *poor* people suggests the person is lacking in something and it highlights the person's deficits. But poor people are not just lacking things, they do have assets. A poor person may have limited financial and physical assets but he may have strong social assets in family, friends, and community. Vulnerable is used instead of poor to denote the fact that when people have few assets they are more vulnerable to economic changes and crises.

Types of and Views About Poverty

Noted development ethicist Denis Goulet (1995) has argued that excessive focus on material poverty has skewed the focus of human development toward economic growth. Goulet challenges the hierarchical models of poverty and he argues that poverty is not simply about material scarcity. In fact, he notes that poverty can be related to one or more of three key areas: material insufficiency, lack of esteem, and lack of control over one's plans and future are the key manifestations of poverty. Impoverished or vulnerable people lack one or more of these components of the good life.

Maslow's well-known model describes human need, and its relative poverty, as hierarchical: people who are materially poor are disabled from attaining other levels of health, for instance in the emotional and spiritual realms. Only by attaining one's basic needs, according to Maslow's theory, can one's emotional needs be achieved, and once those are met, one's spiritual needs or "self-actualization" can be attained. While this might be the case for certain people, it is equally plausible that for other people, deficits in some areas such as material needs are made up in other areas such as social networks and religious faith. Goulet rejects a hierarchical model in that he rejects the idea that material well-being is a prerequisite to emotional well-being. One group may experience one and not the other, while another group may experience the reverse. Meeting one's material needs is not necessarily a means to meeting further human need.

Goulet argues instead that poverty can be manifested in material, emotional, or political form. Material insufficiency is fairly understandable and aligns with much thinking and practice around human development. For instance, the World Bank, based on extensive research in India, has identified US$1.25/day/capita as the threshold of material, sometimes called absolute poverty. However, Goulet's analysis of material poverty goes further when he notes that the goal of development is sufficiency and not superfluity. By sufficiency he refers to a situation in which a person's material needs are met. Goulet distinguishes this from a condition of superfluity, in which excessive material goods are the goal. Moreover, Goulet talks about the importance of non-economic aspects of human need. He notes that people have the need to feel a level of individual and collective esteem. Poverty can take the form of a lack individual or collective esteem and this sense may or may not be connected with material poverty. For instance, immigrants or Indigenous

Peoples in the Global North might have their material needs met but they may suffer from racism that affects their sense of individual and/or collective esteem. But Indigenous Peoples in poor countries may experience both material and esteem forms of poverty. Finally, Goulet notes that people need to have a sense of some level control over their lives. A manifestation of poverty can be a situation in which a person or group feels that they lack any control over their lives. No one person or group has complete control over their lives but Goulet argues another manifestation of poverty is a situation in which a person has very little control over their lives. Domestic servants, indentured laborers, and slaves come quickly to mind. Some of these cases are no longer common but many people around the world have few resources of their own and so are heavily reliant on others for their livelihood and lifestyle.

The terms poor, poverty, and impoverished are sometimes associated with particular assumptions about personal responsibility or character. Sometimes referred to as the "blame the victim" theory of poverty, it assumes that poverty is caused by poor individual choices and personal deficits associated with a particular person or group of people. This book rejects that assumption and takes a broader approach that finds that there can be a variety of personal and structural factors that result in poverty. Personal choice can lead to or aggravate existing impoverishment. But structural factors—also referred to as obstacles, barriers, or constraints—in the form of unequal asset distribution, inequitable social programs, unfair taxation policy, racism, and weak job creation are disproportionately borne by poor people.

Human Capability and Financial Resilience

As with the concept of poverty, there are many approaches to and theories of human well-being. One that has gained considerable traction is the capabilities approach. Sen (1999) and Nussbaum (2006) argue that improved well-being is about removing obstacles that constrain people and communities from achieving their capabilities. "Development requires the removal of major sources of unfreedom: poverty as well tyranny, poor economic opportunities as well as systematic social deprivation, neglect of public facilities as well as intolerance or overactivity of repressive states" (Sen 1999, p. 3). Moreover, improved well-being is about expanding people's capabilities—what they are capable of achieving—and enabling them to improve their self-determined functionings, what they actually do. The capability approach provides a conception of well-being that focuses on self-defined improvements to the lives of vulnerable people.

A lack of financial resilience acts as an obstacle to a person achieving a higher capability or reduces one's capability. Low levels of income or assets or inability to adjust one's finances in the face of exogenous changes can lead to indebtedness and/or asset sales which can stagnate or reduce a person's capability. On the other hand, an expanding financial resilience can be a means to improved human freedom. If one's financial literacy improves and/or if one has improved access to constructive financial services, then one is capable of improved financial management that can stimulate one's human capability and reduce unfreedoms. Credit and finance schemes are examples of efforts to enhance human capability and reduce unfreedoms.

Some of the first studies on the relationship between credit and finance schemes and human capability involved microcredit. Microcredit received a lot of praise in its early years; consider that 2005 was the year of microcredit and Muhammad Yunus won the Nobel Peace Prize in 2006. However, by the late 1990s and early 2000s studies identified limitations associated with microcredit (Buckland 1996; Bateman 2010, 2011) and work by Milford Bateman particularly raised questions about the impact of microcredit which was confirmed through further research (Roodman and Morduch 2014). What about the relationship between other financial services and economic improvement? The World Bank reports on evidence that finds the availability of savings and insurance products supports economic improvements for poor people (World Bank 2014, p. 41). But the World Bank notes:

> [E]ffective financial inclusion means responsible inclusion. ... Financial inclusion does not mean increasing access for the sake of access, and it certainly does not mean making everybody borrow. (World Bank 2014, p. 41)

Finances are a means to the end of improved human well-being and they are not the end in themselves. This is an obvious point but it needs to be said and underscored. This is because there is a tendency for money to become an end. This can be seen in popular culture today in many countries, for instance Western countries obsession for shopping in malls and "big box" stores or the annual Dubai Shopping Festival. Consumerism, discussed below, is an ideology that finds that value is obtained from consumption of material goods (clothing, cars) and services (video games, cellphones). Consumerism encourages us to value material things and to believe that our value is linked to the accumulation of material goods. New clothes, the latest electronics, a shiny car, and a big house are the goals. But financialization moves us into a different if related track in which we are encouraged to value the financial sum of our lives reflected in our financial net worth.

When money becomes the end and not the means, goals become convoluted and strategies lead down dead ends or destructive paths. At an individual level, consumption for its own sake can lead people to accumulate consumer debt that grows and ultimately becomes unsustainable. Ultimately it can only be addressed by reducing consumption, leading to a full circle. At a macro level, an obsession with economic growth through market innovation can lead to rising income inequality, which can lead to social problems associated with poverty and violence. Moreover, the pursuit of economic growth has led to mounting environmental debt, evidenced in habitat destruction, ozone layer depletion, and the accumulation of toxic and non-toxic pollution. When the environment is seen as a tool to foster to economic growth, as opposed to a valuable end in itself, then it is exploited. And there is evidence that economic growth does not necessarily lead to improved human happiness (Kroll 2015). Studies are somewhat conflicted but some find that it is only when one's relative economic position—compared to your neighbor—improves that happiness increases. General income improvements do not necessarily lead to a happier population. This is a win-loose relationship that diminishes the common good. The premise of this book is that as money creeps closer and more comprehensively into people's lives, finances can move more closely into our ultimate purpose.

Saying that finances are only a means to the end of human development is not to say that finances are not important. Finances are an important means and paradoxically, as financialization, among other processes (e.g., commodification), monetizes an ever-increasing share of the human enterprise, the importance of money as a *means* expands. But to say that money is an important means is different than saying it is an end. As a growing means it requires that we learn how to carefully steward it, at the micro and macro levels. This is why financial literacy is so important. Financial literacy is often conceptualized narrowly as teaching individuals to be careful and strategic consumers. This is important but not enough; a broader conception would include understanding how finances fit into life goals and the community and social dimensions of goals (i.e., no one is an island). This will be discussed further in Chap. 3.

Recent History of Money and Banking

It is generally agreed that the origin of formal banking and lending is rooted in the Middle Ages in Europe. However, there is considerable controversy regarding the relationship between banking and lending, on the one hand, and economic well-being on the other. Different views about banking and credit see it as beneficial, ambivalent, or detrimental.

There are different views regarding the origin of money.[6] One theory—the markets-first view—is that organized markets predate money and that money was an innovation created to facilitate market-based interaction. According to this view, organized markets were first associated with barter exchange (Siklos 2004). Here trade was undertaken between two people, where each held items that they wanted to give up in exchange for items the other person had—the "double coincidence of wants" (Graeber 2014, p. 36). This requires a coincidence of interests that is clearly not always going to be the case, although perhaps it is more likely in a simpler economy when households are more self-sufficient and there are fewer goods and services. The markets-first theory holds that during this pre-historical and early historical period, the main means of storing value was gold, other precious minerals, and stones. People who had these precious items would leave them for safety with a goldsmith and get a receipt for their deposit. This receipt became the first type of paper money. Eventually the deposit slip became used for exchange purposes rather than the gold.

For some thinkers, progress through the years has been the result of the expansion of the role of money and credit:

> [P]overty is not the result of rapacious financiers exploiting the poor. It has much more to do with the *lack* of financial institutions, with the absence of banks, not their presence. Only when borrowers have access to efficient credit networks can they escape from the clutches of loan sharks, and only when savers can deposit their money in reliable banks can it be channelled from the idle rich to the industrious poor. (Ferguson 2008, p. 13)

For others money and banking is a lubricant for, but not the engine of, the modern economy. In this view, the true engine of economic growth was the "real" economy, especially industry and manufacturing. Until the 1990s this was the dominant view in the economics discipline.

For yet others, money, banking, and/or credit are the root of structures that aggravate poverty and inequality. Graeber (2014) argues that debt is a "perversion of a promise (p. 391)": the promise of credit is to assist the borrower, but when it is un-repayable it transforms into debt and the borrower is morally in error. Interestingly, Graeber turns upside-down the standard narrative about the beginning of money. For him, credit came first and was the means by which the money economy was invented:

> [Our] standard account of monetary history is precisely backwards. We did not begin with barter, discover money, and then eventually develop credit systems. It happened precisely the other way around. What we now call virtual money came first. Coins came much later, and their use spread only unevenly, never completely replacing credit systems. Barter, in turn, appears to be largely a kind of accidental byproduct of the use of coinage or paper money. (Graeber 2014, p. 40)

Graeber (2014) argues that that the markets-first theory is incorrect and that money predates organized and modern markets. He contends that barter was not a common system in traditional economies (Graeber 2014, p. 29). He notes that Adam Smith, the author of *The Wealth of Nations* (1776), was the one who first penned the theory that barter exchange came first. Smith's classical views were still influencing economists in the nineteenth century, including the neoclassical economist Stanley Jevons in 1871, even though evidence was amassing to refute this notion (Graeber 2014, p. 29). Graeber argues that more common than barter—which he describes as mythical—is the establishment of a money system that is built upon credit.

Ferguson, documenting earliest records of money, for example, in Mesopotamia from around 1700 BC, at least partly agrees with this explanation: "The central relationship that money crystallizes is between lender and borrower" (2008, p. 30). However, the origins of money are debated and the controversy, due to limited historical evidence, will not likely end anytime soon. Perhaps the markets-first account overlooks the important relationship between money and credit. This relationship continues to the present day and is featured in some banks and bank services vulnerable people use, such as payday lending.

The Changing Role of Actors in Credit and Finance Schemes

Since this book is about the relationship between credit/finance schemes and financial resilience offered by different actors, it is prudent to consider how these actors' roles have changed in this regard over the last century or so. One might identify three pronounced periods over the past 100 years: the late colonial period, from the late nineteenth century to the 1940s; the socio-economic state-led period, from the 1950s through the 1970s; and the neoliberal globalization period, from 1980 and continuing, if at a slower pace, today.

In the late colonial period, the state was *the* central actor in economic planning, particularly in the colonized countries. This feature continued into the social and economic state-led period. By 1915 much of the Global South had been colonized by Britain, France, the Netherlands, and some other European countries, although much of Latin America had already moved to independence from their colonial relationship with Spain and Portugal. Economically speaking, this "late" colonial period was characterized by the classical colonial relationship wherein the colony provided raw materials for the colonizer, who provided manufactured goods.[7] The role of banks and producer and/or consumer banking was generally not considered a critical aspect of this latent social improvement process.

During the 1950s and 1960s, colonized Asian and African nations—which included most of them, with the exception of Thailand and Afghanistan—gained their independence from the colonizing nation. This was a period in which the state was considered the central actor, and development—a mixed bag of economic growth and social improvement—was the central goal. Economic development was heavily emphasized, and there were a variety of debates and strategies.[8] A prominent debate played import substitution off against export promotion. The former approach, often linked with a socialist or dependency political perspective, argued that international economy had reproduced the unfair colonial structures so that engaging with it would only undermine national economic development. Import substitution industrialization called for an approach that matched national production with a dynamic focus on national demand. This approach had mixed results and worked for some countries such as India for some periods of time. Export promotion sought to link resources found in the national economy, such as low-waged workers, with international demand, which led the Asian "Tigers", Southeast Asian "Mini Tigers", and China to rapidly expand their light manufacturing and foster rapid economic growth.

Another important component to the social and economic phase was that the goals of the state became more complex and contested. In the

1950s, state-led economic growth that expanded the industrial sector was a very common goal. It was assumed, and often unstated, that this goal would lead to rising incomes, consumptions, and social services for all people. Rising consumption and access to social services, it was felt, would raise human well-being. By the 1970s the relationship between growth and human well-being was seriously challenged. People in the Global South, women, poor people, and Indigenous Peoples were not benefiting enough or at all.[9]

Thinking at this time pitted the "real" economy over and well above the financial system. The "real" economy refers to enterprises that produce tangible goods, such as farming and manufacturing. The financial system is the combination of organizations like banks, insurance companies, and pawnbrokers that provide financial services to "real" producers, organizations, and individuals. The financial system was considered to be a "lubricant" while the "real" economy—industry and agriculture—was the engine. Consumer banking was not seen as important during the social and economic state-led period. However, the role of banks for the purposes of assisting producers was seen as critical for achieving economic development. Access to capital for investment in agriculture and industry was an important contribution of banks to economic development. And since the state was believed to be a central actor, it either directed private banks or set up state banks to finance these efforts. State involvement in banking led to some challenging outcomes, such as low repayment rates that cost the state and its taxpayers (World Bank 2014, p. 1). This led to the rise of early neoliberal critiques, called the Ohio School, which argued for the state to get out of involvement with banking.

While accumulation of capital was seen as a critical component of economic development, financial markets were not the single or even the central means to deliver this capital.[10] For theorists from a variety of schools,[11] the state was a crucial actor in delivering capital to strategic sectors such as industry. Issues addressed regarding finance through the 1970s to 1980s included whether it should be raised through local efforts or through international sources. With the fixation on the state as the chief actor, local capital accumulation issues related to macroeconomic questions such as its source, taxation, printing money, and/or selling bonds. Once again, accessing international finance related to official movements of grants and loans through bilateral and multilateral agencies such as US AID and the World Bank.[12]

Soon after World War II, the so-called Cold War—devoid of one-on-one warfare but associated with a variety of proxy wars worldwide, including in Central America and Southern Africa—raged between the United States and the Soviet Union. This continued until the end of the Soviet Union in 1989. The Cold War and the Soviet Union's collapse had a profound impact on development thinking and practice. During the period in which the Union of Soviet Socialist Republics (USSR) existed, thinking in economic development was quite broad because there were a variety of different ways in which states operated to foster human well-being. The common thread through these models was that they were more state centric that models seen in the world today, but the models ranged from highly centralized states like the USSR to mixed economies with a substantial state and market. Thinking at the time recognized these different models and debates ranged about the superiority of one over the other. With the fall of the Berlin Wall—through the collapse of the USSR and its control of one side of the wall—this alternative model evaporated.

The end of the US–USSR Cold War ushered in a period that has placed less emphasis on the state and more emphasis on the market as a means to foster economic development, and thus the term "neoliberal" has been applied. It is a term that hearkens back to an earlier liberalism, not the state-oriented liberalism that came to dominate many Western countries by the 1970s but the more free-wheeling liberalism of the early twentieth century, before the Great Depression. The market is seen as the central economic agent because it is small, dynamic, and innovative. Conversely, according to this view, the state is large, static, and bureaucratic. Thus the neoliberal view calls for a declining role for the state.

From the 1980s, another important dynamic has been globalization: the growing economic and cultural linkages across countries. Some date globalization to 1492 and some date it much earlier, but many agree that the 1980s was a decade associated with an acceleration of international economic and cultural connections. These connections were facilitated by more homogeneous economic policies around the world, new technologies such as information and communications technologies (ICTs), and rising wage differential between the Global South and North that were increasingly not defended by a productivity differential. The simultaneous rise of neoliberalism and globalization has led some people to term this period as the neoliberal globalization period. Neoliberalism and globalization are processes that have been foundational to the expansion of financialization that was discussed above.

The neoliberal period has also been driven by policies of the Bretton Woods institutions—the World Bank, the IMF—and what was until 1994 called the General Agreement on Tariffs and Trade (GATT), replaced in 1995 by the World Trade Organization (WTO). The international debt crisis of the early 1980s pushed many Global South state borrowers to the WB and the IMF. Commercial banks rapidly increased their lending to Global South governments and corporations, but when interest rates spiked and economic recession depressed demand for Global South exports, many southern nations struggled to finance their debt. The Bretton Woods institutions had already begun structural adjustment lending in the mid-1970s, and this accelerated in the early 1980s. SAPs were an arrangement whereby countries could borrow from the WB and/or IMF, on the condition that the country implement neoliberal policies, including reducing state involvement in the economy and social programs, encouraging the expansion of the market, and increasing the country's engagement in international trade and investment.

The nature of SAPs changed over time but today the logic driving them is deeply engrained in the Bretton Woods institutions. Early critics of SAPs were social science academics, development NGOs, and some UN agencies. For instance, UNICEF's 1987 study, *Adjustment with a Human Face*, was an important and influential early criticism of the consequences of SAPs on the poor. Government cutbacks often hurt the poor first and worst through declining support for social programs, including education and entitlement schemes. The World Bank in particular responded to these criticisms by engaging in reforms to SAPs, leading to such things as the "post-Washington Consensus", involving recognition of some of the limitations of SAPs identified by UNICEF and other reformist critics. The Poverty Reduction Strategy Papers was a process the WB introduced into some of its lending countries to encourage national participation in decision-making around government spending allocation that sought to privilege spending supporting the poor. In response to these and other pressures, including the Jubilee 2000 Initiative calling for writing off of Global South debt, the IMF's Heavily Indebted Poor Countries (HIPC) program was intended to make debt forgiveness conditional on countries' embracing a market adjustment agenda that included an anti-poverty perspective.

SAPs have changed over time as new concerns such as heavy debt loads and weak poverty reduction policies were raised. The term SAP is not used so much by the international lenders but they still engage in pro-market conditionality. The World Bank does not use SAPs anymore but, for instance, refers to Development Policy Financing, which has the goals to reduce the fiscal deficits, strengthen fiscal institutions, and promote fiscal reforms to facilitate sustainable social spending.

In the literature, some argue that financialization has increased income inequality (Van Arnum and Naples 2013; Stockhammer 2012; Kus 2012). Van Arnum and Naples found that across the Organisation for Economic Co-operation and Development (OECD) members from 1987 to 2007, income inequality grew and this was in part caused by financialization. They found that real disposable household income for the top 10% grew almost universally faster than for the bottom 10%. By revaluing the relationship between the owner of capital and workers, financialization in these countries has given the capital holder more value than the worker as compared with the situation before financialization. Examining a number of OECD nations in the 1990s and 2000s, Kus found that financialization lended itself to rising income inequality: "financialization has exerted an upward pressure on income inequality" (Kus 2012, p. 493).

Discussion

Academic analyses of financialization accent different aspects of it and the focus on everyday (and everyone, including vulnerable people) financialization is most useful for this study. Regardless of the theoretical framework most scholars agree that financialization is a real phenomenon affecting most every corner of the globe and has to do with the growth of finances and credit, including credit and finance schemes that are the focus of this study. The concern expressed in everyday financialization is that it exposes vulnerable people to credit and debt and sometimes this is a substitute for a steady—albeit small—stream of income from state entitlement schemes.

Financial inclusion is a state supported effort intended to draw vulnerable people into the mainstream banking system, to enhance their human well-being. Its ability to do so is constrained by the huge asymmetries between large commercial banks and vulnerable people. If we think carefully about poverty and human well-being, as Dennis Goulet has done, we can see that finance-driven economic growth is a means to an end of improved sufficiency, control, and esteem and not an end in itself.

The history of money, credit, and banking is likely more complicated than the standard economic textbook presents, but the last 200 years has witnessed the growth of all three (money, credit, and banking). Financial crises are a regular feature of the global capitalist system and the 2008 subprime mortgage crisis is an example of one that was the result of financial innovation that was fueled by greed.

Notes

1. There have been several other financial crises that involve southern or emerging economies since the 1980s including Asia (1997), Russia (1998), and Argentina (1998).
2. Financialization is related to but distinct from the expansion of markets and trade, sometimes referred to as commodification. Commodification involves linking producers directly with consumers through markets. Commodification transforms goods and services that may have been used by the producer to meet his or her own needs. Instead of consuming the goods that one produces one sells (a portion) of these goods and purchases (a portion) of the goods that one needs for household consumption. As commodification proceeds, the role of finances and financial services will expand through the expanded use of cash, credit, savings, and investments by traders, hawkers, retailers, and consumers.
3. Sandel argues that excessive emphasis on markets is objected to on two general grounds: fairness and corruption (2012, pp. 110–13). The fairness objection highlights the limitations of the market under conditions of inequality or crisis. A person who is chronically poor or acutely struggling because of a natural hazard event might sell his/her land for a deflated price or possibly sell a body part. Inequality in outcomes leads the poor person to a further impoverished state. Not so for the non-poor person who can draw on assets such as insurance. The corruption objection relates to how the good in question is degraded by assigning a price. Allowing people to purchase admission to university, as opposed to meriting it through their academic achievement, is an example of degradation, in this case of the university and its staff. Sandel argues that expanding money incentives crowds out non-market incentives. The example he provides is of a Swiss village that voted on whether to accept a proposal that a nuclear waste facil ity be set up there. Initially the plebiscite was based purely on the notion of civic duty and 51% supported the arrangement. They added monetary compensation to each villager and this led to a decline in support to 25% (p. 115). The motivations were not additive but, in fact, were subtractive. Adding a financial incentive undermined the civic motivation and lessoned the local support for the nuclear waste facility. Adding an avenue whereby wealthy people can "buy" admission to university would lead to a similar effect on prospective and current students (and staff). The knowledge that one can

pay their way in erodes that status, if not the content, of the institution turning some people off university or toward another university. He argues that the erosion effect outweighs the price effect (p. 119). Sandel points out that excessive commercialization changes the nature of the good. When land is given voluntarily by the Swiss community for nuclear waste storage it involves a civic contribution but when money is involved then financial payment gets conflated with civic duty. Moreover, Sandel argues that ethical behavior is not a scarce resource as Arrow and others argue but, in fact, can be an expanding good as one ethical act can lead, through ripples, to a series of other ethical acts, without diminishing the total pie or remaining ethical acts (pp. 126–27). Economists might assume that money can "sweeten the pot" and Sandel might argue the reverse that it corrupts the pot. Arguably context matters so that in some cases money might be additive and in other cases it might be subtractive. For instance, can money enable someone to overcome a barrier and then, once dieting/not-smoking/sending the kids to school, realizes the benefits and becomes motivated. Moreover, Sandel seems to assume that there are no other, and conflicting, monetary influences. Is that true? What about the media that obsesses about food and, in the past at least, romanticized cigarette smoking? Can a monetary incentive to diet (or to quit smoking) counter these pressures? The question of social virtue has been examined quite extensively in the social capital literature (Putnam 1993; Woolcock and Narayan 2003). One interesting conclusion of this literature is that social virtue is often path dependent, in that strong virtues today are the basis for strong virtues in the future.

4. The UNDP estimates that in 2015 there were already 7.1 billion mobile subscriptions (UNDP 2015, pp. 80–81).
5. There are many other interesting indicators of financialization. For instance, Ferguson argues that business schools are growing as more undergraduates anticipate getting a job in a bank: in 1970, 5% of graduates went into finances, whereas this increased to 15% by 1990, and 20 of male graduates in 2007 expected their first jobs to be in banks (Ferguson 2008, p. 5).
6. A related question is, what can be used as money? It is commonly argued that money is whatever people believe it is (Siklos 2004, p. 15; Ferguson 2008, p. 27). But money has traditionally taken the form of coins, paper, and more recently, electronic form in credit and debit cards.
7. For instance, while India's textile sector was beginning to rebound, it produced cotton and exported it to Britain that used it to produce textiles that were in part exported to India. This period also witnessed initiatives—for instance, France's *Animation Rurale* in West Africa and Rabindranath Tagore's Sriniketan—on the part of the colonial state and civil society directly targeting social improvement, and so this period included the roots of development efforts that became ubiquitous in the post-colonial period.

8. For instance, an early debate played a "balanced" approach to economic development that sought to grow a wide range of sectors to an "unbalanced" approach that identified leading sectors that dynamically pull the entire economy forward.
9. In its formative years in the post-colonial period, starting in the post–World War II period, the study of development was deeply influenced by economic theory. Sociology made substantial contributions during this time, but these were less policy related. Anthropology's contribution has more recently been critiqued for its focus on understanding diverse local people for the purpose of drawing them into and being controlled by the colonial and then the modern state system. Both economic theory generally and the subdiscipline of development economics were quite different from economic theory today. The discipline was more diverse, and much economic thinking theorized a much larger role for the state in the economy. The neoclassical school in economics was evident but not as dominant as it is today. It co-existed with Keynesian economics, and Keynesian economics dominated macroeconomics. The neoclassical school co-existed with even more interventionist economic theories such as Marxist theory. While Marxist theory was not considered a part of the canon or economic orthodoxy it certainly influenced economic thought at the time. Development economics, as compared to economic theory, was even broader in its approach in that it encompassed neoclassical economics and spanned Marxist and dependency theories of economic development and underdevelopment. While theoretically diverse compared to development economic thinking today, the role of finances were, as in general economic theory, not central.
10. For instance, in a popular textbook of the period written by Canadian Benjamin Higgins (1968, 1959), *Economic Development*, there are no chapters or subchapters on the topic and in fact "banking" and "finances" do not even appear in the index. The book spends about one-half of its volume on grand theories of economic development and another one-third on policies, with the remaining material on case studies.
11. This includes Marxists, who saw class conflict as the principal cause of poverty and its resolution through revolution as the principal means of development; dependency theorists, who saw North–South exploitation as the root of global poverty and disengaging from the North the ticket to Southern development; and liberal—as distinct from *neo*liberal—theorists, who saw the state the key actor in reforming the market for the common rather than private good.
12. One common foreign capital debate at this time dealt with examining the role and impact of multinational corporations (MNCs) on the Global South. Proponents noted the benefits associated with MNCs including capital and technology inflows, while opponents noted the limitations such as the lack of linkages into the broader economy.

Bibliography

Aitken, Rob. 2007. *Performing Capital.* 1st ed. New York: Palgrave Macmillan.

"The Economist Explains: Why China is Creating a New "World Bank" for Asia | The Economist". 2015. Accessed April 27, 2015. http://www.economist.com/blogs/economist-explains/2014/11/economist-explains-6

Bateman, Milford. 2010. *Why Doesn't Microfinance Work?: The Destructive Rise of Local Neoliberalism.* New York: Zed Books.

———. 2011. *Confronting Microfinance: Undermining Sustainable Development.* Sterling, VA: Kumarian Press.

———. 2015. South Africa's Post-Apartheid Microcredit Experiment: Moving from State-Enforced to Market-Enforced Exploitation. *Forum for Social Economics*: 1–29. http://dx.doi.org/10.1080/07360932.2015.1056202

Boyer, Robert. 2005. From Shareholder Value to CEO Power: The Paradox of the 1990s. *Competition and Change* 9 (1): 7–47. https://doi.org/10.1179/102452905X38623. http://www.ingentaconnect.com/content/maney/com/2005/00000009/00000001/art00002.

Buckland, Jerry. 1996. The Distributional Impact of Income-Generation Programmes in Bangladesh. *Canadian Journal of Development Studies* 17 (3): 385–404.

———. 2012. *Hard Choices: Financial Exclusion, Fringe Banks, and Poverty in Urban Canada.* Toronto: University of Toronto Press.

Caplovitz, David. 1967. *The Poor Pay More: Consumer Practices of Low-Income Families.* New York: The Free Press.

Epstein, Gerald A., ed. 2005. *Financialization and the World Economy.* Cheltenham, UK: Edward Elgar.

Ferguson, Niall. 2008. *The Ascent of Money: A Financial History of the World.* New York: Penguin.

Goulet, Denis. 1995. *Development Ethics.* 1st Publ. ed. New York: Apex Press.

Graeber, David. 2014. *Debt: The First 5,000 Years.* New York: Melville House Publishing.

Higgins, Benjamin. 1968 [1959]. *Economic Development: Principles, Problems, and Policies.* New York: WW Norton Inc.

Hudson, David. 2015. *Global Finance and Development.* 1st Publ. ed. London: Routledge.

Kelly, Sonja E., and Elisabeth Rhyne. 2015. *By the Numbers: Benchmarking Progress Toward Financial Inclusion.* Washington, DC: Center for Financial Inclusion.

Krippner, Greta R. 2005. The Financialization of the American Economy. *Socio-Economic Review* 3 (2): 173–208.

Kroll, Christian. 2015. Global Development and Happiness: How can Data on Subjective Well-being Inform Development Theory and Practice? *Oxford Development Studies* 43 (3, Sep.): 281–309.

Kus, Basak. 2012. Financialisation and Income Inequality in OECD Nations: 1995–2007. *Economic and Social Review* 43 (4, Winter): 477–495.

Lapavitsas, Costas. 2009. Financialised Capitalism: Crisis and Financial Expropriation. *Historical Materialism* 17 (2): 114–148. https://doi.org/10.1163/156920609X436153. http://booksandjournals.brillonline.com/content/journals/10.1163/156920609x436153.

———. 2013. *Profiting Without Producing: How Finance Exploits Us All*. London: Verso.

Lapavitsas, Costas, and Jeff Powell. 2013. Financialisation Varied: A Comparative Analysis of Advanced Economies. *Cambridge Journal of Regions, Economy and Society* 6 (3): 359–379.

Montgomerie, Johnna. 2006. The Financialization of the American Credit Card Industry. *Competition and Change* 10 (3): 301–319.

Nussbaum, Martha C. 2006. *Frontiers of Justice: Disability, Nationality, Species Membership*. Boston: Harvard University Press.

Parthasarathi, Prasannan. 1997. *Religion and Consumption*. United Nations Development Report.

Putnam, Robert. 1993. *Making Democracy Work: Civic Traditions in Modern Italy*. Princeton: Princeton University Press.

Roodman, David, and Jonathan Morduch. 2014. The Impact of Microcredit on the Poor in Bangladesh: Revisiting the Evidence. *Journal of Development Studies* 50 (4, Apr.): 583–604.

Roy, Ananya. 2010. *Poverty Capital*. 1st Publ. ed., 1st ed. New York: Routledge.

Sandel, Michael J. 2012. *What Money Can't Buy: The Moral Limits of Markets*. New York: Farrar, Straus and Giroux.

Sen, Amartya. 1999. *Development as Freedom*. New York: Alfred A. Knopf Inc.

Siklos, Pierre L. 2004. *Money, Banking, and Financial Institution: Canada and the Global Environment*. 4th ed. Toronto: McGraw-Hill Ryerson.

Soros, George. 2009. *The Crash of 2008 and What It Means: The New Paradigm for Financial Markets*. New York: Public Affairs.

Stockhammer, Engelbert. 2012. Financialization, Income Distribution and the Crisis. *Investigacion Economica* 71 (279, Jan.): 39–70.

United Nations Development Program. 1998. *Human Development Report 1998*. New York: UNDP.

———. 2015. *Human Development Report*. New York: UNDP.

Van Arnum, Bradford M., and Michele I. Naples. 2013. Financialization and Income Inequality in the United States, 1967–2010. *American Journal of Economics and Sociology* 72 (5, Nov.): 1158–1182.

van der Zwan, Natascha. 2014. Making Sense of Financialization. *Socio-Economic Review* 12 (1): 99–129.

Villasenor, John, and Darrell West. 2015. The 2015 Brookings Financial and Digital Inclusion Project Report. Brookings Institution Reports. https://search.proquest.com/docview/1787813332

Woolcock, Michael, and Deepa Narayan. 2003. Social Capital: Implications for Development Theory, Research and Policy. In *Elgar Reference Collection. Critical Studies in Economic Institutions*, ed. Elinor Ostrom and T.K. Ahn, vol. 2, 416–440. Cheltenham, UK and Northampton, MA: Elgar; Distributed by American International Distribution Corporation, Williston, VT.

World Bank. 2014. *Global Financial Development Report 2014: Financial Inclusion*. Washington, DC: International Bank for Reconstruction and Development.

Zelizer, Viviana A. 2011. *Economic Lives: How Culture Shapes the Economy*. Princeton: Princeton University Press.

CHAPTER 3

New Areas of Commercial Banking Directed at Vulnerable People: Payday Lending and Mobile Banking

The financial service firm and the consumer are on either side of the financial service relationship. These firms come in many forms; this chapter will examine informal financial providers, fringe banks, and mainstream banks. In addition, this chapter will examine some newer financial products that reflect "everyday" financialization, including payday lending and mobile banking.

Informal financial service providers include corner stores that cash checks, fringe banks such as payday lenders, and mainstream banks that offer mobile banking to poor people. Informal and fringe banks are largely focused on vulnerable people, while mainstream banks see these people as a marginal group with respect to their business model. Informal financial providers are declining in the Global North but are central financial providers in poor rural geographies of the Global South. In the Global North fringe banks, such as payday lenders, are growing in population coverage as the informal sector declines, raising a causation question, discussed below. As mainstream banks, states, and intergovernmental agencies dedicate more resources to promote financial inclusion, one consequence is the rise of mobile banking, particularly prominent in the Global South countries such as Kenya and Bangladesh.

In Canada, the United States and the United Kingdom, mainstream banks have cut back certain services and branches, while fringe banks, in particular payday lenders, have expanded their offerings. These fringe banks operate on the borders of regulation, focus on transactions services, and generally charge large fees that if they were put into an annual interest

J. Buckland, *Building Financial Resilience*,
https://doi.org/10.1007/978-3-319-72419-5_3

rate,[1] like annual percentage rate (APR),[2] would be very high. This chapter will examine fringe banks of the Global North in general and payday lenders in particular.

Meanwhile, in the Global South pawnshops are the fringe bank of note in certain locales, particularly in Asia. But for poor people it is informal financial services, in the form of moneylending or credit/savings circles, that often provide the bulk of their financial services. Microcredit has been a rising player in finance in much of the Global South, and this will be discussed in Chap. 4. Mainstream banks have not been big players in providing banking services for the poor until the rise of mobile banking. This chapter will also examine informal financial service providers and mainstream banks, with a focus on mobile banking.

Firm Motivation, Politics, and Ethical Considerations

Motives and Markets of Financial Institutions

Before looking at the financial services themselves, it is important to first examine the motives of the main suppliers of financial services. Motives vary across informal, fringe, and mainstream banks. Size is a factor as well. Generally speaking, businesses seek to maximize profit, revenue, and/or market share, depending on what type of market they operate within. If the market is perfectly competitive—a rare situation—then the goal of the business is to maximize its profit, but its ability to do so is limited by its co-competitors so that it is only able to obtain a "normal" profit level, which is a level that gives the owners a "reasonable" profit margin. Many, if not most markets, are not perfectly (sometimes called imperfectly) competitive, so that businesses may be able to influence the market in order to obtain higher than normal profits. Or their goal may be to maximize their market share.

Neoliberalism highlights the importance of the "market" as a means of allocating resources, limiting the role of the state to matters such as policing, national defense, and the maintenance of national parks.[3] Neoliberalism highlights the role of the market and downplays the role of the state in terms of economic planning and action. Neoliberalism advances its economic growth agenda through imperfectly competitive firms, associated with large corporations, partly because it is thought that they are more innovative. The evidence on this point is mixed, but the ambivalence of neoliberalism toward oligopolies is clear.

Informal financial providers form a broad category that includes a family member with liquid assets, the local moneylender, and the corner store. Their motives will obviously vary, but consistent across these types of actors is the combination of social and economic motives. Even the moneylender, if he wants to maintain his business, needs to maintain some level of social connection with his clients (Ferguson 2008, p. 4). Informal financial providers seem to face the market that is closest to perfect competition in that the creditor cannot influence the outcome of the market. The exception to this statement would be the large moneylender in a homogenously poor rural area in the Global South. In this case the market may approximate a monopoly.

The fringe banker's motives are more homogenous and are often stigmatized as exploitative. The strong blending of social and economic relations associated with informal banks is not found with this group, at least not to the same extent. This is because fringe bankers charge high fees and engage in other practices, like non-transparent fees, that are criticized. But these providers also face the high costs associated with administering a large number of small transactions. Some fringe bankers, such as small pawnshops, face a fairly competitive market. Meanwhile large multinational payday lenders, by controlling a large share of the market, may experience some market power.

But it is the mainstream banks that are the largest players operating in markets that are clearly not perfectly competitive. The markets they face, generally speaking, involve a few large banks controlling the lion's share of the financial assets. This is certainly the case in parts of the Global North. As a result of their immense resources and market influence, mainstream banks are more able to achieve their financial goals, be they profit, revenue, and/or market share. In fact, the size of mainstream banks creates an important phenomenon, "too big to fail". This phenomenon was powerfully demonstrated during the US subprime mortgage crisis, when the US government bailed out several banks that were about to collapse because, it was argued, their collapse would lead to the demise of both US and global economies. And because of this, the motive of a very large bank might be different than simple profit or sales maximization. With a certain level of protection, the bank might opt for behavior that is too risky for others, because it knows it will be bailed out. An important factor affecting mainstream banks' financial inclusion motives relates to corporate social responsibility or CSR. CSR is an approach taken by some banks and credit unions and involves businesses committing to the "double bottom line", so that they seek to achieve a reasonable financial return while addressing important social and/or environmental goals, such as financial inclusion.

Understanding the motivations of banks, in their various forms, is important when we consider that the "everyday financialization" is increasingly directed toward vulnerable people. Self-interested firms may not be concerned with vulnerability. If these firms have power, discussed below, then this is a recipe for a negative social outcome.

The Political Influence of Financial Institutions

The motives of FIs are largely economic, but they can use their political influence to improve their financial goals. Since the US subprime financial crisis and the government bailout of certain American banks and corporations, quite a lot has been written about the influence that US banks (Johnson and Kwak 2010; Casey 2012), Canadian banks (Livesey 2012) and banks in general exert on their respective governments (Coggan 2012).

Johnson and Kwak (2010) argue that the ten-year period preceding the subprime financial crisis was a period of growing influence of banks on US government. Surprisingly, the crisis did not lead to a diminishment of their influence but rather the reverse—bank influence continued to grow (p. 12). Using metaphors such as "deck-chair shuffling" and "fingers in leaky dams", they argue that President Obama's reforms were marginal in nature and "did little to address the problem at the heart of the financial system: the enormous growth of top-tier financial institutions and the corresponding increase in their economic and political power" (p. 191) An indication of this is that in 1983 the largest US bank, Citibank, held assets worth 3.2% of the US GDP. By 2007, nine banks, Citibank included, each held assets of greater value (than 3.2% of US GDP) (p. 10, p. 203).

In the late 1990s and early 2000s, US Federal Reserve head Alan Greenspan saw financial innovation combined with new information technologies (ITs) as a critical ingredient for a healthy and growing US economy (Johnson and Kwak 2010, p. 7). By 1998, financial sector innovation was considered inherently good for the US economy, and "it was a part of the worldview of the Washington elite that what was good for Wall Street was good for America" (p. 10). This coincidence of interests was related to the influence of Wall Street banks on politicians through intensive lobbying efforts and through the metaphorical revolving door between Wall Street banks and federal government political appointments (p. 11). It is estimated that in 2009 there were just over 1500 lobbyists representing the financial and corporate sectors; meanwhile 4% of these numbers represented consumer groups, unions, and other representatives advocating stronger regulations (Johnson and Kwak 2010, p. 192).

According to Johnson and Kwak, Wall Street banks are America's oligarchs, and they will continue innovating new and risky financial products like subprime mortgages, mortgage-backed securities, collateralized debt obligations, and credit default swaps. According to the World Bank, among others, these innovations can, deliberately or not, favor the banks by taking advantage of the bounded rationality of consumer.

Ethical Issues and Usury

Whenever money is a component of an issue, ethical concerns are not far away. And when money is mixed with poverty and banking, then it is almost certain to involve moral or justice concerns. Studies in the financialization of the everyday highlight this point. For instance, substituting credit for an income stream places a vulnerable person in a potentially more vulnerable position. So responses to this process have come from a variety or quarters.

Consider the long tradition in Western religions that seek to limit usury. The social science literature of the recent past is rich with critical assessments of moneylending and, today, with critiques of payday lending. Ethics plays a role in our response to finances for the poor because it tends to bring together powerless actors—poor people—and (relatively) powerful actors, creditors. Issues that have attracted ethical critique include high interest rates, repeated borrowing (i.e., the debt cycle), unfair disclosure of fees and conditions, and ineffective government regulation. These ethical concerns are often situated within broader concerns around socio-economic division and structural injustice. Much of the ethical critique comes from the literature on fringe banks in the Global North and literature on moneylenders in the Global South.[4]

Usury is the term applied to loan interest rates that are seen to be excessively high and therefore unethical. There is a long history within Western religions and, more recently, within social sciences to ethically critique certain types of lending on the basis of the interest charged. Religious-based critics of usury include early Jewish society, medieval Christian-influenced Europe, and Sharia law-following Muslim countries today. In these contexts, high interest charged on loans was often judged to be unethical. The ethical critique addressed different issues, including fostering unequal relations and perpetuating poverty. For instance, in some cases it was the fact that poor people were borrowing to meet their basic needs from non-poor, who were benefiting well beyond their basic needs. Since traditional moneylenders charge such high interest, from 100% and up, it's not surprising that the relationship attracted ethical critique.

Contemporary critiques of creditors include reference to interest rates and to other factors as well. For instance, Global North fringe banks are often criticized for unfair disclosure, for manipulatively presenting data on their fees and conditions. Fringe banks will often present their fees as several different ones and sometimes mix them up in terms of absolute dollar amount and percentage of the dollar amount, making it very difficult for consumers to understand the full cost they face for a loan. The conditions for a loan might be presented in a contract that is difficult to understand.[5] Of course, this is an approach that many retailers are inclined toward; however, it is exacerbated if government regulation is lacking. And this is certainly the case in many countries with regard to fringe bank products.

Mayer (2003) provides a comprehensive analysis of ethical issues of consumer finance. He defines exploitation as taking "unfair advantage" of someone, and the outcome can be deepening inequality. But, he argues, it is a complicated moral concept as compared with murder or theft, because there is an element of mutual benefit in that even though the exploiter gains much, the exploited person also gains from the relationship but less so (Mayer 2003, p. 199). The ethical problem is the distribution of the gains and the growing inequality that results.

Mayer describes four types of exploitation: neoclassical economic, neo-Marxian, sufficiency, and relative advantage. Neoclassical economic exploitation occurs when the borrower pays an interest rate for a loan that is not the result of competitive forces but determined by a firm or firms that are controlling the market and affecting the interest rate (p. 201). Market control is the result of the lender being a monopolist, oligopolist, or having some type of market power. Conversely, exploitation will not occur if markets are "perfectly competitive", which means that no buyer or seller has market power and that prices are set by a competitive process, not by one actor. So, for instance, in a perfectly competitive market, when a creditor raises the interest rate being charged on her loans, borrowers will move to another creditor offering lower interest rates. This will lead the high interest creditor to lose money, go out of business, or reduce her interest rates in order to win back her clients. In a monopolistic market there is only one creditor and, according to neoclassical economic theory, he/she will restrict the supply of credit which will automatically increase the interest rate, maximizing the creditor's profit. Here the borrower has no alternatives other than to borrow from the one creditor. It may seem that fringe banks fall into the category of neoclassical exploiters, but because it is relatively difficult to obtain data on profit rates of fringe banks, it is often difficult to test whether fringe banks are earning excess profits. Moreover, even if they were earning high profits, they might absorb much of these profits in poor management, what economists call X-inefficiency.

Neo-Marxian exploitation has to do with the disadvantage certain classes have relative to other classes, even within competitive capitalism (p. 201). The existence of a monopoly is unnecessary to achieve exploitation from the neo-Marxist perspective, because exploitation is rooted in the class system that undergirds capitalism. The working class is disadvantaged in comparison to the capitalist class and taken advantage of in various ways. For instance, in the labor market, technological change disadvantages workers as compared with capitalists by making them more redundant, lowering (the growth rate) of wages as compared with profit.

But to understand contemporary fringe bank lending, Mayer points to two more nuanced forms of exploitation he refers to as sufficiency and relative advantage exploitation. Sufficiency exploitation is the common basis for criticizing payday lending in Canada and the United States. This happens when the borrower is absolutely materially disadvantaged and takes out a loan in order to meet his basic needs. By being able to pay a car repair bill to facilitate getting to work, for instance, the borrower may benefit from the loan. But there is still exploitation according to this ethical principle, having to do with the asymmetry in the demand for the payday loan, which is based on the borrower's insufficiency and limited options. Generally speaking, wealthy people will not use a payday loan because they have other, lower-cost options, and when they borrow money it is not for essentials, but instead it is for conspicuous consumption. Payday loans are largely used by people with low and modest incomes:

> Exploitable parties, however, are not always exploited when they decide to take their best option and exchange. If they gain as much or pay as little as

> someone who does not begin with the initial disadvantage, the exploitable party has not been exploited. In sufficiency theory the counterfactual benchmark is an agent with enough of the relevant currency ... We ask what terms those who do possess enough would find acceptable. If the latter would not reasonably consent to the exploitable party's best offer, that offer is held to be exploitative—its mutual advantageousness notwithstanding. The exploitable agent stands to gain too little or pay too much. Hence the exploiter will gain at her expense. (Mayer 2003, p. 204)

Mayer's relative disadvantage principle is linked to the debt cycle, not the interest rate. This principle is based on the idea that while engaging in one loan may not involve exploitation, payday loan clients often find themselves being unable to pay off the loan and so have to take out another loan to pay off the first. This is called a new loan, but there are also repeat loans, rollovers, and no doubt other variations that involve people borrowing multiple loans within a short period. The term relative disadvantage comes from the fact that while one loan was an advantage to the borrower, the repayment period made paying off the loan unlikely and thus necessary for the borrower to get another loan, and so on. Each additional loan involves additional fees that make the loan relatively disadvantageous rather than relatively advantageous.

Another ethical issue, related to Mayer's neoclassical economic exploitation, is tied to the question of whether banks manipulate clients in order to pursue their profit goals at the expense of their clients' personal financial goals. This is an important question, and there are a number of points to consider. Manipulation means that there is an element of exploitation of the other, which causes her/him harm. Let's consider some different examples.

As was discussed in Chap. 2, when comparing mainstream and fringe banks in the Global North, the latter tend to offer more relevant services to vulnerable clients, in more convenient locations, by staff trained to assist them. Is this manipulative on the part of mainstream banks to do poorly in these areas, as compared with fringe banks? Or is the mainstream bank simply pursuing its self-interest? Consider the payday lender that tends to either not disclose or poorly disclose critical information about the product, such as its interest rate. Is this manipulation or justifiable self-interested behavior? Payday lenders resist presenting their fees in the form of an annual percentage rate because, they claim, it is not a one-year loan, it is a two-week loan. They prefer the fee to be presented in the form of $X per $100 loaned. However, for many consumers this fee presentation gets confused with an annual interest rate. Some people assume that $X means X%, which it doesn't—far from it. One study found when prospective clients were told how much a payday loan would cost and how much an equivalent loan from a credit card would cost, payday loan uptake was reduced by 11% (Bertrand and Morse 2011). Simple and comparative information led to more consumers choosing to not take out an expensive credit product. Conversely, complicated and non-transparent information will not enable borrowers to protect their interests as well.

Another relevant study explored how presenting people different information and images affected credit choice (Bertrand et al. 2009). They found that choice was affected by unexpected things, like an image of an attractive person, leading to decisions that were not always rational. As consumer debt increases, according to another World Bank study, consumers become more conscious of interest rates, so creditors keep them low and raise other fees (p. 77). Moreover, financial institutions are more likely to target poor and less educated consumers with risky and costly products, for instance, with mortgages and credit card companies in the United States (p. 77):

> Research has shown that consumers are frequently ignorant about many of the features of products they use; they do not always make good decisions; *and credit providers often exploit the tendency for consumers to make mistakes.* In particular, consumer biases such as the exponential growth bias and cognitive limitations such as the lack of financial literacy lead to inefficient consumer credit market outcomes and overindebtedness [italics added]. (World Bank 2014, p. 75)

These are some common ethical critiques of poverty finance. There are counter-critiques as well.[6] The critiques point out that when credit and poverty are mixed, there is the potential for many ethical issues. Taking a loan is a risky activity because it requires repayment that requires drawing down accumulated assets or a constant income stream and steady spending. But vulnerable people have few assets and their income and spending streams can vary, placing them into a risky situation.

Information Technologies and Banking

Information technologies have and continue to profoundly change banking. The automation of credit scoring, the rise of shadow banking, the emergence of crowdfunding microloans, and the rise of alternative currencies are contemporary examples of IT-shaped finances and financial services. Some of these have direct consequences for poor people while others not so, and with all new products there are strengths and weaknesses, winners and losers.

It is very apparent today that information and communications technologies continue to rapidly change, evidenced by the ubiquitous nature of computers and cellphones, the proliferation of services on the web including banking services. It was not imagined ten years ago that most Kenyans would transfer money through a cellphone, and it is hard to imagine how ICTs will change banking in another ten years. The UNDP describes technological change as "mindboggling" if we consider the devices people purchase: it took Apple just two years to sell 67 million iPads as compared with 24 years to sell as many Mac computers, five years to sell that many iPods, and just over three years to sell that many iPhones (UNDP 2015, p. 82).

The automation of credit scoring, beginning in the 1970s, has had a major consequence for credit access for people in Canada and the United States.[7] Credit scoring automation partly explains the rise of credit card holding in these countries. Automated credit scoring means that no human relationship between creditor and borrower is required. While this has assisted the extension of credit to millions of people, it creates barriers for others. The barriers are the result of the simultaneous shift, by mainstream banks, away from small loans and toward credit cards. While automated credit scoring enables more people to access a credit card, the "catch-22" is that those without a credit report or a damaged credit score cannot be automatically assessed and thus cannot get a credit card. And without small loans and special consideration based on an interpersonal relationship between banker and consumer, the barrier can be substantial. Moreover, unlike a regular loan that involves disbursement and installment repayment, credit cards and lines are open sources of credit and are not aligned with all credit needs. In some cases people prefer the discipline associated with an installment repayment system.

Today there is a proliferation of automation in banking that includes the above-mentioned technologies: automated credit checking, ATMs, Internet banking, mobile banking, and electronic systems to transfer money internationally (remittances[8]).

Information technologies are also important factors behind the growth of the "shadow" banking sector. This refers to "a new network of banks, rating agencies and non-bank actors such as hedge funds or money market mutual funds that are linked through practices of securitization" (Kessler and Wilhelm 2013, p. 249). These shadow banks offer many of the same services associated with traditional banks but without public oversight. It is estimated that in the United States, this sector was worth US$22 trillion in 2012, US$8 trillion more than the "traditional" banking sector (Kessler and Wilhelm 2013, p. 249).

New digital alternative currencies are another example of IT-shaped finances. There are a variety of alternatives to official currencies. Digital currencies are not the first alternative currencies and are small in comparison to official currencies, but some of them are growing. While they are often presented as more "community-oriented", it is not clear, particularly for the higher-tech versions, that they are. Moreover, their connection to the lives of vulnerable people is not strong.

The impetus for alternatives to state currency may come from the perception that the state-based currencies are manipulated by state interests and the proponents of alternatives want greater "community" control. Or the impetus may come from new technologies that facilitate their creation. Official currencies are controlled by state agencies, generally a central bank. The central bank is often at arm's length from the government and is responsible to ensure that short- to long-term monetary and economic goals are achieved. For instance, central banks use monetary instruments (i.e., controlling the money supply or changing the official interest rate) to achieve targets related to inflation, unemployment, and economic growth. State monetary authorities have been criticized over the years for a variety of reasons by sources found across the political spectrum. In the 1980s Western monetary authorities were critiqued by conservatives such as Milton Friedman and Robert Lucas for trying to "fool" people about a short-run relationship between inflation and unemployment. More recently, critics have argued that the bailout of large US banks that were "too big to fail" (because their failure would lead to an even more dramatic economic decline) was a welfare program for elite capitalist corporations.

Traditional versions of alternative currencies include the local economic trading systems (LETS). These establish a local system of accounts for people to trade within. These systems are a popular means to foster community economic development in that they encourage internal trade and exchange. A plumber offers plumbing services, and a teacher offers tutoring services. They do not need a convergence of interests—that is, she needs tutoring and he needs plumbing—to benefit from a LETS. This is because when she offers plumbing within the system and he offers tutoring, it is marked down on the LETS ledger, and this allows them to draw on other goods and services within the system. A challenge with the LETS system, call it the limitation of the local, is that it is restricted by the mutually beneficial trades that can take place among a group of local people. This is a serious limitation, particularly for people in the Global North, who consume goods and services from around the world.

The digital alternative currencies do not suffer from this limitation of the local but face other shortcomings. Some examples of digital alternative currencies include Bitcoin, Apple Pay, Paypal, Google Wallet, and other "alternative coins" spawned by Bitcoin and related to the underlying technology called Blockchain (see Chandran 2015; Chowdhry 2015).

Bitcoin, created in 2009, is the name of both the system and the monetary unit. There are over 13.4 million bitcoins in circulation that have a market value of US$4.6 billion. Today thousands of businesses accept bitcoin for payment (Yelowitz and Wilson 2015). While state-based currencies are controlled by the central bank, Bitcoin is different. It uses peer-to-peer technology and is built on a general program called Blockchain. The total supply is being created over time but is limited to 21 million coins (Weber 2016). The coins can be used to buy and sell items, but they are "created" through a process referred to as "mining". The mining process controls the supply of bitcoins. Coins are regularly released, but to obtain them people must devote computer capacity to solve cryptographic puzzles (or codes) that the system generates. These puzzles are generated when the coin is used in a trade:

> Successful solutions print a time stamp on the transaction, which serves as proof that the transaction is based on a unique "coin" not having been spent by the same user before. The proof is added to a public ledger that contains every transaction in the network, thereby keeping track of all transactions to avoid double spending but without releasing the identity of transaction partners. The updated public ledger is then checked by all other computers in the mining network for correctness of the solution of the underlying puzzle related to each bundle of transactions. If confirmed by the community, the updated version of the public ledger is copied by all network members and serves as a decentralised form of keeping account of the history of all transactions in the network. (Weber 2016, p. 19)

Bitcoin claims that its currency is community-based, free, and open sourced (Weber 2016). However, these claims may be exaggerated.

Certainly, the impact on communities of vulnerable people is limited. Participation in Bitcoin requires, at minimum, a computer and Internet connection that much of the world's poor do not have. Moreover, the Bitcoin system is a complicated enough idea that many people might shy away from it. Weber argues that Bitcoin, rather than promoting community trust, may actually erode it:

> Bitcoin evokes community while aiming at the elimination of the central asset of community governance, trust. In addition, the need for trust is in fact not eliminated, but shifted to different terrains than in established systems (e.g. need to trust in personal technological infrastructure and/or third party providers for wallet services, currency exchange etc.), making users vulnerable to trust abuse which might strike back on the system's legitimacy. (Weber 2016, p. 37)

Financial Institutions That Offer Services to Poor People

Depending on the context, informal finances might be the norm for vulnerable people. This is the case for poor regions in the Global South, where there are few formal institutions that work with the poor. But, through "everyday" financialization, this is changing in many communities and countries of the Global South like Kenya, as mainstream banks and phone companies partner to make mobile banking more accessible. In other cases fringe banks might be heavily relied on by vulnerable people, for instance, in inner cities in Canada and the United States. In some places mainstream banks provide universal coverage and are the go-to institutions for vulnerable people. This is more likely the case in select Northern European nations, where rates of financial inclusion are very high.

Vulnerable people may depend on one type or provider—informal, fringe, or mainstream—or they may simultaneously rely on a mixture of more than one type of provider, or they may shift their reliance over time. In the Global South many people also use microcredit products offered by microfinancial institutions (discussed in Chap. 5). In the Global North, vulnerable people often use services from all providers, simultaneously or sequentially.[9] For instance, sometimes people have a bank account when they are employed, and then, when they lose their job and have to depend on the social welfare system, they rely on fringe banks to cash their check. This is changing in Canada, as the government moves to using direct deposit as a means of entitlement payments. In other instances, people have a bank account and use fringe banks for services such as payday lending and bill payments. And relying on a family member or friend for a small loan or grant is quite common.

It is hypothesized that as everyday financialization proceeds, the informal sources of finance, as a share of the total amount of finance, will decline (Fig. 3.1). It is assumed in this figure that, generally speaking, in moving from left to right, per capita income is rising. During this process it is further hypothesized that the share of finances delivered by fringe and mainstream sources expands. Growth in income and finances are associated with an even faster growth in fringe and mainstream bank products and a decline in demand for informal finance products. More and more people are relying on payday loans or mainstream bank products and, at least as a share of all of their finances, relying less on informal finances.

Informal financial service providers range from family members and friends through moneylenders, credit/savings circles, and small transactions services run by a small store, like cashing a check (Table 3.1). The clientele of these providers are primarily poor people. The general features of these services—perhaps with the exception of moneylending—are that

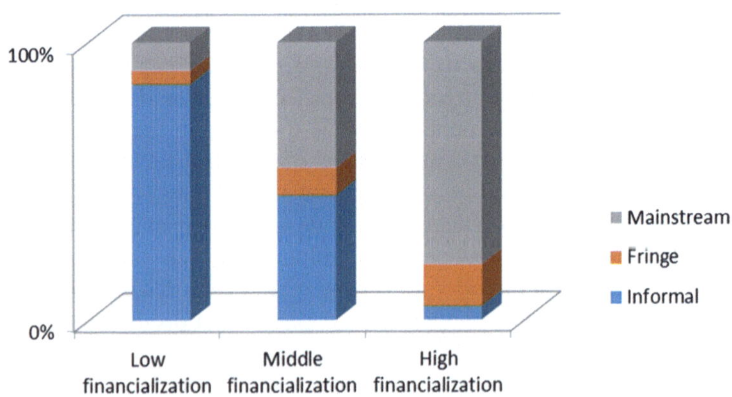

Fig. 3.1 Hypothetical personal banking transition in community or country as financialization increases, as a share of personal financial services

Table 3.1 Examples and features of types of banks typically used by vulnerable people

Type	*Examples*	*General features*
Informal	Traditional moneylenders Traditional social finance: ROSCA, ASCRA Small retailer financial services: check cashing, running a tab	• Poor people as clientele • Very small amounts • Shorter duration • Personal, sometimes "fictive" relationship-based • Are small retailers: provide financial services to support their core business
Fringe	Small loans: title loans, auto loans, payday loans, pawn loans/buy-back schemes, rent-to-own Transaction services: check cashing, money wiring, bill payment, secured credit cards Miscellaneous: tax refund advances, gold purchase	• Primarily poor people as clientele • Small amounts • Shorter duration • Commercial relationships but at times consumer-oriented • Core business
Mainstream	Secured credit cards, subprime mortgages, Islamic banking, retail store banking, mobile banking	• Non-poor people as clientele • Larger $ amounts • Longer durations • Commercial relationships but, at times, consumer-oriented • Core business

the amounts of money are very small, the duration of the service is short, and the relationship with the provider has a social feature, although in the case of moneylenders it is sometimes referred to as a "fictive" friendship, in the sense that the person presents himself/herself as a friend when in fact he/she is not. Again, with the exception of moneylenders, most informal financial service providers see financial services as a side business to support their main business.

Fringe banks are more formalized than informal financial service providers, and financial services are the core part of their business. Their clientele are primarily poor people, but some elements of their business, such as payday loans, may also be used by modest non-poor people. Fringe banks deal in small amounts of money for short durations but possibly larger volumes and durations compared to informal providers. There is not the same social rootedness of the relationship between consumer and operator, but—and this is important—often the fringe bank presents itself as a "friend" to the unbanked. For examples, look at the signs in your local payday lender, or check out their annual report (e.g., DFC Global 2014).

To a poor person, a mainstream bank may appear to be like just another financial service provider, along with fringe and informal providers. But in fact, mainstream banks are very different and are really the only "bank" in this categorization scheme, because they are the only ones that can accept deposits, a basic feature of a bank. Fringe and informal providers cannot do this, and so they must access their capital in another way, for example, borrowing it or accumulating it. Mainstream banks often offer consumer and commercial financial services, but their consumer services are principally focused on middle- and upper-income clients. Furthermore, financial services are their core or only services, and banks are generally most interested in their high-value products such as mortgages, investments, and large loans. They are less interested in small loans and in fact often do not provide them but instead offer credit cards and lines. Bank services of particular relevance to poor people are the simple deposit account, the debit card, the secured or not-secured credit card, and bill payments.

Generally speaking, any adult can open a bank account. But in fact certain people find themselves excluded from the mainstream bank's orbit for various reasons, some of which were discussed in Chap. 2. This includes accessibility, types of services offered, and training of staff. One reason for exclusion has to do with bank location strategies and the phenomenon called "redlining" (Now disallowed in the United States but in the past insurance companies, on their work area maps, physically drew red lines across low-income neighborhoods in which they would not work). An important contextual change that has occurred in several countries in the Global North, in particular the United Kingdom, the United States, and Canada, is the "consolidation" of mainstream bank networks. Consolidation involves reducing the number of physical branches, often justified because of the growing number of alternative means to access bank services, through ATMs, telephones, the Internet, or mobile phone apps. Consolidation may also involve establishing certain larger hub branches with full services and smaller spoke branches with a subset of services. This process began in Canada in the 1980s and continues today. An important side effect of this process is that marginally profitable branches are closed, and those clients are asked to move to another branch. Extensive data has demonstrated that low-income neighborhoods, often located in American and Canadian inner cities, have fared badly by this process, as it has reduced the number of branches in those neighborhoods, while the number of fringe bank outlets has often grown in these same sites (Caskey 1994; Graves 2003; Leyshon et al. 2008; Brennan et al. 2011; Simpson and Buckland 2016).

Financial services are offered through various channels: branches/outlets, automatic teller machines (ATMs), the (land-line) telephone, the Internet, and the mobile phone. The Internet and mobile phone are the newest ways to deliver financial services. No doubt services will be offered through other channels in the future. The advantage of the mobile phone is that the phone is cheap and the needed infrastructure is limited. The disadvantage is that, especially for a basic "non-smart" unit, the phone's ability to build trust and instruct is negligible. On the other end of the spectrum, the ability of a teller in a bank, with proper training, to build trust and instruct a client can be quite high. The problem is that there is an inverse relationship between bank costs and this ability to build trust and instruct. This means that banks want to move clients down the continuum into electronically based services, but clients, at least for some of their services, desire the high-contact services that are expensive for the banks to provide. The implications are that the banks are reluctant to provide labor-intensive "high-touch" services for poor people and would rather rely on digital-based services. This can act as a barrier to financial inclusion.

Some mainstream financial institutions do make particular efforts to remove barriers to poor people using their services. In some cases, mainstream financial institutions do this to meet government regulations (e.g., the US Community Reinvestment Act or the Canadian Access to Basic Banking Regulations), but in other cases it is more internally motivated. For instance, some banks' corporate social responsibility embraces financial inclusion, and/or some banks recognize the medium-term financial benefits associated with encompassing un- and under-banked clients. Eventually some of these clients will find their incomes and assets rising and invest in more lucrative (for the bank) financial products. In Canada and the United States, the credit union system has been quite active in addressing financial inclusion efforts. This becomes clear when one looks at the number of financial inclusion projects they have compared with the big banks, whose financial assets are much larger. Consider the case of Canada:

- Two credit unions—Vancity and First Calgary Financial—and the Desjardins Federation (the credit union system in the province of Québec) are responsible for the only three small-sum short-term loan products that are intended as an alternative to payday loans. No mainstream bank in Canada has developed a payday loan alternative product.
- Credit unions in Canada are also responsible for several special bank branches, including Assiniboine Credit Union's West End and North End mini-branches, and Vancity's (with the Portland Hotel Society) Pigeon Park Savings in Vancouver's Downtown Eastside. Vancouver's Downtown Eastside and Winnipeg's North End are two of the poorest neighborhoods in Canada. Credit union activity in this field compares favorably to only one special project offered by a big bank, RBC's Cash and Save in Parkdale neighborhood, Toronto, a gentrifying community.

Early Roots of Fringe Banks: Pawnshops and Check Cashers

Pawnshops provide small consumer loans that are secured on the pawned good, generally a household item. Pawnshops have ancient roots, as there is reference to making loans based on the commitment of personal property in the Old Testament of the Bible, but they likely first developed in a formal sense in China (Caskey 1994, p. 13). As is so common with credit systems, there has been a strong critique of pawnshops, first from the church and then from secular groups.

In the late Middle Ages in Europe, concerns around usury led to the development of the mont-de-piété, translated as "banks that take pity". Caskey notes that these efforts were spearheaded by the Franciscan order of the Roman Catholic Church, and others, including the church more generally, along with municipal governments and other charitable organizations. As secularization in Europe grew, municipal governments often took over pawnshops from the church. Dawson notes the coexistence of for-profit and not-for-profit pawnshops in Munich, Germany, in the early twentieth century and comments on the benefit of this mixed system:

> [T]he existence of the municipal institutions [not-for-profit pawnshop] is held to have decidedly raised their [for-profit shops'] level, while the police also exercise a more careful supervision than might be the case were there

> no official rivalry. Even so, the municipal pawnshops are far more popular than the private ones, and the reasons given to me were that they enjoy greater confidence, are regarded as more respectable, while those who use them are assured of receiving more generous treatment, alike in the advances made and the interest charged, than could be relied upon in the ordinary pawnshop. (Dawson 1913, p. 251)

Caskey notes that as compared with Europe's public pawnshop tradition, private and for-profit pawnshops were the norm in Britain, but were regulated by the state. Pawnbroking began in the United States before its independence and followed the British model of regulated profit-oriented businesses. Pawnshops grew in number through the end of the nineteenth century, so that they were common in most cities in the United States (Caskey 1994, p. 16). Early critics of pawnshops in the United States denounced them as exploitative, and regulations included monitoring items for stolen property, capping interest charges, and limiting the amount loaned on items. Caskey notes that concerns about pawnshops also led some "civic-minded citizens" to establish philanthropic pawnshops. Their interest rates were lower than the rates of for-profit shops, and if items were sold, surplus income was returned to the patron. The Provident Loan Society of New York is one of the earliest such efforts and continues to operate today.

In Europe today, pawnbrokers are found in the United Kingdom, Germany, Norway, France, Ireland, Austria, Holland, and Belgium (Buckland 2009). In the case of Belgium, the mont-de-piété is the only legal provider of pawn loans and provides approximately 120,000 loans per year. France also has a system of public pawnshops that dates back to the seventeenth century, and these have a social mission. Pawnshops are common in urban centers in Canada and the United States.

Pawning has a long history in China and Southeast Asia. For instance, pawnbroking in Singapore is a growing sector, and the recent move by the government to enter the market is an example of this (Chan and Owyong 2010). The number of pawnshops grew through the Asian financial crisis (1997–1998) and continued through the 2000s, rising from 66 in 1998 to 91 in 2004, while the number of loans rose from around 2 million in 1975 to around 2.9 million in 2003 (Chan and Owyong 2010, pp. 85–87). Pawnshops were banned in China during the communist period but have now returned as a part of what is termed the "shadow banking industry", estimated to be valued at US$4.4 trillion (Pawnshops China 2014). Their growth is seen as a means to support small and medium enterprises to alleviate the recent credit constraints, so they are not necessarily targeting poor consumers. Caskey notes pawnshop traditions in Thailand, Sri Lanka, and the Philippines. Pawnshops are also found in Hong Kong, Singapore, Malaysia, and Vietnam, but, some of this pawn market is targeting the credit-constrained middle class, not poor consumers (Danubrata and Jittapong 2013). Money Max, a Singapore-based pawnshop that asserts itself as "[s]pearheading the modernisation of pawnbroking in Singapore", claims to be the largest chain in the region, with 45 outlets, and offers an electronic appraisal service that begins when the client sends them a photo of the prospective item by cellphone (Money Max 2015).

There is a complex relationship between pawning and Islam. For instance, in Malaysia pawning is offered by non-Muslims. Sulaiman et al. (2014) argue that the standard pawn model is inconsistent with Islam but that are ways to organize pawning to meet Muslim requirements. Pawning was first introduced into Malaya in the fifteenth century by Chinese traders, and even today many pawnshops are run by ethnic Chinese Malaysians, generally not Muslim (p. 58). By the early 1990s there was recognition of the problems for borrowers associated with pawnshops, so that an alternative model was developed that was consistent with Muslim beliefs, the Ar-Rahnu model, first established in Malaysia in 1992. It operates in a similar fashion to the European municipal pawn loan in the sense that fees are minimized, and if the item is not redeemed and its sale exceeds the value of the loan plus fees, the excess is given to the customer. Unlike the European pawn loan, there is no interest charged in the Ar-Rahnu system; however, there is a safe-keeping fee (p. 59).

Pawnshops are surprisingly resilient. Relying on a relatively simple and resilient business model, pawnshops have a long tradition, existed around the world, and continue to find new spaces to operate. The simplicity of the pawn loan helps to explain its long life. The pawnbroker provides a loan to a client secured on that person's household item that is left with the pawnbroker. If the client does not repay the loan, the broker owns and has the right to sell the pawned item. There is no need for any kind of "social collateral", as the risk is addressed by the broker holding the item. Pawn loans have been criticized on some of the ethical grounds discussed above, and religious and value-based alternatives have arisen over time in response.

Check cashing is a service that dates back to the early twentieth century in parts of the Global North. It has been a critical service for many low-income people in the Global North through the latter half of the twentieth century as payroll systems moved from cash to checks. But since the 1970s, automation has led to a decline in the use of checks. Caskey notes that check cashers' rise was related to their realization that they could unbundle the check cashing and savings bundle that mainstream financial institutions offer (Caskey 1994, p. 54). Mainstream financial institutions offer check-cashing services to their customers with savings, so that cashing a check leads to immediate cash, even though technically it is the customer's savings that are financing the cash as the check is "held" for a period of time while it is "cleared". Check cashers separate out the check cashing and are able to operate in this fashion by charging a relatively hefty fee.

The check-cashing transactions at check cashers have been declining, as checks become less common with the rise of direct deposits into one's bank account, payroll loaded onto debit cards, and as hold periods at mainstream financial institutions have declined. For instance, National Money Mart Inc.'s contribution to its parent's revenue from check cashing held steady at around 14.5% from 2006 to 2008, but the contribution of payday lending rose during this same period from 19.5% to 25.7% (Buckland 2012, p. 39). Revenue from check cashing declined from US$164 to US$128, as compared with the growing revenue from payday lending from US$266 million to US$728 million for each year from 2009 to 2013 (DFC Global Corp. 2013, p. 39).

Informal Financial Services

Informal financial service providers are a complicated assortment of retailers, traders, middle persons, friends, and family members.[10] One common thread that weaves across these actors is that they offer some type of financial service, and with the possible exception of the loan shark, they do not provide the financial service as a core part of their business. The financial service is offered as a way of promoting or enabling other business or social goals. Informal financial service providers are in fact the traditional creditor, as mainstream and fringe banks are relatively recent in origin. In fact, most sources find that the history of mainstream banks is fairly informal:

> In the past credit was the domain of moneylenders, pawnbrokers, commodity traders, shopkeepers, landlords, patrons, friends and family. Generally

> speaking, however, these traditional credit providers either had a very limited capacity to lend, or extracted a (proportionally speaking) very high price for their loans, or both. While rotating savings and credit associations were institutionally simple means for pooling the capital of small groups, and offered an alternative source of credit for certain purposes, they were inflexible in terms of the timing and size of the loans, and were not always reliable. (Goenka and Henley 2010, p. 1)

This section considers moneylenders (sometimes called loan sharks) and social finance. These types of informal finance are found in the Global South today, and some are found in the Global North. Another common source of informal transactions and loans in the Global North are corner stores, bars, friends, and relatives. There is little written on this topic, and so it will not be examined here.

Traditional Moneylenders and Loan Sharks

The terms moneylender and loan shark are sometimes used interchangeably and applied to a relatively large and informal lender. While the term "moneylending" is fairly innocuous, "loan shark" suggests something aggressive and exploitative. Indeed, this type of lending was disallowed in Europe in the Middle Ages under the influence of the Christian religion, because the practice was seen as unethical and exploitative.[11] The notion of the exploitative loan shark continued on in Europe through the Middle Ages and was captured in Shakespeare's character Shylock in *The Merchant of Venice* (Ferguson 2008, p. 38). The ethical issues were brought into particular focus when lending involved usury, a rich moneylender, a poor borrower, and a high interest rate loan.

Moneylending is an age-old business that is particularly prominent in a traditional agrarian economy. As a subsistence economy in which people rely on peak and slack seasons of work, investment, and returns, many who have limited assets will need credit. Often there a few people with many assets who need to lend. In some cultures and sometimes the activity was frowned upon but nevertheless took place. In the Indian subcontinent it is common for large farmers to act as moneylenders and loan to landless and near-landless laborers. In some cases these loans are needed by the small farmer to make it through to the harvest. Then he/she is required to sell his/her product the moment it is harvested and when prices are the lowest. This farmer faces the double disadvantage of a low market price and the immediate payment of principle and interest on his/her loan.

Informal moneylending is particularly common in places that lack mainstream banks but where productive activities like farming require access to capital. Moneylenders can be found in rural and poorer parts of Africa, Asia, and Latin America and generally charge 100 to 200% interest per year but can reach as high as 20% per day (Todaro and Smith 2015, p. 792). Examining finances and credit in several Global South countries, Collins et al. (2009) found that while rates are very high, they are not that high in practice because of the unique features of moneylending. They found that while the interest rate was stated to be 125% *per month* (yes, that's not a mistake—per month), it was not so in practice. In one scenario, they noted that the borrower was to make regular repayments on a loan of US$32. In fact, he/she did not make regular payments over 50 days. The payments were elongated over 330 days, but the same total amount was repaid, so that the actual interest rate was 19% *per year* (again, not a mistake) (Collins et al. 2009, p. 141).

While there is evidence of the existence of informal moneylenders in the Global South, there is not so much evidence for the existence of loan sharks in the Global North. Part of the challenge of documenting moneylending in the Global North is that there are usury laws that disallow it and possibly criminalize it. Fringe bankers that charge high interest argue that if they face regulation that is too restrictive, they will go out of business and low-income consumers will have to flock to illegal moneylenders and face higher interest rates and more harmful lending practices.

The controversy surrounding the illegal credit market is not so much about the existence of illegal moneylenders—there is evidence that it exists. For instance, Ferguson reported on the loan shark industry in the United Kingdom, which reportedly lends out £40 million/year, to 165,000 households, at an interest rate of 25% per week (2008, p. 38). The controversy relates to the idea that if fringe banks are more restrictively regulated, then the illegal money trade will dramatically expand to meet the gap in the supply. This is an important point to consider. If this type of substitution was easily possible, one would expect to see evidence of a fairly brisk illegal credit market where usury laws are restrictive, such as in continental Europe, some states in the United States, and Québec, Canada. But the evidence for this is limited, as will be discussed further below. Moreover, the substitutability argument rests on the idea that people will simply shift their credit demand from fringe banks to loan sharks. But there is enough stigma, which is probably partly deserved, that many people would not be interested. Moreover, the substitutability argument also relies on the idea that loan sharks are able to increase their access to capital to finance a growing consumer credit market. Finally, the argument rests on the idea that government regulation is ineffective—that even though their activity is illegal, the loan sharks will expand their lending portfolios and the state will be unable to control it.

An active player in the research into this area is Policis, a research organization based in London. In one of their studies they found that "loan sharks are used by circa 2% of low-income (lowest 50%) households, 5% of those on low incomes refused credit in the last 12 months and 10% of those on low incomes who have experiences serious financial distress" (Ellison et al. 2010, p. 12). They note that the incidence in use of moneylenders in Germany and France is two to three times higher than in the United Kingdom. It is not clear how the figures for Germany and France were estimated, but they (the rates of illegal money) are certainly debated by the German and French academics.

I am not aware of similar measurements of illegal moneylending in Canada and the United States. One interesting US study investigated how different payday lending regulations affected borrowing habits (The Pew Charitable Trusts 2012, p. 16). The study compared responses by consumers in states where payday lenders were outlawed, in states where payday lenders were regulated, and in states where there was no or virtually no regulation of payday lenders. If illegal moneylending was common, one would expect that in states where payday lending is outlawed that people would be more likely to access loan shark credit. The results of the study did not find people are more likely to resort to loan sharks, or internet lenders. Rather, the people cut back on their expenses, borrowed from friends and family, and pawned personal possessions.

Traditional Social Finance

Moneylenders and loan sharks are individuals, some linked to certain groups such as organized crime, who lend to other individuals for the purpose of generating a profit. They are one response to meeting demand for small-scale credit. But there have also been collective approaches to credit, through credit and savings societies. The ROSCA—rotating savings and credit society—is quite common in the Global South but rarely found in wealthy parts of the Global North. It involves a group- or community-based system whereby members make regular payments into a pot that is distributed to members in turn. In this way people make a series of small payments to generate one large payment. An ASCRA—accumulating savings and credit association—is a similar style of collective action that involves group savings and lending, for instance, a burial society. This is a group- and community-based system that accumulates savings from members in order to provide them with loans during a time of need. In the case of a burial society, the time of need is the death of a loved one. Larger versions of burial societies are found in the Global North, for instance, through cooperative burial societies. Since these systems are designed by the community, their terms do better at aligning, as compared with the moneylender or loan shark, the interests of the borrower with the interests of the lender.

Each of these systems has strengths and weaknesses. The strength of these systems is that they are rooted in community need and interest. The weakness of both is that the capital is limited to what is internally generated. Generally speaking they do not access external capital. A further weakness of the ROSCA is the timing of receiving the pot: it may not coincide with the time that one needs it. With the ASCRA, one draws on the capital when one needs it.

Collins and colleagues, in their examination of financial diaries, found that ASCRAs played a critical role for South African participants in the burial and funeral process. The costs a poor South African family faces when a family member dies are substantial, because they include the burial of the body and the hosting of family members and friends around the funeral period. A household with a monthly income of US$155 to US$300 could face a funeral cost of US$1500, up to 81% of their annual income (Collins et al. 2009, p. 76). In order to deal with these high costs, many South Africans were involved in one or more of these schemes, and participation in the informal schemes was twice as common as the formal schemes. They found that the burial societies were competitive with formal insurance plans in financial terms and offered social benefits not associated with the formal ones (p. 79). Even with participating in several schemes, many respondents would still not be covered for the full cost of a funeral, and so they would be forced to find additional finances from other sources (e.g., family members, sales of personal items).

Traditional social finance is an important source of credit for borrowers in the Global South. It builds on local social capital, offers terms that are not exploitative, but has limited financial capital. Social finance is rooted in cooperative capacity, and, through successful implementation, it can build cooperative capacity. Financial inclusion efforts such as increasing mobile banking should be mindful to not undermine these collective efforts because of the positive social outcomes.

New Commercial Financial Services Directed at Low-Income People: Payday Lending and Mobile Banking

Fringe Banks and Payday Lending

Fringe financial service providers are a semi-formal category of financial service provider that have arisen in the last 20 years and continue to grow and change.[12] Fringe banks differ from informal banks in that their core business is consumer finances,[13] but they are similar to informal providers because, generally speaking, they target low-income people with their services. They are distinct from formal mainstream banks in that they do not accept deposits and are not formally recognized as financial institutions by government; rather, they are seen as service providers to consumers.

Fringe banks first formed as one-off or small-chain companies that offer one or a few financial services. For instance, check cashing was an important beginning for fringe banks in Canada and the United States. Later, some of these small firms realized the economies of scale and scope in expanding their outlets and into related services. Some pawnshops, particularly in the United States, have become large multi-outlet operations that offer several financial services. Evidence of the growth of the fringe bank sector includes the balance sheets of growing number of fringe bank corporations. Also, it is interesting to examine studies of the US inner-city retail economy from the 1960s to 1970s (Andreasen 1975; Caplovitz 1967). What is revealing is that in both of these studies, there is no mention of fringe financial services, and in fact the role of credit is not deeply examined. Arguably this is indicative of the weaker role that financial services played in the United States just 50 years ago.

The rise of corporate fringe banks is associated with three characteristics. First, they are no longer small-scale one-unit and one-service companies. Increasingly fringe banks are large corporations with many outlets across the country, offering a variety of services. This is particularly the case in the United States and Canada and also in Europe and increasingly in Asia. Second, these companies are increasingly integrating horizontally by adding new services that are linked with their core business—a payday lender or a second-hand store adds pawning to its service offerings. This horizontal integration allows the company to spread out its costs over a larger number of services, thus lowering its per-unit costs. Third, some fringe and mainstream banks have engaged in numerous partnerships in order to offer several types of products.[14]

In Canada and the United States, payday lenders are one of the largest types of fringe banks; others include pawnshops and finance companies. In Europe, payday lenders are found in some locales, for instance, in the United Kingdom and Eastern Europe, and there are other firms such as subprime lenders and pawnbrokers (Table 3.2).

Payday Loans and Lenders

The root of payday lending in the United States was the informal, early twentieth-century system of third-party lenders providing loans to workers and then receiving repayment by turning up at the plant on payday (Packman 2016). Generally speaking a payday loan is a small sum (e.g., \$500) for a short-term (e.g., two-week) loan. The loan is linked to the borrower's next paycheck. In a broad sense the borrower's paycheck provides a kind of collateral for the lender or at least evidence of the borrower's ability to repay the loan. Generally speaking the loan is paid off in full on payday and until recently, only rarely are there installment repayment options.

"Modern" payday lending is a relatively new type of credit product dating to the 1990s in the United States and 2000s in Canada; it has spread

Table 3.2 Fringe lenders in Europe

Type of provider	*Type of product*	*Location*
Subprime market	Subprime lenders or non-depositing taking lenders	United Kingdom, Ireland, Lithuania, Slovakia, Bulgaria
	Subprime credit card companies	United Kingdom
	Payday lenders	United Kingdom, Bulgaria, Poland
	Mail-order catalogues and rental purchase outlets	United Kingdom, Ireland
Very subprime market	Legal moneylenders (doorstep lenders, home credit companies)	United Kingdom, Ireland, Poland
	Pawnbrokers	United Kingdom, Germany, Norway, France, Ireland, Austria, Holland, Belgium
Illegal market	Unlicensed moneylenders (loan sharks)	Said to be found in most EU states

Source: Corr 2007; Buckland 2009

to the United Kingdom and some countries in Eastern Europe. Some payday lenders began as check cashers, and as the demand for payday loans increased, their business portfolio shifted from reliance on cashing checks to processing loans. Payday lending grew dramatically in the United States in the 1990s and in Canada in the early 2000s. It is estimated that in the United States there are now 20,000 outlets and the value of annual loan volume is US$40 billion (Packman 2014). In Canada it is estimated that there are between 1200 and 1500 outlets and that the market value of the industry is $2.5 billion. Payday lenders sometimes offer other loan products, such as title and auto loans. Title loans are a loan which has as collateral the title of some property, for instance, one's car.

Payday loans are quite controversial for a few reasons. Many studies find that payday loan borrowers have relatively low incomes, that the APR associated with the loan is relatively larger than that associated with a credit card, that lenders often have relatively complicated fee and contract formulae and presentations, and that payday loans can begin or aggravate a borrowers' debt cycle. Points one and two present a troublesome picture: that relatively poor people pay relatively high fees for loans. Payday loan proponents argue that high fees are the result of the high cost of operating outlets, and they tend to emphasize that their clients come from a broad socio-economic continuum. Critics counter that regardless of the reasons for the high fees, it is simply unethical for poor people to pay high fees for small loans and that the evidence is that it *is* largely the working poor who take out payday loans (Mayer 2003).

Perhaps the most controversial issue around payday loans is the question of how one payday loan leads some people into an ongoing reliance on these loans. This problem is well documented in the United States, and there is evidence it exists in Canada. Based on its own research and a review of the literature, The Pew Charitable Trusts noted that "repeat [payday loan] borrowing is the norm" (The Pew Charitable Trusts 2012, p. 15). In Canada the evidence is that repeat borrowing is common, particularly among lower-income clients (Simpson and Bazarkulova 2013).

Qualitative narratives are forceful statements about the negative consequences of the debt cycle. For instance, one story reported in Toronto's *The Globe and Mail*, in a series entitled "Canada's Borrowing Binge", featured a 47-year-old man who took out a $200 payday loan as a part of a special promotional rate for $20 for the two-week term. He then took out a second loan for $300 with a fee of $86 and the third loan for $400 with fee of over $400 (Grant and McFarland 2015). He found himself in a debt spiral where he could not pay for rent and utilities. Although he was able to climb out of the spiral, he then found himself in it again the following year:

> Like many in his situation, he borrowed from one payday lender to pay off another. He says his credit rating is shot. He figures he spent thousands on fees in recent years. Lack of cash meant having to go to food banks. "I was in a terrible loop I didn't know how to get out of." (Grant and McFarland 2015)

Another payday loan client reported, "They do make it pretty easy … They don't check any credit or anything, as long as you have a job, you get the loan" (Grant and McFarland 2015). This comment is particularly interesting considering the insights from behavioral economics about human behavior, specifically the observation that people, through tunneling, sometimes sacrifice their future finances to meet an immediate need. Making access to cash easily without raising awareness of the risks of a debt spiral can be a problem for the consumer.

Other Transactions Services Payday Lenders Offer

There are a series of "transactions" services[15] that everyone needs in order to live in a money-based (as opposed to a barter-based) economy. One cannot pay for milk from a grocery store with one's physical labor or pay for one's cellphone with produce from our vegetable garden. One needs physical cash or, increasingly, digital cash held on a debit card, cellphone, or implanted chip.

The need for transactions services is more pronounced for poor people in rich countries than for poor people in poor countries. Generally speaking, in rich countries poor people are more likely to interact with major institutions like government, large employers, utility companies, and so on. Whether receiving funds or making payments, to interact with these institutions, people need to convert digital payments into cash or cash into digital payments. Poor people in poor countries are more likely to receive fewer government supports and rely less on utility companies for services. But the rise of mobile payments in the Global South is raising the importance of these transactions for poor people in those countries.

Common transactions services in the Global North include check cashing, money wiring/transfer, and bill payments. For people with low income and assets, these services form the bulk of their financial services.

And often these services are provided by fringe banks. Secured credit cards are available for people who have a damaged or no credit history and are therefore precluded from a non-secured credit card. A common problem with these cards is that there are many different types of fees, such as a loading fee, use fee, and administrative fee, so that the cost of operating one can be quite high. Tax refund advances are a loan from the tax return compiler that is based on the forthcoming tax refund. The loan is thus secured on anticipated tax refund. As with other fringe bank services, the fees are high, and in Canada they are regulated through a fee cap.

Services associated with check cashing are declining in most rich countries, as payments are moving to a digital format. For instance, DFC Global Corporation's share of sales from check cashing from 2011 to 2013 declined from 18.3% through 13.1% to 11.4% (Table 3.3).

Other Fringe Banks

Rent-to-own is another common type of fringe bank in the Global North. It is a little different in that its model revolves around renting or leasing furniture. Here the client receives a consumer durable, such as a television or a couch, on a contractual basis that involves both a rent and an ownership option. If the client sticks with the rental arrangement, then she makes a monthly payment until the item is returned. Alternatively, the customer may choose to opt for the ownership option, in which case the "rent" paid counts toward payment of the item.

Table 3.3 Contribution of different services to DFC Global Corporation's revenue, 2011–2013

Service	*2011*	*2012*	*2013*
Sales to unaffiliated customers	*Current US$*	*Current US$*	*Current US$*
Consumer lending	429.2	645.9	728.3
Check cashing	144.1	138.7	128
Pawn service fees and sales	48	80.9	81.9
Money transfer fees	32.1	38.4	36.7
Gold sales	46.5	70.9	63.3
Other	88.5	86.9	84.1
Total sales to unaffiliated customers	788.4	1061.70	1122.30
	788.4	1061.7	1122.3

Source: DFC Global Corp. 2014, *Form 10-K*, pp. 128–30

Except for general consumer protection rules, these firms tend to be unregulated in Canada, where their business amounts to $260 million per year in sales (Moore 2014). Their fees amount to annualized interest rates that are often illegal in parts of the United States and in fact are illegal in Canada (i.e., greater than the criminal rate of interest, 60%). Another problem that has been identified is that rent-to-own firms often do not fully disclose their fees to the customer and sometimes inflate the price of their retail goods (Moore 2014). One Canadian company, Easyhome, describes its work as "providing goods and financial services to the cash and credit constrained consumer" (Easyhome 2014, p. 3). It emphasizes fostering customer respect (p. 22) and has for over ten years consistently grown its revenues and earned a profit, including a 13.3% return on revenue (pp. 25–27). Easyhome anticipates a growing market for its financial products:

> The Company believes that there is significant demand for the products offered by Easyfinancial in the Canadian marketplace. Historically, the consumer demand for these loans was satisfied by the consumer lending arms of several large, international financial institutions. Since 2009, many of the largest participants in this market have either closed their operations or dramatically reduced their size due to changes in banking regulations related to risk adjusted capital reserves, leaving easyfinancial as the only national participant with stated growth aspirations. The Company estimates that the historic Canadian market for unsecured consumer installment loans, consistent with the products offered by easyfinancial, was in excess of $1.5 billion and that this market was serviced by over 600 retail locations. (Easyhome 2014)

Is there a better way to provide consumers with loans for consumer durables? Fair disclosure and rate caps are a start. Or might savings schemes be an alternative? In the past retailers have had lay-away plans whereby the customer pays off the item before getting it, through an installment plan. If these payments could be tracked and used to assist the person to build a credit rating, an additional benefit could be gained. If carefully designed, with short-run bonuses, a lay-away plan might be better aligned with what we know about human behavior from behavioral economics.

The "Corporatization" of Payday Lenders and Fringe Banks

In the last several decades, fringe banks have evolved from simple pawnshop-type businesses to large corporations. Caskey notes that pawning in the United States declined from 1930 through 1970 as a response to the Depression, restrictions on consumer spending during World War II, and, from the 1950s, growing access for middle classes to mainstream bank credit (Caskey 1994, pp. 27–28). But, he notes, from the mid-1970s, "these fringe banking industries grew explosively" (Caskey 1994, p. 36). Pawnshops have grown in certain areas of the United States, such as the south and central mountain regions, and these regions are noted for more liberal regulations of pawnshops (Caskey 1994, p. 47). By the mid-1980s, the "corporatization" of the pawnshop model is evident through the appearance of chain-based pawnshops in lower middle-class suburban neighborhoods (Caskey 1994, p. 53). Chains were established by Cash America Investments,[16] which later purchased a pawnshop chain in the United Kingdom to become an international pawnbroker, making its initial public offering in 1987 with shares valued at $6.67. As of August 2015, these shares were trading for $22.55 (Caskey 1994, p. 54). This corporatization process involves establishing a corporate structure, bundling a series of similar services into a core offering, and creating a store chain.

The corporatization process has occurred with US payday lenders too, including Advance America, Ace Cash Express, Cashland, and DFC Global Corporation (Table 3.4). Not to overstate the corporatization process, this statement by a major US fringe bank corporation is worth noting:

> The pawnshop industry in the United States remains very fragmented, with as many as 14,000 stores nationwide operating in 2014 that were owned primarily by independent operators and, to a lesser extent, by publicly-traded companies. The Company believes that it is the one of the largest operators of pawnshops in the world in terms of pawn loan balances and number of pawn lending locations. The three largest domestic publicly-traded pawnshop companies, First Cash Financial Services, Inc., EZCORP, Inc., and the Company, operated approximately 1500 total pawnshops in the United States in 2014. (Cash America International 2015, p. 10)

This corporatization process has also been occurring among payday lenders in Canada as evidenced in the early 2000s, beginning with National Money Mart Inc., followed by The Cash Store Financial and Cash Canada Group Ltd. (Buckland 2012, pp. 128–29). The Cash Store Financial has since gone out of business, but Cash Canada (now Cashco Financial) continues, and other players include Easy Financial and Cash Money. These corporate fringe banks offer a variety of services across a large network of stores, services that have recently included pawning.

Table 3.4 Corporate-styled payday lenders and other fringe banks in the United States, Canada, and the United Kingdom

Company	*Country*	*Loans*	*Other services*	*No. locations*	*Data source*	*Website*
Ace Cash Express	United States	Installment loan, payday loan, title loan	Auto insurance, bill payments, check cashing, money wiring, prepaid debit card		2006 last 10-K	https://www.acecashexpress.com/
Advance America	United States Also: Canada, United Kingdom	Payday loan, title loan	Secured credit card, money wiring, tax services	2541 "largest non-bank provider of cash advance services in the United States" (p. 4).	2012 10-K	https://www.advanceamerica.net/
Cashland Cash America, Super Pawn, Payday Advance, Mr. Payroll	United States	Auto title loan, installment loans, pawn loan, payday loan	Check cashing, layaway (for pawnshop retail), gold purchase, secured credit card	943 "one of the largest providers of pawn loans in the world (p. 2)"	2015 10-K (But note 10-K may not include all units)	http://www.cashamerica.com/Cashland.aspx/
National Money Mart Inc.	Canada	Pawn loan, payday loan, installment loan	Bill payment, check cashing, currency exchange, money wiring, gold purchase, secured credit card, tax services	>550 "we are the leading alternative financial services company in Canada serving unbanked and under-banked consumers (p. 7)"[a]	See DFC Global	http://www.moneymart.ca/

(*continued*)

Table 3.4 (continued)

Company	*Country*	*Loans*	*Other services*	*No. locations*	*Data source*	*Website*
Cash Money	Canada	Payday loan	Check cashing, currency exchange, money wiring, gold purchase, secured credit card			https://www.cashmoney.ca/
Cashco Financial Carco, Cashco Canada	Canada	Auto loan, installment loan, pawn loan, payday loan, court case settlement loan	Check cashing, loan insurance, money wiring, retail, tax services	50		https://cashcofinancial.com/
Easyhome Easyfinancial	Canada	Debt consolidation loan, installment loan, mortgages, rent-to-own	Secured credit card	> 200	2015 Annual Report	http://www.easyhome.ca/
Wonga	United Kingdom Canada, Poland, South Africa, Spain	Loans				https://www.wonga.com/
DFC Global	International United States, United Kingdom, Republic of Ireland, Canada, and Other Europe (Sweden, Finland, Poland, Spain, the Czech Republic, and Romania)				10-K 2013	http://www.dfcglobalcorp.com/

[a]"We operate the largest alternative financial services retail store network in Canada based upon revenues and profitability, and therefore we believe that we have the largest market share in Canada in our sector" (DFC Global Corp. 2013 10-K, p. 7)

Corporate fringe banks extend beyond the United States and Canada, in part through the operations of American-based multinational fringe banks such as DFC Global Corp., which besides its unit in Canada has operations in the United Kingdom and seven European countries.

DFC Global Corporation

While there are now several fringe bank corporations, there are limited data about their operations. One large company for which there has been more detailed information until recently[17] is DFC Global Corporation, formerly Dollar Financial Corporation and now owned by Lone Star Funds. It is a US-based multinational fringe bank. In the last decade it has grown in terms of revenues, the number of services it provides, and the number of countries it operates in:

> We are a leading international non-bank provider of alternative financial services, principally unsecured short term consumer loans, secured pawn loans, check cashing, gold buying, money transfers and reloadable prepaid debit cards, serving primarily unbanked and under-banked consumers. We serve our customers through our over 1500 current retail storefront locations and our multiple Internet platforms in ten countries across Europe and North America ... Our networks of retail locations in the United Kingdom and Canada are the largest of their kind by revenue in each of those countries. (DFC Global Corporation 2014)

DFC Global's reporting to the US Securities and Exchange Commission, including its Form 10-K, provides a very useful insight into the world of fringe banks. As of 2013 DFC Global operated in the United States and in nine other countries, an increase from three countries in total in 2008. National Money Mart Inc., in Canada, is a subsidiary of DFC Global Corp. and one of Canada's largest fringe banks; it is clearly an important core component of DFC Global's business. More recently DFC Global Corporation has invested in Europe, including in the United Kingdom, Sweden, Finland, Poland, Spain, Romania, the Czech Republic, and the Republic of Ireland.

Both revenue and net income have increased over the ten-year period (2004 through 2013), in both current and inflation-adjusted real dollars (Table 3.5). Real revenue stood at US$271 million in 2004 and increased to US$827 in 2013, and the annual growth averaged at 5.3%. Real net income is quite variable, experiencing both positive and negative years, and stood at US$38.3 in 2012 but dropped to US$0.7 in 2013. Average annual net income for the period stood at US$9.8 million in real dollars.

DFC Global offers a variety of fringe financial services to its clients, including payday loans, check cashing, pawn loans, gold purchase, money transfers, and debit cards. The company has invested in online payday lending so that it currently has "one of the largest online unsecured short-term consumer lending businesses by revenue and loan portfolio in the United Kingdom" (DFC Global Corporation 2014) (Table 3.6). The share of their loan portfolio in "e-commerce" jumped from 15.4% in 2011 to 33% in 2012. This led to a declining share of the "retail" operations, particularly the Canadian retail operations, which declined as a share of the total from 40% to 30%. DFC Global plans to expand its Internet lending capacity and the number of countries in which it is offered, as well as pawn services, including in existing outlets in Canada and the United States. So far the company has invested in pawn operations in Europe and believes it is now the largest pawn lender in Europe, measured by loan portfolio.

DFC Global Corp. explains that the demand for its services, especially in the United States, has been driven in part by the decline in the number of mainstream bank branches, operating hours, and services, particularly in locations where DFC's clients live. It argues that these customers do not provide these branches a sufficient basis to run profitable mainstream bank branches. Mainstream bank strategies have made accessing them less convenient for the typical DFC client. DFC Global also notes that mainstream banks have "tended in recent years to eliminate, or have made it difficult or relatively expensive to obtain, many of the services that unbanked and under-banked consumers desire" (DFC Global Corp. 2014). DFC Global describes its clients in the following way:

> We believe that our customers, many of whom receive income on an irregular basis or from multiple employers, choose to conduct their personal financial business with us rather than with banks or other financial institutions due to the range and convenience of services that we offer, the multiple ways in which they may conduct business with us and our high-quality customer service. Our products and services, principally our unsecured short-term consumer loans, secured pawn loans and check cashing and gold buying services, provide customers with access to cash for living expenses and other needs. In addition to these core offerings, we strive to offer our customers additional high-value ancillary services, including Western Union© money orders and money transfers, reloadable VISA© and MasterCard© prepaid

Table 3.5 Dollar Financial Corporation's revenue and net income (US$)

		2004	2005	2006	2007	2008	2009	2010	2011	2012	2013
Current prices	Revenue		321.0	358.9	455.7	572.2	530.2	633.3	788.4	1061.7	1122.3
	Net income	−28.0	−0.4	0.7	−32.2	51.2	−7.0	−6.0	63.7	51.8	−0.9
	Price level	142.9	150.8	156.9	162.9	175.8	167.1	175.4	189.1	193.1	193.9
Real prices[a]	Revenue	270.6	304.2	326.9	399.8	465.1	453.4	516.0	595.8	785.7	827.1
	% increase		12.4%	7.5%	22.3%	16.3%	−2.5%	13.8%	15.5%	31.9%	5.3%
	Net income	−28.0	−0.3	0.6	−28.2	41.6	−6.0	−4.9	48.1	38.3	−0.7

Sources: For DFC and DFC Global: DFC 2008; DFC Global Corp. 2013

[a]Price level adjustment from the US Bureau of Labor Statistics

Table 3.6 DFC Global Corp. loan portfolio by region, 2011–2013 (US$ millions)

	2011		*2012*		*2013*	
	$	*Percentage (%)*	*$*	*Percentage (%)*	*$*	*Percentage (%)*
E-Commerce	340.3	15.4	985.7	33.0	1021.6	32.7
Canada retail	876.4	39.7	893.0	29.9	922.9	29.5
Europe retail	511.1	23.1	603.9	20.2	648.7	20.7
United States retail	480.8	21.8	507.6	17.0	533.6	17.1
Total	2208.6	100.0	2990.2	100.0	3126.8	100.0

Source: DFC Global Corporation 2014, p. 11

debit cards and foreign currency exchange. (DFC Global Corporation 2014)

DFC Global describes its core clients as coming from two groups: "ALICE" customers, who are working at near minimum waged jobs and have limited assets (Box 3.1) and "ARTI" customers, who are better off but for various reasons have limited liquidity (Box 3.2) (DFC Global Corporation 2014). It claims that these two groups are growing in numbers because of population growth, the growing number of low-income people, and the declining supply of mainstream bank services (DFC Global Corp. 2014).

Box 3.1 DFC Global Corporation's ALICE customers

"Generally, ALICE customers are service sector workers, small business owners, or employees of small businesses. ALICE customers typically hold more than one lower paying job in order to satisfy their monthly bills and living expenses. Many of these individuals periodically require short-term loans to provide cash necessary for living and other episodic or unexpected expenses. They may not be able, or even desire, to obtain loans from banks as a result of their immediate need for cash, the irregular receipt of payments from their employers, a lack of tangible collateral or the unavailability of bank loans in small denominations for relatively short periods of time. For ALICE customers who maintain banking relationships, unsecured short-term loan products can provide immediate access to funds as well as an alternative to the generally high cost of overdraft fees charged by their banks for overdrawn accounts. Individuals within the ALICE demographic who do not maintain regular banking relationships use services provided by us and other participants in our industry for a variety of reasons, including that they lack sufficient assets to maintain minimum balance requirements or to achieve the benefits of savings with banks, do not write enough checks to make a bank account beneficial, have a dislike or distrust of banks, or do not have a neighborhood bank in close proximity to them." (DFC Global Corporation 2014)

Box 3.2 DFC Global Corporation's ARTI customers

"ARTI customers can fall within several income and wealth categories, with the common characteristic among the demographic being ownership of liquid asset collateral, such as gold jewelry, quality watches and timepieces and other items of value. The ARTI demographic includes temporarily unemployed individuals in need of short term credit, individuals and small business owners with the need to access funds in advance of expected income streams, and high net worth individuals with irregular income streams such as commission sales. Unlike the ALICE demographic, which generally does not have tangible assets by which to collateralize their credit needs, we and other participants in our industry allow ARTI customers to leverage the tangible value of their possessions to obtain access to credit on a secured basis for a cost that is generally less than the fees associated with unsecured short term loans, for which we and other lenders in our industry have no security or collateral other than the promise of the borrower to repay the loan." (DFC Global Corporation 2014)

Mainstream Banks and Mobile Banking

Mobile Banking

From the fairly recent establishment of shadow banking and crowdfunding back to the automation of credit checking for accessing credit cards, information technologies have and continue to deeply influence banking. However, many of these IT-induced processes and products have limited direct effect on the lives of vulnerable people. Poor people rarely invest in or receive funding from the shadow banking sector. They are also less likely to receive finance or credit from crowdfunding sources, although this is more likely as compared with shadow banking, considering the proliferation of web-based programs such as Kiva. Vulnerable people are less likely to have a credit card or line than their non-poor neighbors.

However, there is one IT-based product that seems to offer a direct impact on the financial lives of poor people and that is mobile banking. Mobile banking is the processing of banking transactions on one's cellphone. In the Global North the client likely has an app on her smart phone that enables her to do almost as much banking as she is able to do on her Internet bank website. In the Global South it is more likely that mobile banking is intermediated by a simple ("non-smart") phone and be concentrated largely on money transfers. As seen in Chap. 1, the physical expansion of mobile banking has been rapid and those studying its implications are trying to catch up.

While mobile banking is held out as having particular relevance for the unbanked in the Global South, there is also a case to be made for mobile banking as a means to address the needs of unbanked people in the Global North. This stands to reason considering the prevalence in cellphone ownership in the Global North even among vulnerable people, noted in Chap. 1. From the bank's perspective, offering a mobile banking app makes sense, as it is very low cost. If mobile banking is combined with other institutional changes then it could be a means to reduce financial exclusion:

> Such mobile access may be economically feasible for banks, but if not, the social value is such that mobile access should be subsidized or incentivized by the government. Statutes and regulations should be revised to increase financial inclusion via mobile banking. In particular KYC [know your client] requirements should be reduced for small accounts, and deposited funds from trusted sources should be made immediately available to account holders. (Martin Christopher 2015, p. 252)

The mobile banking service is generally provided by a bank, an Internet service provider, or a partnership between them (Vaithilingam et al. p. 5). For instance, bKash, the largest mobile bank in Bangladesh, is majority owned by BRAC Bank and has minority holding by Money in Motion (US company), the IFC, and Gates Foundation (CGAP 2015). M-PESA, the largest operator in Kenya, is operated by Safaricom (Kenya-based) and Vodafone (UK-based), mobile network operators. Because it is seen to have positive development outcomes, donor agencies are supporting mobile banking which include government aid donors (DfID and USAID), intergovernmental organizations (the World Bank, the World Bank's International Finance Corporation, the United Nations Capital Development Fund), and private foundations including the Bill and Melinda Gates Foundation, the Mastercard Foundation, and the Ford Foundation. Consortiums have formed across various stakeholders, including donors, to promote mobile banking, for example, the Better Than Cash Alliance and the Groupe Spécial Mobile Association (GSMA), an industry association for mobile network operators.

In Global North countries like Canada, mobile banking is generally done via a bank app on a smart phone, which allows the client to do as many or more activities (e.g., submitting a check via photograph), as are available via Internet banking, which offers most of the activities that are available through an ATM or bank teller with the exception of obtaining cash. The adoption of mobile banking in the Global North has been slow, partly because there are a variety of other ways to access one's finances: the physical branch, an ATM, or telephone and Internet banking.

In poorer countries in the Global South, mobile banking operates through regular cellphones, uses text messages (short message service, SMS), and offers a limited number of services such as money transfers. However, the potential exists for the number of services to increase: "m-banking has digitized the concept of money, enabling users to store monetary value in accounts linked to their mobile phones, convert cash in and out of these accounts, and transfer funds between accounts by using a set of short messaging services (SMS) and personal identification numbers (PINs)" (Vaithilingam et al. 2013, p. 5).

One cash-to-digital money framework theorizes four stages in the transition from a cash-centered economy to a "cash lite" economy (Better Cash Alliance 2015, p. 4). Stage 0, the "cash heavy" stage, is characterized by reliance on paper cash, as exemplified in Haiti and Niger. Stage 1, the "bulk payer transition" stage, is characterized by the shift on the part of bulk payers—government and large business—to electronic payments, as exemplified in Colombia. Stage 2, the "increasing e-usage" stage, is a stage when individuals embrace electronic payments to transfer money and make payments, as exemplified in Kenya. The final stage, stage 3, is the "cash lite" stage, when almost all payments are done electronically, as in the United States, Canada, and Northern Europe.

This is an interesting framework, but we might consider a few important nuances. First of all, in one way Canada is not further along the cashless transition than, say, Kenya, a country with a fraction of Canada's per capita income. In Kenya, mobile phone-based transfers are far more common than in Canada. So a sequential transition from one stage to the next does not entirely hold. Second, countries in stage 0, the "cash heavy" stage, might actually not be very cash heavy, particularly in lower-income portions of the economy such as the informal economy, the rural economy, and other remote parts of the economy. In these locations, cash might be quite uncommon as people are poor and have little income or assets; instead they may rely on in-kind and inter-family activities such as family-based farm support, child care by a family member, and so on.

The Better Cash Alliance identifies barriers to moving toward more electronic transfers: distrust and misunderstanding on the part of consumers, lack of appropriate products, and the perceived and actual high costs of electronic transfers (Better Cash Alliance 2015, p. 11). They note that trust is a critical ingredient for the success of mobile banking and that building it is harder than losing it:

> Trust is an outcome of many variables—most importantly, individuals' experiences of a system over time. Trust is easy to lose; if it is not sustained by an enabling legal environment throughout the stages, it can be difficult and slow to rebuild. (Better Cash Alliance 2015, p. 11)

Another important factor limiting the growth of electronic payments and mobile banking, particularly when there are multiple actors, is interoperability or the ability of these different systems to communicate and interact with one another. Whereas cash is accepted by virtually all consumers and businesses, transferring money from one mobile banking provider to another is not easy or even possible.

The mobile banking market is large and growing. In 2014 there were 255 mobile bankers operating in 89 countries (Scharwatt et al. 2014, p. 8). There were 2.3 million mobile money agents in 2014, up from

1.4 million in 2013 (Scharwatt et al. 2014, p. 20), and 300 million mobile money accounts, up from 225 million in 2013. Africa is in the lead in terms of mobile banking coverage. Eighty-one percent of sub-Saharan Africa's markets are covered by mobile money as compared with 75% for South Asia, 65% for Latin America and the Caribbean, and 63% for East Asia and the Pacific. Estimates find that 10% of mobile money services are delivered over the counter, that is, without the use of a personal mobile phone (In this case the mobile money provider uses his/her mobile phone to undertake the transaction.) (Scharwatt et al. 2014, p. 31). In terms of volume of banking, much of the transactions relate to paying for one's cellphone airtime, and in terms of the value of transfers, almost three-quarters of transactions are for transfers to other persons. Although mobile banking penetration in certain countries like Kenya and Tanzania is quite high, it encompasses a "small minority" of all payments, especially for proximate transactions (Parada and Bull 2014, p. 9).

On many scales, mobile money is most successful in sub-Saharan Africa, one of the poorest world regions. Why is that? The following are some factors that are commonly suggested to explain this:

- The lack of physical infrastructure in sub-Saharan Africa—telecom, banks, and ATMs—has led to what some call "leapfrogging" over Global North countries (Vaithilingam et al. p. 6). Since the physical infrastructure is absent, there are fewer alternatives to cash and in-kind transactions, and this raises the attractiveness of mobile banking: "M-banking is also the preferred choice of banking for communities living in remote areas, where access to traditional banking services is scarce" (Vaithilingam et al. 2013, p. 5).
- Related to physical infrastructure, there are also relatively low levels of Internet connectivity in sub-Saharan Africa (Vaithilingam et al. 2013, p. 5). This means that Internet banking, retailing, and payments are relatively scarce options, once again raising the attractiveness of mobile banking.
- The technological and production changes have led to a dramatic reduction in the cost of mobile phones, so that "the mobile phone is the fastest growing ICT among the marginalized communities in the developing world" (Vaithilingam et al. 2013, p. 5). Since the mobile phone is the hardware for mobile banking, the reduction in its price has had a major impact on the price of mobile banking and its subsequent demand. ICT technological change in general has lowered

the costs of hardware and software for, and the transmission of, digital data.

- There are a number of prominent proponent donors with a high level of interest in mobile banking, perhaps reflecting a certain "trendiness" element to mobile banking.
- Supportive government regulation in some countries in sub-Saharan Africa (such as Kenya) and elsewhere (as in Bangladesh) is also a factor that explains mobile banking's success there. This will be further discussed in Chap. 5.

GSMA (Groupe Spécial Mobile Association) also tracks the growth of insurance, savings, and credit products delivered via mobile banking. Insurance is not popular, particularly among vulnerable people, due in part to the high cost of provision. Mobile banking might reduce costs, but this might also reduce client knowledge about the product. In 2014 there were 17 million mobile insurance policies in sub-Saharan Africa, South Asia, East Asia and the Pacific, and Latin America and the Caribbean (ranked by number of services by region) (Scharwatt et al. 2014, p. 52). There were 10 million mobile savings accounts in 2014 and growing (Scharwatt et al. 2014, p. 55). And some deposit-taking institutions are developing savings products to be delivered over mobile phones, for example, M-Shwari in Kenya (Scharwatt et al. 2014, p. 61).

Regarding lending, some argue that mobile banking can complement microcredit and deliver credit to remote locations (Parada and Bull 2014, p. 16). Currently there is a small absolute amount of credit delivered by this channel, but it is growing (50% this year). Credit scoring models are being developed to assess potential borrowers in order to reduce creditor risk. For example, the non-performing loan share for M-Shwari loans is 2.2%, which favorably compares with the Kenyan average of 4.9% (Parada and Bull 2014, p. 62). Parada and Bull note that this is a growing trend because digital finance leaves a "fingerprint" that allows for the collection of individual data (2014, p. 13).

Mobile Banking: Constraints to Adoption and Contribution to Broad-Based Economic Development

The literature on mobile banking is in its infancy, largely focusing on descriptive issues in two principal areas. The first area is narrowly concentrated on identifying constraints to adopting mobile banking, while the second area examines the broader relationship between mobile banking and economic development.

The question of constraints, which is primarily rooted in the business sciences, begins with the assumption that financial innovation is a critical and positive means to achieving improved financial well-being. Mobile banking is considered a prime example of a financial innovation that will automatically benefit poor people and countries, an assumption that may or may not be explicitly stated in this literature. For instance, several studies examine characteristics of mobile banking adopters and/or barriers to adopting mobile banking (Vaithilingam et al. 2013; Bajpai 2010; Yang 2009; Jerold 2008; Sayid et al. 2012; Uppal 2012).

A second body of literature is broader in scope, examining the relationship between mobile banking and economic development. In some cases the focus is on the individual adopter, while in other cases it highlights the consequences of adoption for national development; in some instances the research considers both of these issues. This body of literature examines how mobile banking relates to development, including policy connections (Duncombe 2012), the relationship to an individual's sense of well-being (Graham and Nikolova 2013), and female empowerment (Buvinic and Furst-Nichols 2014). Tobbin (2012) argues that mobile banking can be a means to financial inclusion and human betterment, but that uptake by the poor will be limited until "other barriers to having a bank account, which include affordability, trust, convenience, and documentation are addressed effectively in its deployment" (p. 103). Mbiti and Weil (2011), in their survey of M-PESA users, found that participation in M-PESA—the main mobile banking provider in Kenya—lowered participants' use of informal financial services such as rotating savings and credit associations (ROSCA) and increased their likelihood of getting a bank account. This raises a question about the consequences of people relying less on informal financial services. Does this raise or lower their vulnerability to challenges such as financial fraud? The existing literature has not yet addressed the particular challenges facing poor people in poor countries with regard to mobile banking.

M-PESA and bKash

Probably the best known mobile banker is M-PESA in Kenya. Another important one is bKash of Bangladesh. M-PESA, owned by Safaricom, a mobile phone network, began its operations in 2007 (Economist 2015). It is one of the fastest growing and largest mobile phone providers in the Global South. The 17 million Kenyans who use the system can access cash via Safaricom's 40,000 agents. In Bangladesh, mobile banking got started in 2010 when 28 providers received government approval to offer this service, and there are currently 19 providers currently offering mobile banking (The Mobile Money Revolution 2015). The largest mobile banker is bKash, a subsidiary of BRAC Bank, and BRAC—one of the largest development NGOs in the world—is BRAC Bank's largest shareholder with 44.6% of the Bank's shares (BRAC Bank Ltd. 2015). BKash opened in July 2011 and reached 11 million clients by 2013 (Chen 2014). By 2015 there were 23 million mobile bank clients across all service providers (The Mobile Money Revolution 2015). BKash has 100,000 agents throughout Bangladesh, and customers can also use 300 BRAC Bank automatic teller machines to access some services (bKash 2015). Total daily transactions amount to Taka 3.3 billion (US$56.7 million), and the average transaction ranges from Taka 600 to 5000 (US$8 to $65) (The Mobile Money Revolution 2015).

Problems Identified with Mobile Banking

Certain limitations have been identified with mobile banking. For instance, using financial diaries research methodology, researchers from Microfinance Opportunities tracked a group of 92 M-PESA clients in three locations for eight months to learn, among other things, about the impact of M-PESA on low-income households. Their results were interesting. They found that low-income clients use M-PESA in an instrumental and limited way that mimics the way in which they use cash (Stuart and Cohen 2011). For low-income and geographically dispersed Kenyan family members, M-PESA provides a valuable service, with the majority of transfers moving from city to country and from wives to husbands. Clients use M-PESA to transfer money to family members in other locations and generally do not use it to accumulate savings.

The researchers note that "cash is still king" (Stuart and Cohen 2011, p. 10), as M-PESA transfers amount to just under 6% of average household transfers. Moreover, the research found that for 75% of the time, when funds were received through M-PESA, they were cashed out, often the same day, by the entire amount (Stuart and Cohen 2011, p. 11). The researchers conclude that the "e-money loop"—"the number of times that a unit of e-money travels from one person to another before it is cashed out, is short" (Stuart and Cohen 2011, p. 11). This is noted by the authors because greater frequency in cashing in and out increases the operational costs of mobile banking. The authors predict that the M-PESA can continue to grow for distant transactions while cash still dominates proximate transactions, yet it is the latter where there is the greatest potential for e-money growth. For this growth to occur, Stuart and Cohen argue, the fee structure will need to be changed, and clients' trust that the system will work as well with a retailer, for instance, as with their family member, will need to be demonstrated.

While mobile banking is in its infancy in Bangladesh, there are growing reports about its success and some reports of its challenges. For instance, certain problems have been identified, including operators not keeping records of transactions, and customers having been scammed by fraudulent messages that enable third parties to withdraw money from their wallet (The Mobile Money Revolution 2015). Reporting on preliminary results of field research, Lee notes that without assistance fewer people signed up for a bKash account, but when given the option of receiving help to sign up, most participants did so and found that, at 10 minutes, signing up did not take long and was convenient as it could be done at any bKash outlet (Lee 2014). She hypothesizes that the cause for the slower uptake rate (than M-PESA) may have to do with the network effects: that the incentive to sign up to bKash grows the more members of one's network are members.

A critical issue about mobile banking for this study is its ability to assist poor people to improve their livelihoods. Too often new technologies stimulate economic growth without benefiting poor people. What are the risks that vulnerable people face in using mobile money? McKee et al. (2015) compiled results from a series of field studies that examined the riskiness of mobile banking for the customer. Nationally representative quantitative surveys and deeper level qualitative surveys were undertaken in several countries in Africa, Asia, and Latin America. They identify seven categories of risks faced by mobile bank clients (Table 3.7). These include the inability to undertake one's transaction because the network is not working, the inability to obtain cash from agent as she has none, a complicated user interface, poor customer service in the face of problems, non-transparent fees and terms, consumer fraud, and inadequate data privacy and protection. The first two sorts of risks are faced by all customers and do not, apparently, have a differential effect on different groups of people such as the poor. The last five types of risks do have the potential to negatively affect the poor more, and it is these five that we shall focus on here (Table 3.7, column 3).

Regarding the user interface, McKee et al. identify three problems: complicated operating instructions that are in English or a formal version

Table 3.7 CGAP identified risks faced by mobile banking clients in the Global South

Risk	*Type of risk*	*Greater impact on poor persons*
Inability to transact due to network/service downtime	Power outage/Technical problem	No
Insufficient agent liquidity or float, which also affects ability to transact	Financial problem	No
User interfaces that many find complex and confusing	Technical problem	Yes
Poor customer recourse	Customer service issue	Yes
Non-transparent fees and other terms	Information and protection problem	Yes
Fraud that targets customers	Agent manipulation issue	Yes
Inadequate data privacy and protection	Information and protection problem	Yes

Source: McKee, Katherine, Michelle Kaffenberger, and Jamie M. Zimmerman. 2015. *Focus-Note-Doing-Digital-Finance-Right-Jun-2015.pdf.* Washington, DC: Consultative Group to Assist the Poorest

of the national language; sharing the PIN with other people, including the operator; and keystroke errors. All of these risks are greater for someone with less experience in using the operating language and ICTs. Generally speaking, this is more likely the case with a poor person as compared to a rich person. Moreover, the authors note that some clients cope with a complicated procedure by seeking assistance from the operator, friends, or family members. This opens the door to manipulation by these people. Regarding the complicated menu, one person commented, "I'm not that educated, therefore, I don't understand the mobile menu" (Pakistan man, McKee et al. 2015, p. 7).

The next type of risk factor deals with poor customer recourse when he faces a problem. The issues identified include vague, expensive, and time-consuming procedures and limited agent capacity to address the problem. People are often unaware of what they can do if they face a problem, and if they find out what to do, it may be time-consuming and ineffective. These problems are compounded when people have to wait a long time to get through on the phone when facing a potential fraud. The fraudster takes advantage of this delay to complete her fraud. One person commented: "If I call … the manager … the reply is that we have to be careful about transactions ourselves" (p. 10).

A third type of risk for poor clients relates to non-transparent fees and contracts. There were two types of problems identified here: vague/non-transparent fees and suspicious overcharging. One person noted: "The charging rate is not standard ... the way [the fees are listed on posters] is different from what the agent says" (woman in Tanzania, McKee et al. 2015, p. 11). On the latter point related to suspicious overcharging, a fourth type of problem identified that the poor particularly face is general fraud against the customer, including fraud by the financial company staff or by the agent (McKee et al. 2015, pp. 13–14). Examples of the former include SIM swaps, social engineering scams, caller ID spoofing, counterfeit ATMs, and unauthorized account access. An example of agent fraud includes breaking a single transaction into several. Finally, the authors note data privacy and protection issues, including accessing personal information about the client, concern about the use of consumer data, and problems such as identity theft and money laundering.

Pilot Survey Results

To investigate the issue of mobile banking and riskiness for poor Bangladeshis, a pilot study of mobile banking was undertaken in July and August 2015 in Sylhet District, Bangladesh. It involved interviewing 21 clients and five key informants.[18] The clients were purposively selected because they were poor, and we used simple criteria to determine this, including if they were an asset-less unskilled worker or riskshaw puller. Key informants were bKash operators in the city of Sylhet. Clients were asked to explain how they use bKash, what benefits they get in using bKash, and what challenges they face in using it. Key informants were asked to explain how the system works and what the challenges from their perspective are. BKash operators are independent businesses that offer the bKash service, along with a number of other services not linked with bKash such as utility (natural gas and electrical) bill payments and photocopy services.

One-half of the client respondents were from a rural area, and the other one-half were from the city of Sylhet. One-third of the respondents were female, and two-thirds were male. Two-thirds of these respondents worked in unskilled labor or rickshaw jobs, while female respondents were primarily employed as house workers. Only one-third of respondents had other sources of income outside of their principal occupation, and for most of these, the incomes were low (less than Taka 55,000/year). Respondents, on average, had approximately five dependents. Only one respondent had a bank account, eight were participating in a microcredit program, none were involved in an informal credit or savings circle, and one relied on a moneylender for credit. One-half of the respondents had a mobile phone.

All respondents used bKash[19] as their mobile banking provider, and on average, they had been using it two times per month for just over three years. All respondents used the service to transfer money, and on average the transferred funds amounted to just over Taka 2000/transaction. One respondent used the service to save money, and six respondents used it to pay down debt. All respondents used the bKash agent, not their mobile phone, to transfer the funds. While clients understood the basic fee for the service, Taka 20 per Taka 1000 sent, there was some confusion around certain aspects of it.[20]

In terms of the client assessment of bKash, all clients were satisfied with the service as it meets a need they have to quickly transfer funds. All but two respondents said that it is unequivocally better than previous systems. All but two respondents said that they would continue to use the bKash service and that they would recommend it to their friends and family members. Two-thirds of respondents said that they would use new financial services if they were offered by bKash. Respondents had previously used a variety of services including a private courier system, a post office service, delivery by a family member, and self-delivery.[21] Key informants also mentioned that funds can be transferred through physical bank branches. The fees for these services vary—some less and some more than the bKash fee—and they all take longer than bKash.

Clients and bKash operators were asked about challenges that they faced with using or providing the service. Twelve clients stated they had no problems with the service, while the remaining clients identified a number of problems. For instance, four clients found that agents had insufficient funds; five clients found times when the network was not working; and four other clients had other challenges (Table 3.8). Two respondents said that the fees they were being charged were inconsistent and that, in addition to the standard fee, they were also charged another fee.

Key informants identified a similar set of challenges. Most commonly they identified the problems of the network being down and the funds getting lost or sent to the wrong destination (Table 3.9). Some of these bKash operators also noted problems associated with balance limitations that prevent the fund transfer, stolen PINs, and scam calls that remove funds.

Table 3.8 Problems clients experienced in using bKash service

Problem	*Frequency*
No problems	12
Network is down	5
Agent has insufficient cash	4
Funds are lost or sent to the wrong mobile phone number	2
Inconsistent and excessive fees	2
Agent is too busy	1
Scam calls	1
Total comments	27

Table 3.9 Problems bKash operators experienced in providing bKash service

Problem	*Frequency*
No confirmation message due to network being down	3
Funds are lost or sent to the wrong destination	3
Cannot transfer money into account because it contains > maximum	2
Stolen PIN	2
Scam call removes funds	1

The advent of mobile banking presents new opportunities and benefits for poor people around the world. But as with all new technologies, there are also risks and costs. Deliberate efforts are needed to minimize the risks and costs and maximize the opportunities and benefits and to ensure that vulnerable people are indeed benefiting from mobile banking. These deliberate efforts might be undertaken through a development practitioner who can act as an intermediary between vulnerable people and mobile bankers. To be effective, the practitioner seeks to understand the goals, needs, and interests of vulnerable people on the one side and the mobile banker on the other. An effective practitioner understands the asymmetry of power between these two groups and seeks to inform each actor about the other.

Based on their field work, McKee et al. (2015, p. 16) identify several ways to address the supply side of the mobile banking equation. These include strengthening the reliability of the network; strengthening agent quality, management, and liquidity; making customer interface more user

Table 3.10 Mobile banking risks for poor clients and responses

Risk[a]	*Mobile banking improvements*[a]	*Individual and collective capacity building*
General	Strengthen reliability of network Strengthen agent quality, management, and liquidity	Build full financial literacy that includes means-ends analysis and broader economic literacy Build financial literacy that includes exposure to current and future mobile banking services Build strong communities of practice through literacy and connections with specialists
User interfaces that many find complex and confusing	Make the customer interface more user friendly	Build literacy related to interfaces
Poor customer recourse	Improve handling of complaints, queries, and redress	Build literacy around consumer rights
Non-transparent fees and other terms		Build literacy around types and common formulae (e.g., APR) for fees
Fraud that targets customers	Combat customer-affecting fraud	Build literacy related to common fraud scams
Inadequate data privacy and protection		Build literacy related to knowledge of what is, and why it is, private

[a]Source: McKee, Katherine, Michelle Kaffenberger, and Jamie M. Zimmerman. 2015. *Focus-Note-Doing-Digital-Finance-Right-Jun-2015.pdf*. Washington, DC: Consultative Group to Assist the Poorest

friendly; and improving handling of complaints, queries, and redress (first two columns, Table 3.10). Deliberate efforts are needed to communicate with vulnerable people about their mobile banking experiences and carefully relay this information to mobile bankers in order that these services can be improved. McKee et al.'s survey is a useful benchmark, but the market and the vulnerable clients will continue to change. Ongoing communication is critical so that mobile bankers can modify their services to meet the needs of vulnerable people.

In addition to work on the supply side, deliberate efforts are needed on the demand side by seeking to financially empower vulnerable consumers. This can be done by assisting people to become more intentional and goal-oriented and by educating them on the financialization of the economy. Intentional goal orientation is more necessary in a fast-paced changing economy as compared with a static traditional economy. By assisting individuals and groups to think more deliberately about their life and financial goals, and about financial knowledge, skills, and helpful attitudes, their interests and goals regarding mobile banking will become clearer. If vulnerable individuals and communities become more goal-oriented, then their goals can better influence the mobile banker, not vice versa.

If poor people are to integrate into an expanding mobile banking system, then they need literacy that will enable them to utilize it to achieve their goals and to reduce their vulnerability. First of all, it is important that financial literacy curriculum is comprehensive in scope, so that it includes basic concepts and practices such as saving, budgeting, and tracking spending and includes broader topics such as means-ends analysis and economic literacy. Means-ends analysis involves having participants examine personal life goals and relate these to financial goals and financial means. This is necessary to encourage participants to see their finances as a means to larger life goals. Broader economic literacy involves curriculum that considers broader economic changes affecting one's economy such as industrialization, commercialization of farming, the economic consequences of information technologies, and processes including globalization, financialization, and neoliberalism. This material is important because these economic changes can happen without people being aware of or fully understanding them. Both of these points will motivate people to improve their financial literacy. Other financial literacy topics include mobile bank–user interface, consumer rights, common business practices regarding fees and awareness of important standard formulae, common practices regarding fraud scams, and the importance of data privacy and protection.

Adoption rates of mobile banking are high in countries such as Bangladesh which is evidence that there are tangible benefits to users of mobile banking. While the main service that is supported at present is cash transfers, there is scope for offering more bank services. The risks and costs associated with mobile banking for vulnerable people are tied to the consumer's own limited resources, structural inequality, and the asymmetry of power and resources the consumer faces vis-a-vis mobile bank suppliers. Some of these have been well documented by field work (McKee et al. 2015). Deliberate development efforts can play a critical role in managing these risks and costs so that vulnerable people benefit from mobile banking. This will improve the likelihood that poor people benefit, that adoption by others continues, and that mobile banking contributes to national-level development.

Discussion

Banking around the world is delivered by informal, fringe, and mainstream providers. It is hypothesized that as financialization increases, often associated with rises in per capita income, that mainstream banking's share of the total personal financial services rises the most and fringe banking's share also rises. Informal financial services decline as a share of the total during this process. But everyday financialization argues that without per capita gains in income, vulnerable people's use of financial services is expanding. Thus even the most vulnerable people are exposed to a growing number of banking products and providers.

Some types of informal finances offer safeguards through peer monitoring and support associated with the ROSCA model. This is not the case with traditional money lenders and loan sharks. There is little evidence that fringe bank products are an improvement over informal finances in terms of impact on vulnerable people's finances. Arguably, vulnerable people are best served by having the option to engage with the mainstream banking system because it is relatively less expensive, more consumer-friendly, and has transactions and developmental financial services. Restricting fringe and informal financial service providers can serve vulnerable people when these are combined with requirements that mainstream bank expand their scope. Some have already done so, for instance, select credit unions in Canada, via bKash and BRAC Bank in Bangladesh. Because of the relatively lower average incomes in the Global South, financial inclusion will likely involve a substantial increase in mobile banking and modest increase in physical banking. In the Global North, where incomes are relatively higher, financial inclusion will involve a more substantial and strategic increase in physical banking and a modest increase in mobile banking.

Without analysis, including evaluation results, it is difficult to say if commercially driven finance and credit schemes help or harm vulnerable people. What would be most useful are both quantitative results on economic impact and qualitative results that enable one to understand what clients think about these products and their views on how they affect their lives.

Notes

1. An annual interest rate is a tool to present the full cost of a credit product for a one-year period. Providing the interest rate in this form allows the person to compare different credit products. In some cases loans are for one year so that the interest rate presented by the creditor is an annual rate. In other cases the loan is for longer than one year, for instance, a large loan or a mortgage, and once again, it is helpful to provide the borrower with the annual interest rate. In many cases of credit for vulnerable people, the credit term is for less than one year, for instance, pawn loan or payday loan. Again, to enable comparing prices across products, an annual interest rate is helpful.
2. Annual percentage rate, APR, is a formula that enables the conversion of an interest rate for a short term into an interest rate for an annual term. This allows the prospective borrower to compare credit products of different durations such as a payday loan and a credit card. APR is a linear and non-compounding method using a formula akin to the following: APR = (loan fees/loan principal) (365/12). Effective annual rate, EAR, is another formula to convert term interest rates into annual interest rates and involves compounding. It involves a formula akin to the following: EAR = [((loan principal + loan fees)/loan principal)$^{(365/T)}$−1][100%].
3. Economic thinking and policy are partly responsible for this confusion. Neoclassical economics is the dominant or orthodox theory in the economics discipline today. This school of thought focuses on increasing efficiency or boosting economic growth and encompasses many central assumptions, and it regards markets as the most effective means to organize much of the economic realm, with the role of the state and civil society as being secondary. Neoclassical economic theory informs economic policy, that is, the rules, regulations, and laws that govern economic interaction. The dominant economic policy today is neoliberalism, dominating most of the world. (North Korea is an exception, and China embraces some but not all aspects.) The orthodox approach applies limited thought to the relationship between economic and human goals, Amartya Sen being an important exception. Sandel notes that the scope of the economics discipline has expanded in the last 30 to 40 years, and this is an important indicator of financialization. He notes that a key textbook in economics in the 1960s was Paul Samuelson's *Economics* and that in the 1958 edition it defined economics, relative to today, narrowly, with a focus on "prices, wages, interest rates, stocks and bonds, banks and credit, taxes and expenditure" (Sandel 2012, p. 84). Sandel notes that the scope of economics has dramatically expanded today as evidenced in Greg Mankiw's, a prominent economist today, expansive definition, "An economy is just a group of

people interacting with one another as they go about their lives" (Sandel 2012, p. 85). Further evidence is the rise of the use of the word *incentive* that was rarely used in economics in the past but is now common fashion in economics and popular culture. According to Sandel the use of the term increased by over 400% between the 1940s and the 1990s (Sandel 2012, p. 86).

4. The microcredit literature has tended to downplay ethical issues. However, there is a small body of literature that examines ethical issues, including high interest rates, damaged social relations within borrowing circles, and stressed intra-family gender relations. These points will be dealt with in Chap. 4.
5. A finance professor colleague with expertise in consumer finance and payday lending was presented with a payday loan contract and reported being "baffled'" by it. I certainly could not understand the contract. If that was our experience, imagine how a typical low-income consumer feels.
6. There is an interesting circle of ethical critique. Critics of poverty finance might themselves be critiqued for "blaming the business", that is, blaming the creditor even though he/she may simply be operating a business. For instance, in interviewing a pawnbroker, I shared with him the critique that pawnshops were charging excessive fees for loans to very poor people. His response was that he was simply running a business and that in comparison, mainstream banks were earning much higher profits and were therefore more exploitative. There is also the counter-critique of fringe bank consumers that says they are making unwise decisions and that their use of fringe banks is their own fault. Interestingly, I have heard mainstream bankers voice this notion when asked about the existence of payday lending. This is sometimes referred to as blaming the victim. A more general ethical critique is that it is not the borrower or the lender but the system that is exploitative. In this case, the borrower may be doing her best, and the lender may be doing his best, but because of structural inequalities the borrower is harmed or helped much less than the lender.
7. In Canada the automation of banking accelerated in the 1980s (Brennan et al. 2011). Automation was one trend, and, second, banks reduced and consolidated their branch networks. There is evidence in some cities in Canada that this branch network rollback process led to a particular decline of branches in low-income neighborhoods.
8. International remittances are a growing feature of the global economy, and it is estimated that they were valued at $401 billion in 2012 and intra-country remittances (from urban to rural, etc.) were valued at "several times more than that" (World Bank 2014, p. 55). The use of remittances, according to the World Bank, holds the potential to foster financial inclusion.

9. In interviews that I have done with low-income people in Canada, I find it significant that often respondents will not distinguish between what I refer to as mainstream, fringe, or informal financial service providers. For these respondents, there is little difference between the types of banks, and the issue is simply the different types of services they provide.
10. An excellent source of material on informal financial services in the Global South is the book *Portfolios of the Poor* by Daryl Collins et al. (2009). It is a book that distills key insights from an intensive panel research methodology called the financial diaries. This methodology carefully tracks participants' income, spending, saving, and dissaving over the course of an entire year and was undertaken with poor people in Bangladesh, India, and South Africa.
11. Islam and historical Judaism share prohibitions on interest charges. Within the Jewish tradition there is even a resolution to debt-led impoverishment: the year of jubilee takes place every 49 to 50 years and involves returning land that had been lost—for example, sold off to pay off debt—to its original owner.
12. Where did the market for fringe financial services come from? One theory is that fringe banks have expanded into the market previously controlled by informal financial service providers such corner stores offering check-cashing services and bars offering credit services. A second theory is that the fringe bank market opened up when mainstream banks consolidated their branch networks and services and pulled out of many low-income neighborhoods. The truth probably encompasses elements of both of these points, recognizing that payday lenders offer services to modest middle-income customers who are credit constrained. So consumerism is a factor that should be kept in mind.
13. The rent-to-own model is a little different in that it is associated with directly linking consumer purchase with a loan option.
14. For instance, National Money Mart Inc. and Western Union Canada and Western Union Canada, Scotiabank, and BMO/Interac
15. "Developmental" services include savings, investments, mortgages, credit repair, and credit building.
16. Cash America claims to be one of the largest pawnbrokers in the United States, offering services through a number of names and has grown by 260 outlets in the last five years, for a total of 943 outlets in 2014 (Cash America 2015, pp. 2–3). Its main service is pawnbroking, but it also offers second-hand sales, payday loans, check cashing, money wiring, and so on. It recently sold off its pawn locations in Mexico and formed a new company, Enova, to run its online payday lending services. In 2014 Cash America's pawn loans were over six times the amount as its consumer loans (p. 36). The company operates 7% of pawnshop outlets in the United States, with

a total of 14,000 pawn outlets in the country. In its latest 10-K report, it noted that it continues to "de-emphasize" non-pawn "consumer lending" in order to focus on pawn loans (p. 39).

17. Until 2013 DFC Global and its forerunners were publicly traded US corporations that regularly reported to the US Securities and Exchange Commission. Since Lone Star Funds purchased it, these data are no longer available.
18. This section is based on research completed by Jerry Buckland and Iqbal Ahmed Chowdhury (2015).
19. Alternatives to bKash include other mobile bankers like Dutch-Bangla Bank, but these respondents have no experience with that bank.
20. Clients were charged Tk 20 to send Tk 1000, but some of them understood that this charge was rounded up from the official charge of Tk 18.50 per Tk 1000. Clients understood that if they were to send their funds via their mobile phone to the recipient's mobile phone, the fee would increase by Tk 5, for a total of Tk 23.50.
21. Other options for wiring money include the post office money order which, according to some respondents is cheaper, at Tk 12 to send Tk 1000, but slower as it takes up to one week for the money to reach its destination. Money courier is another option which is fast but costly at Tk 63 to send Tk 1000. The clients have also used an informal system to send money. This system requires more elaborate planning, or a coincidence of interests, and is particularly useful if several neighbors or family members are sending money from the same location to the same home destination. The arrangement is that one community member takes the money home for the group.

Bibliography

"The Mobile Money Revolution is Transforming Bangladesh Global Voices". 2015. Accessed August 5, 2015. http://globalvoicesonline.org/2015/01/08/the-mobile-money-revolution-is-transforming-bangladesh/

"China's SMEs Head for Pawnbrokers as Credit Tightens". 2014. Accessed January 23, 2018. http://www.chinaeconomicreview.com/china-sme-lending-shadow-banking-pawnshop-credit

"The Economist Explains: Why China is Creating a New "World Bank" for Asia". 2014. *The Economist*. Accessed April 27, 2015. http://www.economist.com/blogs/economist-explains/2014/11/economist-explains-6

"The Economist Explains: Why does Kenya Lead the World in Mobile Money?". 2015. *The Economist*. Accessed July 6, 2016. http://www.economist.com/blogs/economist-explains/2013/05/economist-explains-18

Andreasen, Alan R. 1975. *The Disadvantaged Consumer*. New York: Free Press.

Bajpai, Bhavna. 2010. E-Banking Management: Impact, Risks, Security. *International Journal of Research in Commerce and Management* 1 (6, Oct.): 132–136.

Bertrand, Marianne, and Adair Morse. 2011. Information Disclosure, Cognitive Biases, and Payday Borrowing. *Journal of Finance* 66 (6, Dec.): 1865–1893.

Bertrand, Marianne, Sendhil Mullainathan, Dean Karlan, Eldar Shafir, and Jonathan Zinman. 2009. What's Advertising Content Worth? Evidence from a Consumer Credit Marketing Field Experiment. Economic Growth Center, Yale University, Working Papers.

Better than Cash Alliance. 2015. The Journey Toward 'Cash Lite': Addressing Poverty, Saving Money and Increasing Transparency by Accelerating the Shifts to Electronic Payments: Better than Cash Alliance.

bKash: Making Remittances Easier in Bangladesh | CGAP. 2015. Anonymous a.

bKash. 2015. Home | bKash. Accessed August 5, 2015. http://www.bkash.com/

BRAC Bank Limited. Knowing BRAC Bank 'Company Profile' Shareholding Structure. Accessed May 8, 2015. http://www.bracbank.com/Shareholding-Structure.php

Brennan, Marilyn, Brian McGregor, and Jerry Buckland. 2011. The Changing Structure of Inner-City Retail Banking: Examining Bank Branch and Payday Loan Outlet Locations in Winnipeg, 1980–2009. *Canadian Journal of Urban Research* 20 (1, Summer): 1–32.

Buckland, Jerry. 2009. *Affordable Credit Options for Vulnerable Consumers: Identifying Alternatives to High-Cost Credit in Australia, Belgium, Canada, France, Germany, the UK, & the US.* Ottawa: Office of Consumer Affairs/Industry Canada.

———. 2012. *Hard Choices: Financial Exclusion, Fringe Banks, and Poverty in Urban Canada*. Toronto: University of Toronto Press.

Buckland, Jerry, and Iqbal Ahmed Chowdhury. 2015. Managing Mobile Banking to Address the Needs and Protect the Vulnerability of Poor People in Bangladesh: SSRN.

Buvinic, Mayra, and Rebecca Furst-Nichols. 2014. Promoting Women's Economic Empowerment: What Works? The World Bank, Policy Research Working Paper Series: 7087.

Caplovitz, David. 1967. *The Poor Pay More: Consumer Practices of Low-Income Families*. New York: The Free Press.

Casey, Michael J. 2012. *The Unfair Trade: How Our Broken Global Financial System Destroys the Middle Class*. New York: Crown Business.

Cash America International. 2015. *Form 10-K*.

Caskey, John P. 1994. *Fringe Banking: Check-Cashing Outlets, Pawnshops, and the Poor*. New York: Russell Sage Foundation.

Chan, Selina Ching, and David T. Owyong. 2010. Pawnshops in Singapore: Traditional Microfinance in a Modern Society. In *Routledge Studies in the Growth Economies of Asia*, ed. Aditya Goenka and David Henley, 84–94. London and New York: Taylor and Francis; Routledge.

Chandran, Nyshka. 2015. Can Bitcoin Help the World's Unbanked? Accessed July 8, 2015. http://www.cnbc.com/id/102720768

Chen, Greg. 2014. bKash Bangladesh: What Explains its Fast Start? | CGAP. Accessed July 7, 2015. http://www.cgap.org/blog/bkash-bangladesh-what-explains-its-fast-start

Chowdhry, Bhagwan. 2015. Show Me the (New) Money. *Zocalo Public Square + » Show Me the (New) Money*, Mon, 29 June.

Coggan, Philip. 2012. *Paper Promises: Money, Debt and the New World Order.* London: Allen Lane; Penguin Books.

Collins, Daryl, Jonathan Morduch, Stuart Rutherford, and Orlanda Ruthven. 2009. *Portfolios of the Poor: How the World's Poor Live on $2 a Day.* Princeton and Oxford: Princeton University Press.

Corr, Caroline. 2007. *Alternative Financial Credit Providers in Europe.* Brussels: Directorate-General for Employment, Social Affairs and Equal Opportunity, European Commission.

Danubrata, Eveline, and Khettiya Jittapong. 2013. Pawnshops Hit Paydirt as Southeast Asians Sweat before Pay Day | Reuters. Accessed July 8, 2015. http://www.reuters.com/article/2013/09/10/us-asia-pawnshopsidUS-BRE98908520130910

Dawson, William Harbutt. 1913. Municipal Pawnshops. *The Economic Journal* 13 (50): 248–251.

DFC Global Corporation. 2008. *Form 10-K.* Berwyn, IL: DFC Global Corporation.

———. 2013. Form 10-K.

———. 2014. *Form 10-K.* Berwyn: DFC Global Corp.

Duncombe, Richard. 2012. An Evidence-Based Framework for Assessing the Potential of Mobile Finance in Sub-Saharan Africa. *The Journal of Modern African Studies* 50 (3, Sep.): 369–395.

Easyhome. 2014. *Annual Report.* Mississauga: Easyhome.

Ellison, Anna, Tony Dignan, Rob Forster, and Claire Whyley. 2010. *Interim Evaluation of the National Illegal Money Lending Projects.* London: Policis.

Ferguson, Niall. 2008. *The Ascent of Money: A Financial History of the World.* New York: Penguin.

Goenka, Aditya, and David Henley, eds. 2010. *Southeast Asia's Credit Revolution: From Moneylenders to Microfinance.* Routledge Studies in the Growth Economies of Asia. London and New York: Taylor and Francis; Routledge.

Graham, Carol, and Milena Nikolova. 2013. Does Access to Information Technology Make People Happier? Insights from Well-being Surveys from Around the World. *Journal of Socio-Economics* 44 (June): 126–139.

Grant, Tavia, and Janet McFarland. 2015. Payday Loans: Predatory Loan Sharks Or Crucial Fix in a Pinch?—The Globe and Mail. Accessed July 27, 2015. http://www.theglobeandmail.com/report-on-business/payday-loans-predatory-loan-sharks-or-crucial-fix-in-a-pinch/article24463029/

Graves, Steven M. 2003. Landscapes of Predation, Landscapes of Neglect: A Location Analysis of Payday Lenders and Banks. *The Professional Geographer* 55 (3): 303–317.

Jerold, V.A. 2008. Financial Inclusion and Literacy in India—A Critical Study. *Indian Journal of Finance* 2 (3, July): 25–33.

Johnson, Simon, and James Kwak. 2010. *13 Bankers: The Wall Street Takeover and the Next Financial Meltdown*. New York: Pantheon Books.

Kessler, Oliver, and Benjamin Wilhelm. 2013. Financialization and the Three Utopias of Shadow Banking. *Competition and Change* 17 (3): 248–264.

Lee, Jean. 2014. Bangladesh's bKash Adoption Puzzle | Financial Access Initiative. Accessed August 5, 2015. http://www.financialaccess.org/blog/2014/04/bangladesh's-bkash-adoption-puzzle

Leyshon, Andrew, Shaun French, and Paola Signoretta. 2008. Financial Exclusion and the Geography of Bank and Building Society Branch Closure in Britain. *Transactions of the Institute of British Geographers* 33 (4): 447–465.

Livesey, Bruce. 2012. *Thieves of Bay Street*. Toronto: Random House.

Martin Christopher, Catherine. 2015. Mobile Banking: The Answer for the Unbanked in America? *Catholic University Law Review* 65: 221–252.

Mayer, Robert. 2003. Payday Loans and Exploitation. *Public Affairs Quarterly* 17 (3): 197–217.

Mbiti, Isaac, and David N. Weil. 2011. Mobile Banking: The Impact of M-Pesa in Kenya. National Bureau of Economic Research, Inc., NBER Working Papers: 17129.

McKee, Katherine, Michelle Kaffenberger, and Jamie M. Zimmerman. 2015. *Doing Digital Finance Right*. Washington, DC: Consultative Group to Assist the Poorest.

Money Max. 2015. Money Max Home Page. https://moneymax.com.sg/

Moore, Holly. 2014. Rent-to-Own Practices in Canada would be Illegal in Parts of U.S.—Manitoba—CBC News. Accessed June 8, 2015. http://www.cbc.ca/news/canada/manitoba/rent-to-own-practices-in-canada-would-be-illegalin-parts-of-u-s-1.2850023

Packman, Carl. 2014. *Payday Lending: Global Growth of the High-Cost Credit Market*. Palgrave Pivot 1st ed., 2014 ed. New York: Palgrave.

Packman, Carl, ed. 2016. *A Short History of Payday Lending*. Vol. 81. http://www.historyworkshop.org.uk/a-short-history-of-payday-lending/

Parada, Marcia, and Great Bull. 2014. *In the Fast Lane: Innovations in Digital Finance*. Toronto: The Mastercard Foundation.

Pew Charitable Trusts. 2012. *Who Borrows, Where They Borrow, and Why: Payday Lending in America*. Pew Center on the States.

Sandel, Michael J. 2012. *What Money Can't Buy: The Moral Limits of Markets*. New York: Farrar, Straus and Giroux.

Sayid, Osman, Abdelghani Echchabi, and Hassanuddeen A. Aziz. 2012. Investigating Mobile Money Acceptance in Somalia: An Empirical Study. *Pakistan Journal of Commerce and Social Sciences* 6 (2): 269–281.

Scharwatt, Claire, Arunjay Katakam, Jennifer Frydrych, Alix Murphy, and Nika Naghavi. 2014. *2014 State of the Industry: Mobile Financial Services for the Unbanked*. London: Groupe Speciale Mobile Association, GSMA.

Simpson, Wayne, and Dana Bazarkulova. 2013. *Payday Loans Consumer Profile Based on the 2009 Canada Financial Capabilities Survey*. Winnipeg: University of Manitoba.

Simpson, Wayne, and Jerry Buckland. 2016. The Dynamics of Financial Institution Location in Toronto: Who is Serving the Inner City? *Economic Development Quarterly*: 1–29. (forthcoming).

Stuart, Guy, and Monique Cohen. 2011. *Cash in, Cash Out Kenya: The Role of M-PESA in the Lives of Low-Income People*. Washington, DC: Microfinance Opportunities.

Sulaiman, Nor Surilawana Hj, Siti Fatimah Kassim, Ibrahim Alzoubi, Khaled Ashaboul, and Mashitah Zainol Abidin. 2014. The Comparison between Ar-Rahnu and Conventional Pawn Broking. *Global Business and Economics Research Journal* 3 (5): 57–65.

Tobbin, Peter. 2012. The Adoption of 'Transformational Mobile Banking' by the Unbanked: An Exploratory Field Study. *Communications and Strategies* 86: 103–120.

Todaro, Michael P., and Stephen C. Smith. 2015. *Economic Development*. 12th ed. Boston: Pearson.

United Nations Development Program. 2015. *Human Development Report*. New York: UNDP.

Uppal, R.K. 2012. M-Banking Services—A Milestone for Customers. *International Journal of Business Economics and Management Research* 3 (11, Nov.): 19–31.

Vaithilingam, Santha, Mahendhiran Nair, and Balachandher Krishnan Guru. 2013. Do Trust and Security Matter for the Development of M-Banking? Evidence from a Developing Country. *Journal of Asia-Pacific Business* 14 (1): 4–24.

Weber, Beat. 2016. Bitcoin and the Legitimacy Crisis of Money. *Cambridge Journal of Economics* 40 (1, Jan.): 17–41.

World Bank. 2014. *Global Financial Development Report 2014: Financial Inclusion*. Washington, DC: International Bank for Reconstruction and Development.

Yang, Ann Shawing. 2009. Exploring Adoption Difficulties in Mobile Banking Services. *Revue Canadienne Des Sciences De l'Administration/Canadian Journal of Administrative Sciences* 26 (2, June): 136–149.

Yelowitz, Aaron, and Matthew Wilson. 2015. Characteristics of Bitcoin Users: An Analysis of Google Search Data. *Applied Economics Letters* 22 (13–15): 1030–1036.

CHAPTER 4

Financialization and Consumer Behavior

Consumers are a critical ingredient in the credit and finance scheme relationship. They are increasingly influenced by financial markets, for instance, being exposed to advertisements for financial products like subprime mortgages. Consumers are also agents of financialization in that they are increasingly motivated by money and engage in the demand for financial services, for instance, by collecting one more credit card, microloan, or engaging in payday lending. The growing use of the term "consumer", or possibly "creditor"—as opposed to citizen, person, or worker—is itself evidence of growing financialization. People are conceived as consumers and creditors rather than citizens or workers. Of course most people carry many of these identities, but as financialization proceeds the economic identity rises to the top.

But what economics is finding is that consumers do not behave in ways that the economic model predicts, that is, they do not rationally maximize their self-interest. In some cases this unexpected behavior is aligned with social needs and interests, and in other cases it is associated with simple short-sightedness. Thus the consequences of financialization on the consumer are quite complex.

This chapter examines consumerism and debt accumulation as root causes of consumer financialization and considers how advertising can stimulate the money motive. The chapter then considers how consumer debt affects mental health. The lion's share of the chapter is devoted to critically examining assumptions in economics about human rationality and

J. Buckland, *Building Financial Resilience*,
https://doi.org/10.1007/978-3-319-72419-5_4

decision-making about finances. While economic orthodoxy assumes that people are rational and self-interested, evidence from a variety of fields including behavioral economics and sociology find this is not the case. The research on the related concepts of scarcity and tunneling are particularly enlightening when considering the impact of everyday financialization on vulnerable people.

While sociologists point to the cultural dimensions of money and focus on how people and culture shape money, neoclassical economics, on the other hand, focuses on the practical aspects of money. Economists identify three purposes of money: a medium of exchange, a store of value, and a medium of account (Siklos 2004, p. 17).

For consumers, money as a medium of exchange allows them to make exchanges in order to obtain those goods and services that they demand. Instead of bartering, associated with a barter system, or working, associated with an indentured labor system, people within a capitalist system earn income and then use it to pay for goods and services. But their immediate needs and wants do not always align with their income, and that is where personal finance issues enter, discussed below. As a medium of account, closely related to the medium of exchange function, money allows the consumer to make value comparisons between goods and services. Coarse rice costs this much, and fine rice costs that much; my family's needs are X amount with a budget of Y, so I'll buy the coarse rice:

> A personal computer can sell for £600 or $1000, figures that everyone living in Britain and the US can understand. In a barter system, we need to know a computers' worth against the full range of products that might be on offer—a horse, two cows, four sheep, and so on. Expressing the price of all goods and services with relations to one denominator is much easier. (Coggan 2012, p. 25)

As a store of value, a slightly different role, money acts as an asset or liability, and this points to the subject of personal finances. Personal finances are the strategies that individuals and households take with their income, spending, savings, and borrowing to achieve their financial and life goals. Money's various purposes can assist households in achieving these goals. In a capitalist economy, consumers need financial services in order to meet their material needs. These are lumped into two types of services. Transactions services, which are those that are needed for daily finances, involve small amounts of money and short periods of time.

Cashing a check, accessing cash for a small purchase, paying a bill, and transferring money to family members are all examples of transactions services. Developmental financial services seek to assist the consumers to build their assets so they can improve their financial and life goals. These include saving for large assets, saving for a house (mortgage), investing, and building a credit rating. These services can assist the consumer to save, invest, and borrow.

It is commonly thought that household finance changes over a person's life, in keeping with the life cycle theory of finances or savings. According to this view, a young adult dis-saves, as his/her income is low but her potential future income is high, so she borrows through family, bank, student loans, and so on. As the individual approaches middle age, she has paid off her debt and is increasingly saving money for retirement. Finally, in retirement, she dis-saves again, but at this point drawing on savings that were accumulated during middle age.

Consumerism

Consumerism is defined in the Oxford English Dictionary as "the preoccupation of society with the acquisition of goods". A consumerist society is one that places high value on consumption and material growth. This characterization of Western societies dates back to the work of Thorstein Veblen in his *The Theory of the Leisure Class* (1889) (Spechler 1990) and later in the work of John Kenneth Galbraith (1992). Veblen argued that wealthy people have a tendency to pursue ostentatious consumption in order to impress their peers. Galbraith, in his highly challenging book *The Affluent Society*, argued that consumers are not "sovereign" as economic theory suggests but are manipulated by corporate advertising.

> The long history of consumer credit within US society ... is indicative of the predominant role debt plays in "financing the American dream." The consolidation of mass consumerism in the post-war period strengthened the role of credit within the USA's emerging consumerist society. The boom in consumer durables, such as white goods and furniture as well as cars, is intimately linked to the growing availability of consumer credit in the immediate post-war period. These credit practices, themselves, were not necessarily unique to this period as instalment plans already existed for most consumer goods, particularly automobiles, at the turn of the twentieth century. What is unique about consumer credit in the post-war period is its growth in scale

> and scope, as well as its inter-connections with the emergence of other key pillars of US consumer society. For instance, the first universal third-party credit card was invented during the same decade as the first McDonald's, the first fully enclosed shopping mall, the first mass-produced suburban housing development (Levittown, New York), the mass production of televisions and the opening of Disneyland. (Montgomerie 2009, pp. 14–15)

The 1980s witnessed a movement away from the old Keynesian regime of state macroeconomic management toward the new neoliberal regime, which involves greater accent on the market and less emphasis on the state. Neoliberalism calls for markets to be freed from collective entities such as unions and excessive state intervention that would distort markets. Thus the influence and status of unions have declined, as has the role of the state. The Keynesian view that labor income makes up an important component of aggregate demand, associated with the Fordist model,[1] also declined. In contrast, the neoliberal regime places more emphasis on entrepreneurship and shareholder value and less on labor's share of the economic pie. Meanwhile, globalization has continued to march forward, possibly accelerating with the collapse of the communist bloc. This has led to an accelerated migration of highly labor-intensive industries from the Global North to the Global South. This process further undermined the position of labor in the West. As a result of these various processes Western nations such as the United States and Canada have seen a rise in income inequality. This includes a stagnation or slowdown in the growth in income for modest middle-income workers. Montgomerie argues that the consequence of moving from the state-led Keynesian model to a market-oriented model with rising income inequality is that increasingly, Anglo-American countries rely on consumer debt accumulation in order to stimulate aggregate demand to keep economies running smoothly (2007).

There is little debate that Western economies today are characterized by consumerism. Although the growth of information technologies and social media has led to the characterization of the West as an "information economy", a cursory review of social and public media (Migone 2007) provides further evidence of the growth of consumerism, sometimes referred to as hyper-consumerism. Migone (2007) describes consumption today as hedonistic in that it is oriented toward the very short term; after being enjoyed once, consumer goods are quickly discarded, to be replaced by new ones. Hyper-consumerism makes consumption a way of life in which buying and consuming become like religious acts (Lebow 1955, cited in Migone 2007). Migone observes that consumerism has spread rapidly into high-growth economies of Asia and Latin America and is rising in lower-growth economies in Africa, Asia, and Latin America. Through *frugal innovation* consumerism even reaches to the poorest people in the world including those in South Asia and sub-Saharan Africa. Frugal innovation is the concept assigned to the rapid growth, particularly in India, of developing products and services such as cheap cellphones and cooking stoves for the world's poorest consumers (Prahalad 2010; Slavova 2014). Consumerism has also affected the most remote peoples and places, for example, the Tibetan people of Ladakh, India (Norberg-Hodge 1991).

Consumerism offers its follower's benefits, but these benefits are based on relative position and are short-lived. Frank (1999) used the notion of "positional competition" to explain why we continue to consume after our needs are met—it is in order to out-compete others with our goods (Migone 2007). This point was discussed in Chap. 1 regarding the relationship between economic growth and happiness. Migone notes the transient nature about the benefits from consumerism:

> After biological desires are fulfilled, consumers must consistently reinvent new desires to keep consuming. A self-replicating cycle of dream, desire, acquisition, and disillusionment is then established within which the search for novel products is really a proxy for the quest for psychological satisfaction of the desire. Because of the nature of the process, disillusionment sets in after consumption, and new products must be found and consumed. (Migone 2007)

As Montgomerie has noted consumerism can lead to the accumulation of personal debt, which will be considered next. And the consumption system is maintained through advertising, which will be discussed in the last portion of this section.

Consumer Debt

Consumers and households operate with particular budgets that are bounded by their income, assets, and credit worthiness. Leaving aside for the moment life cycle changes, discussed below, people generally seek to keep their spending in line with their income. When needed, people can spend in excess of their income by either drawing down on their assets (sell your sailboat or new aluminum pot) or borrow money based on their credit worthiness or leveraged on their equity (i.e., collateralized loan). Historically in the West and in informal economies in the Global South today, access to credit is limited to informal sources such as pawnbrokers, moneylenders, informal savings and credit societies, and family members. In these cases the credit relationship is based on collateral (e.g., pawnbroker), high fees (e.g., moneylenders), or social relations (e.g., family members).

This informal system of consumer credit has a built-in mechanism to ensure that debt, generally speaking, is kept within sustainable levels. This is because (1) pawn loans are limited by one's collateral, and (2) other informal credit like small-group-based credit and family loans are limited by one's social capital. Point number 1 simply means that one's pawn-based loans are limited by the items available to pawn. Social capital, referred to in point number 2, refers to one's social networks and norms that can be drawn upon to access credit. Here social networks refer to friends, neighbors, and family members who have assets that one can tap into either in a one-on-one relationship or through a credit circle. Normative behavior is another important feature because if the normative attitude about repayment is distrust, or if the borrower has a bad track record of repayment, then having rich friends is of little assistance. Distrust will prevent the network from engaging in group lending and/or one-on-one lending.

But over the last few hundred years in the West, commercial banks have established increasingly consumer-oriented loan products, beginning with small loans such as car loans and then moving in the 1950s to credit cards (Cross 2015). Along with increasing availability of consumer loans, debt levels in Western nations have been rising in the last ten years (IMF 2012; Ryoo and Kim 2014; Kartashova and Tomlin 2013). There is some debate about what has caused the debt to increase and whether the debt has reached unsustainable levels or not. In a recent review of debt levels in advanced economies, the International Monetary Fund found that the ratio of household debt to income increased from 99% to 138% between 2002 and 2007. Household debt as a share of GDP in the United States rose from 45% in 1975 to 100% in 2006 (Ryoo and Kim 2014), holding at about 140% of disposable income in 2013 (Cross 2015, p. 4). Debt-to-disposable income in Canada increased from 100% in 2001 to 150% in 2015 (Cross 2015, p. 4). Debt levels were even higher in some Northern European countries—near 200%, for the Netherlands, Ireland, and

Iceland—and have also risen for some former Eastern European nations such as Hungary, Latvia, and Lithuania (IMF 2012, p. 89).

The cause of the rapid rise in consumer debt is somewhat contested. Cross (2015) argues that consumer debt has grown in Canada ever since the innovation of the credit card and that consumers use credit in a completely rational way that allows them to take advantage of sales on goods, smooth consumption, and invest in their productive capacity. Moreover in the Canadian context, asset prices, notably housing, have grown faster than consumer debt, meaning debt-to-asset ratios have dropped so that consumer debt is not problematic. While this analysis is interesting and helps to explain some aspects of consumer debt in Canada, it misses some important dimensions, including the role of inequality in explaining debt and the risk of declining asset prices as has happened in the United States. Ryoo and Kim (2014) argue that consumer debt has grown, in part, to allow people facing stagnating income to maintain or expand their consumption levels:

> In particular, a social reference group is a key determinant for consumption behavior. Moreover, advertising and sales promotion in the mass media tends to expand the reference group for lower-income households beyond their peers to include the upper income class. The lower income households' desire to emulate the richer may provide a strong motivation for borrowing to finance their desired consumption. (Ryoo and Kim 2014, p. 586)

So for Ryoo and Kim, consumer debt does not result from a purely rational choice to organize a more efficient life but is influenced by less rational motives where one is trying to "keep up with the Joneses", at a time when the Jone's income is outpacing one's own. Accumulating debt allows a short-term way to raise one's lifestyle.

The consequences of consumer debt growth are also debated. If acquiring debt is a rational choice, as neoclassical theory would posit, it supports smoother household spending and more investment, and the consequences are positive. On the other hand, if consumer debt is not fully rational and if the debt has reached unsustainable levels, then the consequences for the macro-economy could be severe. For instance, if asset prices were to rapidly decline, as they did in the US subprime mortgage crisis, then the sustainability of consumer debt would rapidly deteriorate. Moreover, evidence has mounted that an economy that experiences a recession will be worse off if it had been characterized by high consumer debt prior to the recession than if it had been an economy with low consumer debt. "The findings are also broadly consistent with the more general finding in the literature that recessions preceded by economy-wide credit booms—which may or may not coincide with household credit booms—tend to be deeper and more protracted than other recessions … This conclusion is also consistent with evidence that consumption volatility is positively correlated with household debt" (IMF 2012, p. 96).

Consumer Debt and Mental Health

A relatively new and expanding area of study examines the psychological consequences of financialization, consumerism, and debt accumulation (Mullainathan and Shafir 2013; Sweet et al. 2013; Zurlo et al. 2014; Klontz et al. 2015). Studies rooted in behavioral economics have identified the notion of scarcity to explain the effect of financial troubles of people's cognitive capacity. Some early studies have found a link between consumer debt and depression, and finally, there are some interesting studies examining a new field called financial therapy.

According to Mullainathan and Shafir (2013), when people are confronted with pressures in one area, for instance, money, they are less able to attend to other issues. They call this a scarcity process. This relationship will be discussed in more detail below. Mullainathan and Shafir argue that poverty creates a kind of pressure on people that reduces their capacity to analyze and make good decisions. Assuming this relationship holds—that financialization can, like poverty, act as a kind of pressure on people—then financialization creates its own kind of scarcity. In other words, the growth of financialization means that people have less "bandwidth", available for psychological, social, religious, and non-financial economic matters such as quality of work, and even intellectual capacity.

But arguably the impact on human psychology might be more profound than that, because financialization does more than divert our attention away from non-financial issues, as the scarcity process suggests. Financialization may actually increase the importance of money in our minds, thereby diminishing the role of non-money issues—call it a substitution process. The scarcity process diminishes our capacity in a variety of ways, but the substitution process diminishes our valuation of non-money matters in favor of money matters. The scarcity effect makes it more difficult to focus on anything, including money issues. The substitution effect makes it more difficult to focus on anything, but money matters. To exaggerate the process to make the point clear, the substitution process causes us to obsess about finances which divert our attention from other human endeavors.

As discussed above, we know that financialization has been correlated with growing income inequality. This adds another feature to the psychological impact of financialization. For those experiencing a relatively declining income standard, the psychological impact might be magnified. For instance, as introduced in Chap. 1, happiness studies have identified that subjective happiness does not increase when one's income rises with one's peers' income (Kroll 2015). Happiness does increase, however, when one's income rises relative to one's peers' income. These processes might be compounding for those with declining relative incomes: as their income declines relative to their peers' income, they feel the scarcity and substitution effects of financialization. Moreover, as money becomes more central in people's lives and minds, it is plausible that this relative competition intensifies and undermines the pursuit of happiness.

Studies investigating consumer debt and human health reveal a close relationship between the two. Drawing on a US national survey on adolescent health, Sweet et al. (2013) find that household debt is highly correlated with health outcomes (p. 7): "Indeed we found that high relative debt (debt-to-asset ratio), whether subjectively assessed or calculated based on reported debt and asset values, was associated with higher perceived stress and depression and worse self-reported general health, even when accounting for life-course health and economic conditions and other indices of current socioeconomic position" (p. 8). The study found that blood pressure was higher for respondents with a subjective—not necessarily actual—debt-to-asset ratio.

A study by Zurlo et al. (2014) examining national survey data for a sample of Americans over 51 years old found a positive relationship between holding unsecured debt and depression as well as poor psychological well-being. Moreover, respondents who felt in charge of their finances were less likely to experience depressive symptoms and negative psychological well-being (p. 467). A national survey in the United Kingdom of families with children examined household debt and psychological well-being and found a strong correlation between depressed state and perceived financial problems. A meta-study by Richardson et al. (2013) examined 65 papers on the relationship between personal unsecured debt and health. They found that the existence of unsecured household debt increases the likelihood of poor health and that in many cases, more debt leads to worse health outcomes (p. 1154):

> The results of the meta-analysis largely confirm the results of individual studies, showing a strong relationship with overall mental disorder, depression, suicide completion or attempt, problem drinking, drug dependence, neurotic disorders and psychotic disorders. The only variable which was not significant was smoking. Odds ratios demonstrate more than a three-fold risk of a mental disorder in those with debt, or alternatively a three-fold risk of debt in those with a mental disorder. Even stronger effects were shown for suicide with completers having nearly an eight-fold risk of debt. (p. 1154)

An indication of the growing realization about consumer debt's effect on human health is the rise of ***financial therapy***. Financial therapy is a relatively new field that is "interested in the evaluation and treatment of cognitive, emotional, behavioral, relational, and economic aspects of financial health" (Klontz et al. 2015, pp. 3–4). It is related to financial literacy education, but its scope deliberately encompasses emotional well-being with the goal to improve financial well-being and quality of life. It uses various types of "financial" therapies such as cognitive behavioral and psychodynamic to understand and assist people with their financial challenges. The literature in this field is new, but there is evidence of a fairly rapid increase in the use of the term in the popular media (Klontz et al. 2015, p. 5). It is unique from the areas of financial planning, financial counseling, and financial coaching:

> If the client's financial stress is not associated with significant psychological distress (e.g., anxiety, depression, relationship problems), then traditional financial planning may be all that is needed to help the client achieve financial health. If traditional financial planning advice does not lead to permanent changes in financial behavior, then financial coaching—which might entail identifying and exploring money scripts—could be beneficial. If the client's financial stress is associated with significant psychological distress at the outset of the engagement and/or if financial coaching is not sufficient to facilitate financial health, [it is] suggested that financial therapy targeting "unresolved emotions and dysfunctional thoughts that keep maladaptive behaviors in place" would be recommended. (Klontz et al. 2015, p. 6)

There is growing evidence that finances, financialization, and debt can affect people in many ways including emotionally. Some of these affects can be harmful, so much so that a new area of study and practice is emerging, financial therapy.

Consumption and Advertising

It is often assumed that advertising provides more information for the consumer to enable him/her to make sound decisions, but the evidence is that much advertising is less interested in information and more interested in influence or framing. Insights from behavioral economic experiments demonstrate how we are affected by framing—the way in which an idea, a problem, or a good is presented to us.

One type of framing that has been studied in the literature is how providing certain information or images influences decision-making. Some studies reinforce what marketers have known all along that these images sell products. Placing images of attractive people in advertising will boost sales. Thaler and Sunstein (2008) find that framing something positively—choose drug A, and there is a 90% chance you will survive—as compared to negatively, choose drug B, and there is a 10% you will die, will lead to very different decisions. Even though the outcomes are identical, if given the choice, most people opt for drug A.

Van Tuinen notes that spending in advertising is very large, and this is hard to square with the advertising-as-information argument. More than half a trillion US dollars is spent annually on advertising, and one-half of this is spent in the United States (van Tuinen 2011, p. 215). That the spending level is so high is evidence of its influence over consumers. Moreover he argues that rising advertising and corporate profit levels in the last 20 odd years are evidence of both the growing influence of advertising and the growing irrationality consumers (p. 216):

> We have seen how the manipulation of preferences encourages private consumption and work at the expense of spending time with one's family, social activities, self actualization, philanthropy or the provision of public goods. These effects stem from the superior power of the commercial sector in the manipulation of preferences ... We therefore need to analyse the manipulation in terms of the relative power to manipulate preferences for private consumption as opposed to other purposes. This manipulation overrules the sovereign consumer as the ultimate constitutor of the evolution of the economic process in so far as it causes actual preferences to differ from authentic preferences. (Van Tuinen 2011, p. 223)

Consumerism, consumer debt, debt-related ill-health, and consumer-oriented advertising has been examined in this section. There is evidence of a rise in indicators of all of these factors: rising consumption, more consumer debt, increasing debt-related mental illness, and growth in advertising. This is particularly the case in the Global North and the BRICS and to a lesser extent in the Global South. The causal relationships among these factors are complex and have not been untangled here. The analysis is suggestive that advertising can stimulate consumption which can, when incomes are stagnant, drive up debt and that this can lead some people into periods of mental ill-health.

Unpacking Human Rationality

Neoliberalism and financialization make the individual consumer a central economic actor alongside business. In the highly idealized neoclassical model, these two actors behave in economically rational ways and interact in perfectly competitive and frictionless markets. Perfect competition means that there are many buyers and sellers and that none of them have power over any other player. Sadly for the ideal, particularly in the Global North, most markets are imperfectly competitive, and it is generally the case that one or more firms that are large may have power in the market.

The remainder of this section examines three central assumptions in the neoclassical theory that has a direct bearing on the consumer. First we examine the idea that the consumer is an independent agent and not linked in any economically important way to groups, collectives, or identities. Next we consider the concept of the frictionless market in light of evidence that vulnerable people face many barriers to, for instance, banking. Finally, we consider in more detail the rationality of human decision-making with reference to household finances.

Collective Behavior

Neoclassical economic theory focuses on the individual consumer behavior rather than collective behavior (Zelizer 2011). The state is assumed to have a minimal role to play at the national level—preserving a declining list of public goods like the police and the military—but beyond that the model does not admit a role for collectivities such as gender, class, and identity. This means that all individuals, regardless of their income, employment, gender, and identity, are assumed to behave mechanistically to pursue their self-interest and that their self-interest is not shaped by collective characteristics. Neoclassical economics assumes that the economy is the sum of the individuals within it. Markets organize sectors of the economy that allow for and indeed foster a series of mutually beneficial transactions between buyer and seller. So the neoclassical model assumes that a middle-income, formally educated, middle-aged white male enters into these markets in the same way that a low-income, informally educated, young Indigenous female would. This assumption is problematic when we realize that it is particular groups of people—often single-women parents, Indigenous People, and immigrants—who face particular economic challenges. Neoclassical theory simply abstracts from this real-world problem. In doing so, and in encouraging all consumers to behave in one mechanistic way, neoclassical theory can cause misunderstanding in a couple important ways.

Firstly, there is a difference in the knowledge and experience of these two people. While each person's knowledge and experience is valid, one set of experiences empowers certain people to engage more self-interestedly with markets. Generally speaking a middle-aged white male has more knowledge and experience with, say, urban middle-income markets than a young Indigenous female. Considering the axiom "knowledge is power", then it becomes clear that this particular male can probably negotiate in a self-interested way more effectively than this particular female. Consider, for instance, negotiating terms on a mortgage. This particular male is more likely to have done this type of negotiation before and to realize that there is some room for movement on interest rate. In the face of this, he is more likely than this particular female to assume and undergo negotiations.[2] The implications are that markets (contrary to the operating assumptions of the neoclassical model) are not neutral toward class, gender, and identity. This helps to explain why, for instance, more unbanked people in Canada and the United States are poor.

Secondly, through real (e.g., workplace, neighborhood) and virtual networks (e.g., media, social media), we engage in community and social relations with colleagues, family, friends, neighbors, peers, and many others. These social relations shape our values, and this affects our economic behavior. Social capital was a concept first proposed by James Coleman (1988) and then popularized by Robert Putnam (1993). It provides a framework for understanding the economic implications of social relations. Putnam defined social capital and the sum of networks in the society combined with cooperative and trusting relationships that are manifested in it. "Networks and norms" became a popular explanation of the existence of side-by-side wealth and poverty like northern and southern Italy or northeast and southern Brazil.[3] Putnam argued that in regions that were economically advanced, such as northern Italy and southern Brazil, the dense social networks and normative behavior of trust and reciprocity helped to create the economic strength. On the other hand, in the less advanced regions, such as Ssouthern Italy and northeast Brazil, norms were less trustful, and networks were less dense.

One's relative power and social network influence one's access to resources and one's economic outcomes. That is to say that society and economy are more closely linked than the economic model allows. Next, consider structural barriers as a reality many vulnerable people face.

Structural Barriers

The neoclassical model assumes that independent agents interact in a frictionless market. This means that there are no barriers or costs for people seeking to interact in these markets. Of course this is far from the reality for many vulnerable people who face barriers of "omission", for instance, they have inadequate income or employment, and obstacles of "commission", for example, bank staff incentives that encourage them to favor better-off clients as compared to less well-off ones.

For instance, poor people in the Global North make calculations about banking options that are quite rational. And these decisions take into account the real obstacles and opportunities that they face. This leads to some poor people using mainstream banks and fringe banks in various ways. The banking decision is based on a number of general factors including access, fees, product design, and bank staff culture. Access relates to the proximity of the outlet to one's home or work and its operating hours. The proximity issue has been particularly well documented in the United States, the United Kingdom, and Canada, where it has been found many times that mainstream banks are under-represented and fringe banks are overrepresented in low-income neighborhoods, sometimes increasingly over the last 20 years. The fee issue is complicated, but generally speaking poor people prefer up-front and transparent fees, even if they are sometimes higher. People complain about how mainstream banks can apply fees to accounts without notification. Vulnerable people have particular financial needs, associated with small amounts of money. Fringe banks have developed services such as check cashing and payday lending that meet these needs but at a high cost. Although mainstream banks have these services, they do not do a good job at packaging and marketing them to poor people. Often vulnerable people feel disrespected and find that bank staff take less time and effort for them as compared to non-poor.

These bank barriers encourage vulnerable people to choose financial services that may not be ideal. The barriers raise the relative benefits and lower the relative costs of fringe banks as compared with mainstream banks. The result is that to choose fringe bank services, from an economic perspective, is now rational. However, it must be remembered that the choices are not neutral but are the result of government and bank policies. Different policies could lead to different results. The outcome for the vulnerable consumer who relies on fringe banks is convenient services, but they are expensive, and they lock him into relying on fringe banks.

Rational Behavior

As first discussed in Chap. 1, neoclassical economic theory is the dominant school of thought in the discipline of economics in the United States and Canada and increasingly around the world. It is also arguably the most influential school shaping the neoliberal economic policy regime. Neoclassical economics is a sophisticated theory in that it has a number of facets that come together in welfare economics to make universal claims about human behavior and prescriptions for improvement. It uses highly quantitative methods that rely on abstract theory to generate equilibrium and dynamic models that replicate some aspect of our world, which are then analyzed using large datasets with econometric tools. An important critic, Viviana Zelizer notes[4]:

> In my opinion, economics has paid a stiff price for its current scope and precision. It has, on the whole, located its central causes in the decisions of largely autonomous individuals who operate within constraints set by well-defined resources and institutions … Such an approach has the virtue of parsimony. But it almost entirely neglects the incremental negotiation of shared understandings and interpersonal relations that lie at the center of alternative, more sociological, analysis of economics processes. (Zelizer 2011, p. 9)

While it is sophisticated, it can be argued that neoclassical theory is not self-reflexive like disciplines such as anthropology or geography—in other words, it does not critique itself and explore alternative ways to address self-identified weaknesses. The reason for this gap is not entirely clear. One argument is that since economics is more closely linked with the neoliberal policy regime, it holds more power and thus is more resistant to critique.

In order for neoclassical theory to develop a sophisticated mathematically oriented framework, it must begin with certain assumptions about human nature. These assumptions allow the discipline to model human and market behavior through the above-mentioned mathematical equations. Without these assumptions, the model-building process could not proceed. Neoclassical economics supposes that humans are rational animals, or *homo economicus* (economic man), eloquently described by Thaler and Sunstein: "If you look at economic textbooks, you will learn that *homo economicus* can think like Albert Einstein, store as much memory as IBM's Big Blue, and exercise the willpower of Mahatma Gandhi" (2008, p. 6).[5]

The concept of *homo economicus* assumes that humans are very intelligent, knowledgeable, committed, and self-interested, able to make optimal decisions to achieve the greatest satisfaction in life. People know their interests, they know all their options to achieve those interests, and they choose the correct option to achieve their goals. This means they can gather important data for their short-, medium-, and long-term future, analyze it, and make decisions so as to bring them the greatest happiness. Moreover, this information is available, and they can understand the information and how it affects their lives. *Homo economicus* has the willpower to choose the best options for his present and future, and she resists the temptation to make decisions that will undermine her future. Self-interest is the final component of *homo economicus*. While self-interest is generally equated with selfishness, this is not necessarily the case because a self-interested person can include within her interests the interests of others, including family, community, and society. However, generally speaking self interest tends to boil down to selfish behavior.

The fact is that people are not completely informed, perfectly knowledgeable, always committed, and completely self-interested. Most neoclassical economists would not likely disagree. But the disagreement has to do with what assumptions are needed to form the basis of viable theory. Since neoclassical economics uses a modeling methodology, rather than say, inductive theory, they require restrictive assumptions. Assuming people are rational fits nicely with a modeling methodology. Building abstracted mathematical models on the assumption that people are irrational would be much more challenging.

Until the recent rise of behavioral economics, the assumption regarding the rationality of consumers was not contested in mainstream economics. There were some exceptions. Interestingly, in the 1980s, Keynesian macroeconomics was criticized for assuming workers were irrational regarding how inflation affects their real wages (see below). Institutional economics is another important source within economics for examining human rationality. There have also been more visionary critiques within economics of the neoclassical model including the work of Daly and Cobb. But it is outside of economics, in the social sciences more generally, where many of these critiques are rooted, for instance, the work of Viviana Zelizer. Let us review some of these examples.

Keynesian macroeconomics assumed a trade-off between inflation and unemployment rates that was based, according to Robert Lucas (Lucas and Sargent 1981), on people forming expectations about the future state of the economy in an imperfectly, or adaptive, and not rational, way. The essential idea, according to Lucas, was that Keynesian macromanagement involved "fooling" people to accept declining real wages because of state action that was stimulating inflation. Lucas argued that the breakdown of the inflation-output trade-off was because people were not adaptively rational but were fully rational. Once people figured out that prices were rising, they began to demand that their wages keep pace which led to declining output growth and stagnating unemployment.

A rich source of discussion and debate on this topic is rooted in new institutional economics and in particular how it relates to the theory of cooperation. The neoclassical economic view is that competition, not cooperation, is the norm as it enables people to more effectively achieve their self-interest. This view sees cooperation as an irrational distraction to self-fulfillment (Axelrod 1984). Yet there is evidence that cooperation is more common that this view would predict (Ostrom 1990). Ostrom presents evidence of a variety of local approaches to common pool resource (pasture or forest) management that work. Todaro and Smith (2015) note the sustainability of cooperative control of common pool resources and what they call club goods, goods like vaccination campaigns and microfinance delivery that require local input and innovation.

So does engaging in collective behavior mean that people are irrational? Indeed not, according to those who point to the role of collective action for individual success. In an interesting study of the history of cooperation, Bowles and Gintis (2011) note:

> Many observers of experimental games have interpreted the fact that people sometimes sacrifice material gain in favor of moral sentiment as an indication of irrationality, the term "rationality" being misused as synonym for "consistent pursuit of self-interest." But subjects appear to be no less rational when deciding to cooperate and punish than when they compare prices to decide what to cook for dinner. This suggests that preferences that lie behind their social behavior are consistent with the basic axioms of rationality ... (Bowles and Gintis 2011, p. 32)

There have been more foundational critiques of the neoclassical economic model from within the discipline (e.g., Daly 2008; Schumacher 1973). Daly and Cobb (1989) critiqued the notion of *homo economicus* on a philosophical basis, because of its assumption of single-minded human self-interest and individualism and how this conceptualization reinforces harmful action. They argue that this is a partial truth but that it is misleading, not to mention misdirecting. *Person-in-community* is the concept they present as a counterpoint to *homo economicus*. This alternative characterization highlights the fact that individuals live within communities and society and that they do not just think about their own interests—they consider others too. And the authors argue that given the global challenges we are facing—multiple environmental challenges and limited or negative returns to human well-being from economic growth—the concept of *homo economicus* must be changed in order to address these problems.

The social science literature outside of economics involves a nuanced if contested view of consumer rationality. Zelizer's (2011) sociological theory of money argues that consumers are influenced by the culture in which they live. Rationality is not static, and it is not a simple mathematical calculus. She notes that recent scholarship finds that the "rigid concept of 'homo economicus' as a rusty, old-fashioned notion ready for retirement" (Zelizer 2011, p. ix). She notes that the sociological examination of money and economics looks not at psychological behavior but the "cultural and structural grounding of individual economic preferences" (p. x). She notes that people's spending habits are deeply influenced by social relationships. She presents a critique of the neoclassical model and behavioral economics because she argues that neither approach digs into understanding the underlying social relations that leads to consumer behavior. The sociological theory of money presents an insight into why, contrary to the neoclassical model, money is not a "seamlessly fungible medium in which each unit is identical to each other unit" akin to mental accounting, discussed below (Zelizer 2011, p. 89).

Another source of critique of the neoclassical model is rooted in gender or identity analyses (Hewitson 2013; Feiner and Roberts 1999). These approaches challenge the neoclassical concept of rationality as being rooted in a particular worldview and consequently limited. For instance, Indigenous Peoples embrace worldviews that are often quite distinct from the worldview that undergirds neoclassical economics. In many cases their worldview is more intimately tied to nature, more holistic, and their livelihoods are interconnected with spirituality. What are Indigenous Peoples experiences with banking?

Some studies in Canada have examined poor Indigenous Peoples experiences with banking (Martin et al. 2006; Bowles et al. 2011). These studies have found that that Indigenous People, perhaps to a greater extent than non-Indigenous People, rely on fringe banks as opposed to mainstream banks. Fringe banks such as pawnshops and payday lenders offer services that are more accessible than mainstream bank services. There is evidence that Indigenous People feel less comfortable—as compared with non-Indigenous People—with mainstream bank staff which compels them even more to use fringe banks (Collin 2011). Fringe banks offer their services but for a high price, further eroding Indigenous Peoples economy. There is evidence that mainstream bank staff is under-represented by Indigenous Peoples in Canada which adds a further hurdle to inclusion (Sexsmith 2006).

Indigenous views of money have dramatically changed over the past century among Indigenous Canadians: from a more collective understanding to one that is more consistent with mainstream culture, particularly for young Indigenous People (Buckland et al. 2016). In her examination of Indigenous Australian's relationship with money, and drawing on Zelizer's theory of money, Godinho found that while Indigenous Australians see money imposed on them from outside, they have adapted to it in unique ways (Godinho 2014, p. 87). She finds that particularly among more remote peoples, money moves easily among extended family members. This suggests that large family size acts as a financial resource in terms of pooling, income smoothing, and access to family-based credit. She argues that the ongoing disconnect between Indigenous Peoples and money partly explains the higher levels of financial exclusion among Indigenous vs. non-Indigenous Australians:

> Money is disconnected from many important elements of participants' social and cultural world-view, including traditional knowledge, cultural values and norms, and their sense of cultural identity. This feeling of disconnect may be at the heart of why Indigenous people have greater difficulty in accessing banking and developing financial skills, and are more likely to be excluded, irrespective of location. (Godinho 2014, p. v)

Collective behavior, structural barriers, and limits to human rationality present challenges to understanding the consequences of financialization of human development on consumers. The independent and economically calculating agent operating in a frictionless market does not exist in the real world.

Unpacking Bounded Rationality

Human behavior is complex and cannot easily fit into the *homo economicus* box. Most of the remainder of this chapter examines insights about human financial knowledge and behavior from two major literatures: financial literacy studies and behavioral economics. These literatures provide evidence of human limitations and complex rationalities and irrationalities. We focus on these literatures because there are many interesting and relevant studies that relate to consumer finances. We recognize that these studies, coming from orthodox and behavioral economics, have limitations. They accept many of the principal assumptions in orthodox economics, except for full human rationality. In fact two powerful proponents, Thaler and Sunstein (2008), embrace libertarianism as articulated by Milton Friedman but modify it through the concept of "choice architecture". Some of these limitations are discussed further at the end of the chapter.

Measuring Financial Literacy

There is a growing literature on the theory and measurement of financial literacy and the policy and practice of financial literacy education. We discuss the former issue here while the topic of financial literacy education will be addressed in Chap. 6. This measurement literature presents evidence of substantial illiteracies with regard to finances. When this is combined with misplaced self-confidence—as it sometime is—it can give rise to harmful financial decision-making.

Studies on financial literacy measure literacy rates, explain these rates, examine the relationship between financial literacy and other variables such as economic growth, and consider whether financial literacy education is the most effective way to improve financial well-being. Measurement of financial literacy is done at the individual level using a number of indicators, including objective and subjective ones, individual variables and indexes, indicators of knowledge, skill, and attitude. While financial literacy needs vary by type of economy (agricultural vs. information economy), age (life cycle), income level, and financial goals (financially ambitious people have greater financial literacy needs than the voluntary simpleton), financial literacy is generally measured using a universal threshold. Using a universal threshold often finds that people engaged in a more basic economy, young and old people, poor people, and financially less aggressive people, are the least financially literate.

What is financial literacy?[6] Generally speaking it means having the knowledge, skills, and attitude to manage one's finances effectively. Knowledge refers to what an individual knows about finances, such as the risk-reward relationship regarding investments or the percentage rate formula to calculate an annual interest rate for a loan product. Skill refers to the ability to collect data—on risks, rewards, fees—and to apply concepts such as risk-reward trade-off or annual percentage rate in order to make the best decision to achieve one's financial goals. Attitude relates to the outlook on one's finances that allows one to achieve one's goals. For instance, an attitude that critically examines financial options and is careful with debt is an attitude of "hopeful skepticism". An unquestioning attitude that accepts financial information at face value or assumes that debt can be accumulated without negative consequences is probably more harmful. Life goals and economic knowledge are also important. Often definitions of financial literacy leave out its ultimate purpose: why does one need financial literacy? Presumably it is a means to effectively meet one's life goals. This requires the competency needed to determine one's self-defined life goals. Finally, financial literacy is often devoid of a critique of the economic system, which can prevent people from understanding systemic and underlying causes of economic swings. Thus financial literacy must also include literacy about the economic system (Stanford 2015).

In their literature review, Lusardi and Mitchell (2014), using a set of objective questions, find that a large share of adult and young Americans are financially illiterate and that this is documented in other Western nations. They note that people tend to be overconfident in their financial literacy self-assessments but that this is a bigger problem for men compared with women. Women do worse than men, poor people do worse than rich people, and ethnic minorities do worse than majorities in assessments of US financial literacy.

Another interesting issue that arises in the measurement of financial literacy relates to how it is measured. Typically survey respondents are asked a standard set of objective and/or subjective questions that cover a number of aspects of financial literacy, some more basic and some more advanced. Basic financial literacy is about needs that everyone has including budgeting, tracking expenditure, and planning ahead. Advanced financial literacy relates to needs for people who have more sophisticated finances, for example, mortgages and the risk-reward investment trade-off idea. Measurement studies find that better-off respondents out-perform worse-off respondents in advanced financial literacy indicators but not in basic ones (Lusardi 2008; Kempson and Atkinson 2009; Buckland 2011). This supports the notion that people invest in financial literacy that they need. In their cross-country assessment of financial literacy, the World Bank found a similar relationship between country income level and financial literacy: "low-income countries tend to be at the bottom end of the performance rankings" (World Bank 2014, p. 75). While these results find an inverse relationship within and between countries re income and financial literacy, they can be misleading. This is because financial literacy needs vary across different demographics within a country, not to mention between countries. A farmer in Bangladesh has different financial literacy needs as compared with a lawyer in Canada.

An interesting study in the United Kingdom examining the relationship between self-control, financial literacy, and over-indebtedness found that consumers with high debt levels lacked self-control, heavily discounted future spending, and exhibited low levels of financial literacy levels (Gathergood 2012). This is an example of how financial literacy studies are connecting with behavioral economic studies.

Financial literacy measurement is generally drawn from national survey data and presents financial indicators for an entire national population. In the next section we examine evidence of complex rationalities from behavioral economics. These results are often the result of experiments that economists undertake with a limited number of participants.

Rules of Thumb That Go Wrong

Thaler and Sunstein's book *Nudge* (2008) is an important behavioral economic study as it presents a comprehensive framework and details on common financial mistakes individuals make. The study draws particularly on evidence from middle-class Americans which suggests a limitation in its data sources. Thaler and Sunstein identify the ways in which humans commonly make choices is less than reflective and more automatic ways and point out how this behavior deviates from *homo economicus*. They find that rather than collecting and analyzing salient data before making decisions, humans often use heuristics or rules of thumb, like the following:

- *Anchoring*, whereby we make assessments about a new question or issue based on something we are familiar with. For instance, we guess at the size of a city by "anchoring" that guess on the size of our own city. Financially speaking, before the subprime mortgage crisis, we might expect the stock market to behave like it did in the previous ten years.
- *Availability*, similar to anchoring, is where we base an assessment of an unknown situation on what we know. After the 9/11 terrorism event, many people assessed the risk of terrorism as being higher than it was. People's ideas about payday loan interest rates are generally way out of line with the reality. We know that most credit products have interest rates in the 10 to 20% range so when we see a payday loan fee at $17 per $100, we think that is the interest charge, when in fact it is, 17/100 × 365/12 = 517% (annual percentage rate).
- *Optimism and overconfidence* are characteristics of human behavior that lead to common errors. Financial literacy surveys often find people make mistakes on simple calculations but identify themselves as financially literate. We often think we know more about money markets than we do and then are surprised when we have to work longer than planned before retirement.
- *Status quo bias* is a human characteristic that leads us to prefer the known current state over an alternative, even if the alternative might be better. People may rely on expensive fringe bank services, but they are well-known to them, staff may be minimally respectful, and mainstream bank services are less expensive but are remote and unhelpful. Status quo bias suggests that supports are required for a movement from the former to the latter.
- Neoclassical economics assumes that money is fungible, that is, a dollar a consumer uses for groceries is the same as a dollar that is used for car repair, which is the same as the dollar used to pay tuition and book a hotel for a holiday. However, behaviorists argue that real

people don't treat money this way. In fact people use *mental accounting*, a heuristic whereby people place income and expenditure into different categories and these categories do not mix. For instance, in a two-income earning household, one paycheck may be used for the rent and the other paycheck for food and utility bills. Or the salary may be assigned for rent and food, income from an entitlement program may be assigned to larger purchases such as clothes, and income from irregular sources may be used as savings.

These concepts point to nuanced ways in which people behave with money. We don't always collect all the relevant information, fully analyze it, and then make the optimal choice. We take short-cuts, and sometimes these can undermine our financial and overall interests.

Borrowing Behavior

There have been a number of interesting behavioral studies focused on finances of poor people. These studies find that poor people, like the non-poor, make financial decisions that seem to be at odds with their interests. This is demonstrated with microcredit and payday loans. These studies are useful because the focus is on the reality of poor people, a reality that can diverge from middle-income people's.

As we will see in Chap. 5, microcredit has become a powerful force of financialization in the Global South. Bauer et al. (2012), using a behavioral economic experiment, examined why microcredit recipients in India do not simply save, to finance their spending or investment, instead of borrowing. What they find is that microcredit borrowers, as compared with non-borrowers, are biased toward the present. Present-bias is a common feature of the focus on poor people and will be discussed below with respect to scarcity. Present-bias means that people are preoccupied with addressing today's issues so that they cannot deal with tomorrow's. Expressions such as "living hand to mouth" describe the phenomenon. They are unable, relative to non-poor and non-borrowers, to save for the future. Credit is seen as an alternative. Poor people find it difficult to save as compared with their neighbors who are non-borrowers. Microcredit provides the borrower the structure to "discipline their financial lives" (Bauer et al. 2012, p. 1137). Bauer et al. point out that the success of microcredit is linked with the combination of peer mentoring, the provision of immediate money, and a regular repayment process. It is the combination of these features that has aligned microcredit with the needs of poor people and helped to make it so successful.

Moving from microcredit to bank credit, Bertrand et al. (2009) undertook a very interesting behavioral economic experiment on the uptake of loans from a South African lender that exemplifies this point. The lender agreed to send out flyers about a loan product. The flyers came in different forms and included different information. The authors found that recipients did not always behave rationally and did not always pick the loan at the best interest rate and conditions but were influenced by other factors. While people were responsive to the interest rate, they were also influenced by things such as simplified loan presentations and photos of attractive people. Their conclusion is not surprising: "non-informative advertising may play a large role in real consumer decisions" (Bertrand et al. 2009, p. 6).

Finally, consider a study undertaken by Bertrand and Morse (2011) dealing with payday loan uptake in the United States. Payday loans are short-term and small-sum loans that are "collateralized" on a paycheck or other type or regular payment (e.g., a welfare payment). They are quite popular among some people in Anglo-American countries. In this case the authors were studying the effect on payday loan uptake of providing prospective clients information about fees in different formats. The information was provided to clients using an experimental design including the following: a standard statement of how much is due and when; a statement of interest rates for payday loan and comparable loans such as car loan and credit card loan; and, a statement of the dollar cost of a payday loan versus credit card costs for two weeks, one month, and so on. The study's results are, once again, most interesting and reinforce the importance in understanding the ways in which we make decisions. People were less inclined to take up a payday loan when they were provided with salient information about the relative costs of payday lending. In particular, when they learned about the relative dollar cost of payday loans as compared with credit card advance for different time periods, there was an 11% decline in uptake relative to the control group (p. 1867). They conclude, "getting consumers to think more long term about the adding up of the dollar costs over time, putting the loan in the context of comparative products to increase its evaluability, and, to a lesser degree, disclosing information on the typical profile of payday loan refinancing significantly reduces the frequency and amount of payday borrowing" (p. 1889).

These studies demonstrate, from a variety of contexts, that people do not behave precisely as the neoclassical model suggests. Present-bias and the use of different types of advertising—non-informative and comparative—demonstrate how people make decisions that are based on limited scope and assessment, but when data are evenly presented, it can enable better decision-making. *Homo economicus* is not a sufficiently nuanced concept to encompass human behavior. And consumer behavior is affected by the behavior of the firm. If the firm presents influential yet irrelevant information to the consumer, it might feed into human limitations.

Savings Behavior

An early behavioral contribution investigated why people seemed to save less than was rational (Shefrin and Thaler 1993). This work, *behavioral* life cycle, challenged the orthodox economic theories of the time which were Milton Friedman's permanent income hypothesis and Franco Modigliani's life cycle theory. Modigliani framed this into his life cycle theory in which young adults borrow, in order to make investments into employment and education, then middle-year adults repay and save, and finally elderly people dis-save to finance their retirement.

Behavioral theory finds that citizens are often too present focused and lack the self-control to save for the future and developed the behavioral life cycle theory to explain this by integrating elements of behavioral economics into the standard life cycle hypothesis. The consequences are that people do not behave rationally and tend to under-save. Also, the life cycle theory assumes that people are able to compute a complicated problem, when "Without computer software, even a trained economist would find this problem daunting" (Thaler and Sunstein 2008, p. 104). The theory also assumes that people have the willpower to undertake major savings projects like retirement savings. But many people fail both of these tests at least some of the time.

Behavioral life cycle theory helps to explain patterns like under-saving. Thaler and Sunstein's solution is what they call "choice architecture". The basic idea behind choice architecture is to structure policies and programs that, allow people to opt in or out and make some choice within the program, but that the default setting is for more savings, more education, and less high-fee debt. Moreover, choice should be simplified, and salient information be provided without excessive and misleading detail. Other examples of choice architecture include "unless otherwise indicated" provisions (that presume consent for organ donation), providing clear information about car fuel economy, and easily joined charitable contribution programs.

Benartzi and Thaler (2004) add an important institutional dimension to the behavioral life cycle approach. They point out that certain savings institutions do not require constant self-discipline on the part of the saver. Without the need for self-discipline, the likelihood of successfully saving is enhanced:

> One fact that underscores the important role of self-control is that the typical middle-class American household accumulates retirement wealth primarily in three forms: social security, pensions, and home equity. Neither social security nor defined-benefit pension plans require willpower on the part of participants, and once a home is purchased, the monthly mortgage bill provides a useful discipline in building up equity. (Benartzi and Thaler 2004, p. 615)[7]

There are other institutions that can facilitate savings, for example, banks. Mullainathan and Shafir (2009) investigate the advantages for savings to having a bank account. People with low incomes are less likely to have house equity and private pensions, thus leaving them to rely on public pension schemes. Consider two people, one with a bank account receiving funds through direct deposit and second receiving funds through a check. The first person has the money in an account and is therefore less likely to spend it. The second person, dependent on their income from a check, is quite possibly going to cash it at a check casher and therefore hold on to the cash, which is more likely to be spent (Mullainathan and Shafir 2009, p. 127). Unbanked people are more likely to be poor, and even though they want to and do save, their savings may be more limited and less effective (not earning any interest) as compared with a person with a bank account (Mullainathan and Shafir 2009, p. 127).

Formal banking institutions also provide implicit planning: credit card companies provide reminders about payments owing, and banks provide statements about investment status. Through ATMs, Internet banking, and mobile banking, one can access one's bank information readily.

Banks can also assist people to engage in small-to-big transformations, for example, small regular deposits to accumulate larger savings for purchasing things, or to repay an installment loan (Mullainathan and Shafir 2009, p. 130). Lottery tickets are an example of a less-than-rational solution to the small-to-large transformation problem. A local credit club is another example from the Global South. Mullainathan and Shafir argue that based on their behavioral analysis, holding a bank account is a means by which poor people can more ably save. They add that the use of multiple accounts and the naming of these accounts (e.g., emergency fund, holiday fund) tie in with the reality that most people, poor people included, use mental accounting—that is, compartmentalizing different sources of income into different types of spending and assets. For instance, a child tax benefit payment might be thought of as a source of savings. They note that this naming of multiple accounts mimics traditional savings schemes such as Christmas Clubs, Education Funds, and so on.

Scarcity and Tunneling

There is a growing literature in behavioral economics examining the unique economic behaviors of the poor in relation to finances and so this literature is instructive to understanding the impact of everyday financialization on vulnerable people (World Bank 2015; Jantti et al. 2014; Mullainathan and Shafir 2013). To be clear, this literature does not find that poor people are uniquely irrational but begins with the premise that all people behave irrationally at times. Do poor people face particular challenges with regard to their economic behavior?

Mullainathan and Safir's book *Scarcity: Why Having Too Little Means So Much* (2013) explores this phenomenon, arguing that poor people face a particular type of scarcity—the inability to meet their material needs—and that this scarcity, in a variety of ways, reduces the person's capacity to pursue his interests. They are focused primarily on scarcity caused by poverty. While recognizing that context matters, by poverty they mean a situation where a person is unable to meet her basic material needs (p. 149). Other types of scarcity can operate in a similar fashion: scarcity of time, lack of friends, and so on. Scarcity "captures the mind", and the result is that mental "bandwidth", or capacity, is undermined. They find a number of ways in which material poverty places a "tax" on a person's bandwidth. Finally "tunneling" is the consequence of the bandwidth tax, causing the person to narrow his focus on a limited set of issues and taking his attention away from other pressing matters. As a result cognitive capacity and executive control can be diminished. Mullainathan and Shafir liken the bandwidth tax to demanding a software program that is running in the background of your computer that slows down its processing capacity.

Mullainathan and Shafir present numerous examples and results from experiments and seek to do so from a number of regions around the world, Global South and North.[8] Two particularly interesting studies relate to cognitive tests applied to people who are either facing or not facing scarcity in a New Jersey mall and in an Indian farming community. In the mall example, people from a variety of income levels were presented with two scenarios, both related to news that they needed a car repair, the first costing \$300 and the second costing \$3000 (p. 49).[9] After being presented with the scenario, the participants were asked to complete Raven's Matrices problems, an intelligence test. The results found that with the $300 repair there was no statistically significant difference between the performance of the rich and poor participants. They repeated the experiment but bumped up the cost of the repair bill to $3000. The results changed: now the poor participants performed worse than the rich. The authors explained these results by stating that the $300 bill was not constraining for rich and poor alike; while the $3000 bill for the rich was not constraining, but it was for the poor, taxing the bandwidth of these participants: "A small tickle of scarcity and all of a sudden they looked significantly less intelligent. Preoccupied with scarcity, they had lower fluid intelligence scores" (p. 51).

A second interesting example in *Scarcity* relates to farmer performance around the harvest period in India (p. 57). This carefully designed experiment examined cognitive capacity of sugarcane farmers before and after their harvest. The authors chose sugarcane farming where the harvest rotates around the year so that the processor has a steady supply of the highly perishable product. In this way, the study controlled for special events, such as harvest festivals, related to certain peak harvest periods. The important factor for this experiment was to examine food-secure Indian farmers' response to physical and emotional stress before harvest as compared to the low-stress post-harvest period. As hypothesized, the authors found that farmers performed worse before the harvest than they did afterward. As with their mall experiment, they found a substantial cognitive tax on the scarcer group: "The same farmer fared worse on fluid intelligence and executive control when he was poor (preharvest) than when he was rich (postharvest)" (p. 58).

These two experiments reveal some of the effects that poverty or scarcity can have on cognitive capacity or bandwidth. In addition to "tunneling"—a narrowed focus on a particular issue at the expense of problems—by Mullainathan and Shafir (2013), other consequences of the bandwidth tax include:

- Reduced cognitive capacity, raw or fluid intelligence, as measured by with Raven's Progressive Matrices and more generally by IQ (p. 47)
- Reduced executive control. Executive control helps to "direct attention, initiate an action, inhibit an intuitive response, or resist an impulse (p. 53)" and is strongly linked with self-control (p. 52)
- Increased distraction, forgetfulness, and reduced impulse control (p. 65)
- More mistakes in planning and giving in to temptation (p. 82).

The quantitative impact of bandwidth tax is substantial:

> By that measure our effects correspond to between 13 and 14 IQ points. By most commonly used descriptive classification of IQ, 13 points can move you from the category of "average" to one labeled "superior" intelligence. Or, if you move in the other direction, losing 13 point can take you from "average" to a category labeled "borderline deficient." Remember these differences are not between poor people and rich people. Rather, we are comparing how the same person performs under different circumstances … *The poor responded just like the rich when the car cost little to fix, when scarcity had not been rendered salient* (italics added). (p. 52)

Mullainathan and Shafir propose a number of responses to address the problem of material scarcity faced by poor people:

- More carefully designed programs that fit the needs of poor people
- Subsidized daycare; carefully designed education programs[10]
- Financial products that address small net income variations
- Reminders/encouragements to repay/save
- Encouraging impulse savings through a savings card at the grocery store checkout
- Loan repayments that include a portion that goes toward savings
- Require payday lenders to provide actual dollar costs for loans compared with actual dollar costs for a similar loan from a mainstream bank lender.

Datta and Mullainathan (2014) provide another set of suggestions to help people to overcome scarcity. They call for programs and policies that economize on people's scarce mental resources by:

> reducing the need for self-control (e.g., by making payments in smaller units rather than in large sums), the use of commitment devices to overcome self-control problems (e.g., by providing restrictive bank accounts), choosing default options intelligently (e.g., making automatic transfer into a savings account the default option), recognizing the power of micro-incentives (e.g., giving a small amount of grain as a reward when a child is brought to an immunization center), not being shy of continual reminders (e.g., to make deposits into savings accounts), or paying attention to the framing of government messages (e.g., emphasizing what people lose by not participating in a program rather than by stating what they gain). (Datta and Mullainathan 2014, cited in Jantti et al. 2014, pp. 2–3)

From Bounded Rationality to Deliberate Decision-Making
Consumers, particularly in wealthy countries, face many choices regarding consumption. The sheer number of decisions leads us to sometimes take short-cuts, and this can undermine our best interests. How can one avoid irrational pitfalls? One way is to promote a more deliberate process of making choices. Decision-making can be more rational if one can be more deliberate, know oneself better, frame the issue carefully, gather available data, and make decisions on that basis, for instance:

- Identify the decision or choice that is needed
  - Clarify the goal behind a current decision or choice.
  - How does this goal relate to one's overall financial goals? How does this goal relate to one's life goals?
  - What are the different means to achieve the goal, and how do they (the means) rank with one another?
- Know your decision-making biases
  - Which biases are you more likely to be subject to such as status quo bias, anchoring, ideological bias, and so on?
  - Consider if your biases are influencing your decision-making on this particular decision or choice.
  - Frame the decision-making carefully: for instance, try framing it "positively" and "negatively" to see how it affects the outcome.
- Gather available data that can assist in the decision
  - Understand the context
  - Simplify options in terms of

    Number of options
    Identify key and salient factors to base decision-making on
    Exclude non-essential factors
    Exclude marketing features

  - Collect data including third-party information (e.g., from consumer rights groups)
  - Identify unknowns
- Make the decision.

Anchoring, availability, representativeness, overoptimism, loss aversion, status quo bias, and mental accounting are examples of ways in which people behave in irrational ways. What can individuals think or do differently to counteract these common challenges? Again, thinking more deliberately about one's decision and how different types of biases may affect it would be a useful first step. Policymakers aren't the only ones able think more rationally. If anchoring is a challenge, consider talking with a friend who might have a different perspective and possibly knowledgeable about the issues (Table 4.1). If optimism or overconfidence is an issue, assume you're decision is wrong and determine what it would cost you.

Discussion

Behavioral economics has provided us with rich insights about actual human behavior. As the foregoing discussion has shown, we behave differently than what neoclassical economics supposes. This analysis demonstrates a limitation of neoclassical economic theory. But critics of behavioral economics have pointed out its weaknesses. For instance, it is argued that by concentrating on individual limitations, behavioral economics disempowers individuals in favor of the state and corporate sectors. But, as we shall see in Chap. 5, when the behavioral light is applied to policymakers, bounded rationality is the result.

This chapter has examined some correlates of consumer financialization including consumerism, consumer debt, and advertising. It has sought to understand the concept of rationality from various economic and sociological perspectives. Finally the chapter has examined evidence of human rationality in thought and action. Human decision-making is complex and cannot be easily boiled down to *homo economicus*. There is too much evidence at odds with this characterization. Bounded rationality, from an economic perspective, might be due to one or more of the following: decision-making short-cuts, social relationships, and structural barriers.

What are the consequences of "irrationality" on the consumer? It depends on the reason for the particular decision. If the decision is economically irrational but socially rooted, then it's likely rational within a broader meaning of the word. On the other hand, if the irrationality is driven by business practices such as advertising, fee disclosure practices, or outlet location strategy, then the decision might injure the consumer. This chapter has concentrated particularly on the situation in which short-sighted behavior, due to tunneling, status quo bias, anchoring, and so on, has led to decision-making that has harmed the consumer. These

Table 4.1 Countering common types of behavioral bias

Type of bounded rationality	*Individual response*
Anchoring: a rule of thumb whereby we make assessments about a new thing based on something we are familiar with. For instance, we guess at the size of a city by anchoring that guess in how large or small we think it is compared with our own city (p. 23)	1. Ask the question: are you anchoring—making a decision by comparing it with another decision that was quite different? 2. Ask a knowledgeable person about relevance of comparison 3. If anchoring, collect more quality information and/or ask an expert: consumer's bureau, Better Business Bureau, Consumers Reports
Availability: where we base an assessment on an unknown situation based on what we know. For instance, after the 9/11 terrorism event, many people assessed the risk of terrorism as being higher than it was (p. 25)	4. Collect information from quality source 5. Talk with a specialist
Representativeness: a heuristic often followed whereby we believe that we identify a pattern when no pattern exists. For instance, basketball fans often think that players have shooting streaks when they continuously score baskets, but this is not the case (p. 31)	6. Be skeptical about patterns that you see. They may be white noise that looks systematic 7. Ask a knowledgeable person about what you see
Optimism and overconfidence: a characteristic of human behavior that leads to common errors. For instance, we often think we know more about money markets than we do, and then when our retirement savings under-perform, we blame someone else (p. 31)	8. Assume there is a good chance that your analysis justifying your decision is incorrect. What would it cost you?
Loss aversion: the phenomenon whereby people are more averse to loosing something than they are pleased to gaining something of equal value. For instance, we place a higher value on an item we have as compared to that same item that we do not have (p. 33)	9. Consider the benefits of losing something, for example, you no longer have to maintain it or worry about losing it 10. Understand sunk costs
Status quo bias: a human characteristic that leads us to prefer the known current state over an alternative even if the alternative might be better (p. 34)	11. Realize the temporary nature of most things, including our lives
Mental accounting: a heuristic that has people assigning their assets in different mental categories as opposed to the NE assumption that we only think of total asset amount (p. 49). For instance, one source of money, say our salary, may be assigned for rent and food, while another source of money, say income from some entitlement program, may be assigned for savings	12. Remember that money is fungible

behaviors can lead to harmful consequences among vulnerable people flowing from everyday financialization. Payday lending is an interesting case in which structural barriers and opportunities—that underplay mainstream banking in favor of fringe banking—align with people who are tunneling. The consequence for these consumers is a debt cycle that is hard to break out of.

A common prescription for the "irrational consumer diagnosis" from the behavioral school is to nudge them into making a choice that is in their best interest. Save more, borrow less, and choose the better credit product are common outcomes of presenting the consumer with "choice architecture". This issue will be explored further in the next two chapters. Based on analysis in this chapter, two problems need to be addressed to effectively provide choice architecture. First, who decides what is in the consumer's interest? Second, and related to the first question, if it is the policymaker who decides, and given policymaker's own bounded rationalities, how can it be ensured that the default choices are in the consumer's interests?

The discussion of bounded rationality has limitations, and this is an important point to raise. As we will see in Chap. 6, bounded rationality is not limited to vulnerable people but is a universal challenge. In order to determine if finance and credit schemes benefit people, it is important to gain both quantitative insights on its economic impact and qualitative insights on what participants think about these products and the impact on their lives. This latter insight is important, regardless of bounded rationality, and it is most likely achieved through dialogue between the finance provider and borrower.

Notes

1. This was the view, popularized by the actions of early twentieth-century automobile manufacturer Henry Ford, that the demand for his Model T car would increase if the production costs were brought down, through the introduction of the assembly line, thus allowing the price of the car to be within the reach of his factory workers.
2. This is precisely what I learned in interviewing Canadian bank executives a few years ago: that non-poor clients are more aggressive than poor clients in negotiating interest rates (Buckland 2009).

3. One important nuance is that some social capital is exclusive and harmful toward others, while other social capital is inclusive and possibly helpful toward others.
4. Zelizer adds a critique of her own discipline, sociology with the following, "Sociologists, to be sure, pay the opposite price: a potpourri of theories and observations so various that a researcher can rarely be sure that a new finding actually fits with or contradicts previously accumulated understandings of the economic process at hand" (Zelizer 2011, p. 10).
5. It is interesting to note that classical political economists had a more nuanced and varied view about human rationality. Adam Smith's 1776 work on the wonders of the free market in *The Wealth of Nations* was informed by his earlier work, *The Theory of Moral Sentiments.* Humans are rational and a part of a morally minded society. Malthus argued that the pursuit of pleasure by people with limited discipline led them into a vicious cycle of poverty (Spechler 1990).
6. In some cases the term "financial capability" is used instead of or synonymously with "financial literacy". When it is used this way, it generally refers to financial literacy and responsible financial behavior. In this sense, financial capability brings together the concepts of financial literacy and financial behavior.
7. Note that all three of these sources of retirement income are under pressure from various pressures, including financialization. Public retirement pensions in Canada, and I imagine elsewhere, are threatened because the rising share of retired to working people. Private pensions are increasingly defined contribution plans, and home equity is threatened by home equity loans and reverse mortgages, for example.
8. Many of examples and experiments come from either the United States or India. While these two countries have very different socio-cultural-economic contexts, they do not represent an international perspective so that this is a limitation of Mullainathan and Shafir's study.
9. Mullainathan and Shafir make an interesting observation about the differences in how poor and non-poor value money (p. 89). Neoclassical economic theory hypothesizes that people will value a dollar the same regardless of the context and the study supported this in the case of the poor. But in the case of the poor what the study found is that the value placed on money depended on the context. To save \$35 on a \$100 DVD player is valued more highly (the same) than to save \$35 on a \$1000 laptop by the rich (poor) (p. 89).
10. Regarding education, many people—policymakers and poor alike—support more education as a means to address material scarcity. But rather than being offered in a linear and sequential manner, financial literacy

could be taught using stand-alone modules with multiple and staggered start times, focusing on good rules of thumb (p. 174–75). This allows less bandwidth for each class and allows participants to experience early and ongoing success.

Bibliography

Axelrod, Robert. 1984. *The Evolution of Cooperation*. New York: Basic Books.

Bauer, Michal, Julie Chytilova, and Jonathan Morduch. 2012. Behavioral Foundations of Microcredit: Experimental and Survey Evidence from Rural India. *American Economic Review* 102 (2, Apr.): 39–1118.

Benartzi, Shlomo, and Richard H. Thaler. 2004. Save More Tomorrow: Using Behavioral Economics to Increase Employee Saving. *Journal of Political Economy* 112 (1, Part 2): S187.

Bertrand, Marianne, and Adair Morse. 2011. Information Disclosure, Cognitive Biases, and Payday Borrowing. *Journal of Finance* 66 (6, Dec.): 1865–1893.

Bertrand, Marianne, Sendhil Mullainathan, Dean Karlan, Eldar Shafir, and Jonathan Zinman. 2009. What's Advertising Content Worth? Evidence from a Consumer Credit Marketing Field Experiment. Economic Growth Center, Yale University, Working Papers.

Bowles, Paul, D. Ajit, Keely Dempsey, and Trevor Shaw. 2011. Urban Aboriginal use of Fringe Financial Institutions: Survey Evidence from Prince George, British Columbia. *The Journal of Socio-Economics* 40: 895–902.

Bowles, Samuel, and Herbert Gintis. 2011. *A Cooperative Species: Human Reciprocity and its Evolution*. Princeton: Princeton University.

Buckland, Jerry. 2009. *Passing the Buck? Examining Canadian Banks Approaches to Financial Exclusion*. Winnipeg, Canada: Institute of Urban Studies, The University of Winnipeg.

———. 2011. *Money Management on a Shoestring: A Critical Literature Review of Financial Literacy and Low-Income People*. Ottawa: Task Force on Financial Literacy.

Buckland, Jerry, Dion McKay, and Nolan Reimer. 2016. *Financial Inclusion and Manitoba Indigenous Peoples: Results from an Urban and a Rural Case Study*. Winnipeg: Canadian Centre for Policy Alternatives.

Coggan, Philip. 2012. *Paper Promises: Money, Debt and the New World Order*. London: Allen Lane; Penguin Books.

Coleman, James S. 1988. Social Capital in the Creation of Human Capital. *American Journal of Sociology* 94 (Supplement): 95–120.

Collin, Dominique. 2011. Aboriginal Financial Literacy in Canada: Issues and Directions. Canadian Task Force on Financial Literacy. Accessed May 18, 2015 http://www.financialliteracyincanada.com/documents/consultation-2/Collin-09-02-2011-eng.pdf

Cross, Philip. A Longer-Term Perspective on Canada's Household Debt—Longer-Term-Perspective-on-Canadas-Household-Debt.Pdf. Fraser Institute. Accessed May 20, 2015. http://www.fraserinstitute.org/uploadedFiles/fraser-ca/Content/research-news/research/publications/longer-termperspective-on-canadas-household-debt.pdf

Daly, Herman E. 2008. *A Steady-State Economy*. London, UK: Sustainable Development Commission.

Daly, Herman, and John B. Cobb. 1989. *For the Common Good: Redirecting the Economy Toward Community, the Environment, and a Sustainable Future*. Boston: Beacon Press.

Datta, Saugato, and Sendhil Mullainathan. 2014. Behavioral Design: A New Approach to Development Policy. *Review of Income and Wealth* 60 (1): 7–35. https://doi.org/10.1111/roiw.12093. http://onlinelibrary.wiley.com/doi/10.1111/roiw.12093/abstract.

Feiner, Susan F., and Bruce B. Roberts. 1999. Hidden by the Invisible Hand: Neoclassical Economic Theory and the Textbook Treatment of Race and Gender. In, ed. April Laskey Aerni and KimMarie McGoldrick, 43–65. Ann Arbor: University of Michigan Press.

Frank, Robert. 1999. *Luxury Fever: Why Money Fails to Satisfy in an Era of Excess*. Princeton: Princeton University Press.

Galbraith, John Kenneth. 1992. *The Culture of Contentment*. Boston: Houghton Mifflin Co.

Gathergood, John. 2012. Self-Control, Financial Literacy and Consumer Over-Indebtedness. *Journal of Economic Psychology* 33 (3): 590–602.

Godinho, Vinita. 2014. Money, Financial Capability and Well-being in Indigenous Australia. RMIT University.

Hewitson, Gillian. 2013. Economics and the Family: A Postcolonial Perspective. *Cambridge Journal of Economics* 37 (1, Jan.): 91–111.

International Monetary Fund. 2012. *World Economic Outlook*. Washington, DC: IMF.

Jantti, Markus, Ravi Kanbur, and Jukka Pirttila. 2014. Poverty, Development, and Behavioral Economics. *Review of Income and Wealth* 60 (1): 1–6.

Kartashova, Katya, and Ben Tomlin. 2013. House Prices, Consumption and the Role of Non-Mortgage Debt. Bank of Canada, Working Papers.

Kempson, Elaine, and Adele Atkinson. 2009. *Measuring Levels of Financial Literacy at an International Level*. Paris: Organization for Economic Cooperation and Development.

Klontz, Bradley T., Sonya L. Britt, and Kristy L. Archuleta, eds. 2015. *Financial Therapy: Theory, Research, and Practice*. Heidelberg: Springer International Publishing.

Kroll, Christian. 2015. Global Development and Happiness: How can Data on Subjective Well-being Inform Development Theory and Practice? *Oxford Development Studies* 43 (3, Sep.): 281–309.

Lucas, Robert E., and Thomas J. Sargent, eds. 1981. *Rational Expectations and Econometric Practice*. Minneapolis: University of Minnesota Press.

Lusardi, Annamaria. 2008. Household Saving Behavior: The Role of Financial Literacy, Information, and Financial Education Programs. National Bureau of Economic Research, Inc., NBER Working Papers: 13824.

Lusardi, Annamaria, and Olivia S. Mitchell. 2014. The Economic Importance of Financial Literacy: Theory and Evidence. *Journal of Economic Literature* 52 (1, Mar.): 5–44.

Martin, Thibault, Amelia Curran, and Judith Lapierre. 2006. Banking in Winnipeg's Aboriginal and Impoverished Neighbourhood. *The Canadian Journal of Native Studies* XXVI: 331–359.

Migone, Andrea. 2007. Hedonistic Consumerism: Patterns of Consumption in Contemporary Capitalism. *Review of Radical Political Economics* 39 (2, Spring): 173–200.

Montgomerie, Johnna. 2009. The Pursuit of (Past) Happiness? Middle-Class Indebtedness and American Financialisation. *New Political Economy* 14 (1, Mar.): 1–24.

Mullainathan, Sendhil, and Eldar Shafir. 2009. Savings Policy and Decisionmaking in Low-Income Households. In *National Poverty Center Series on Poverty and Public Policy*, ed. Rebecca M. Blank and Michael S. Barr, 121–145. New York: Russell Sage Foundation.

———. 2013. *Scarcity: Why having Too Little Means so Much*. New York: Henry Holt; Times Books.

Norberg-Hodge, Helena. 1991. *Ancient Futures: Lessons from Ladakh for a Globalizing World*. San Francisco: Sierra Club Books.

Ostrom, Elinor. 1990. *Governing the Commons: The Evolution of Institutions for Collective Action*. Cambridge: Cambridge University Press.

Prahalad, C.K. 2010. *Fortune at the Bottom of the Pyramid: Eradicating Poverty with Profits*. Upper Saddle Hall: Pearson Education Inc.

Putnam, Robert. 1993. *Making Democracy Work: Civic Traditions in Modern Italy*. Princeton: Princeton University Press.

Richardson, Thomas, Peter Elliott, and Ronald Roberts. 2013. The Relationship between Personal Unsecured Debt and Mental and Physical Health: A Systematic Review and Meta-Analysis. *Clinical Psychology Review* 33 (8): 1148–1162. https://doi.org/10.1016/j.cpr.2013.08.009. http://www.ncbi.nlm.nih.gov/pubmed/24121465.

Ryoo, Soon, and Yun K. Kim. 2014. Income Distribution, Consumer Debt and Keeping Up with the Joneses. *Metroeconomica* 65 (4, Nov.): 585–618.

Schumacher, E.F. 1973. *Small is Beautiful: Economics as if People Mattered*. New York: Harper and Row Publishers.

Sexsmith, Kathleen. 2006. *Aboriginal Employment in the Banking Sector in Manitoba*. Edited by Kathleen Sexsmith. Canadian Centre for Policy Alternatives.

Shefrin, Hersh M., and Richard H. Thaler. 1993. The Behavioral Life-Cycle Hypothesis. In *Economics and Psychology*, ed. Shlomo Maital and Sharone L. Maital, 166–200. Cheltenham, UK: Edward Elgar.

Siklos, Pierre L. 2004. *Money, Banking, and Financial Institution: Canada and the Global Environment*. 4th ed. Toronto: McGraw-Hill Ryerson.

Slavova, Milanka. 2014. Consumerism as a Source for Innovation and Product Development. *Economic Alternatives* (2): 5–19.

Spechler, Martin C. 1990. *Perspectives in Economic Thought*. New York: McGraw-Hill Publishing Company.

Stanford, Jim. 2015. *Economics for Everyone: A Short Guide to the Economics of Capitalism*. 2nd ed. Ottawa: Pluto Press.

Sweet, Elizabeth, Arijit Nandi, Emma Adam, and Thomas McDade. 2013. The High Price of Debt: Household Debt and its Impact on Mental and Physical Health. *Social Science and Medicine* 91: 94–100.

Thaler, Richard H., and Cass R. Sunstein. 2008. *Nudge: Improving Decisions about Health, Wealth, and Happiness*. New Haven and London: Yale University Press.

Todaro, Michael P., and Stephen C. Smith. 2015. *Economic Development*. 12th ed. Boston: Pearson.

van Tuinen, Henk K. 2011. The Ignored Manipulation of the Market: Commercial Advertising and Consumerism Require New Economic Theories and Policies. *Review of Political Economy* 23 (2, Apr.): 213–231.

World Bank. 2014. *Global Financial Development Report 2014: Financial Inclusion*. Washington, DC: International Bank for Reconstruction and Development.

———. 2015. *World Development Report 2015: Mind, Society, and Behaviour*. Washington, DC: World Bank.

Zelizer, Viviana A. 2011. *Economic Lives: How Culture Shapes the Economy*. Princeton: Princeton University Press.

Zurlo, K.A., W. Yoon, and H. Kim. 2014. Insecured Consumer Debt and Mental Health Outcomes in Middle-Aged and Older Americans. *Journal of Gerontology, Series B: Psychological Sciences and Social Sciences* 69 (3): 461–469.

CHAPTER 5

Credit, Cash, Savings, and Financial Literacy Delivered Through Civil Society

Introduction

This chapter looks at examples of human development efforts in which money plays a central role, including microcredit, cash transfers, asset-building programs, and financial literacy and empowerment programs. These programs are popular in the Global South, the Global North, and worldwide. The fact that these programs are so popular, and that taken together, they are found around the world, demonstrates the important role that money now plays in human development programming. This rising role for money offers both benefits and risks for vulnerable people.

Microcredit is one of the best examples of everyday financialization. In its most basic form, it provides individuals with small loans to invest in and strengthen their microbusiness. Its social dimension, generally speaking, is that the loan is directed to poor people who would otherwise not have access to formal sector credit. It is a financialized initiative because it uses finances—credit in this case—to enable the greater efficiency and or growth of small businesses operated by poor people. The cost of the loan is sometimes subsidized, adding to the cost of providing the credit, but the movement toward commercialized microcredit adds another dimension to its financialization, discussed below.

Roy (2010) argues that the rise of microcredit around the world is an example of the democratization of finance, aligned with Van der Zwag's everyday style of financialization discussed in Chap. 2:

J. Buckland, *Building Financial Resilience*,
https://doi.org/10.1007/978-3-319-72419-5_5

> Microfinance, as it reaches poor women…is an example of the democratization of capital. It seeks to transform hitherto exclusionary systems of finance into those that include the poor. In addition, it facilitates flows of philanthropy and investment—from foundation in the prosperous global North to organizations that serve the poor in the global South. (Roy 2010, p. 3)

Roy argues that microcredit was inspired in Bangladesh and has made important contributions there but she is critical of how some international agencies, associated with the "Washington consensus of microcredit", have sought to commercialize microcredit. She argues that the Bangladesh model of microcredit is multipronged, perhaps best exemplified by the work of BRAC, and well aligned with an anti-poverty approach (Roy 2010, p. 113). Minimalist approaches to microcredit, she argues are supported by some international agencies, are poorly aligned with poverty reduction and better oriented toward commercial schemes (Roy 2010, p. 110).

Regional Variations in Socially Oriented Financial Programs

Through a series of non-governmental organizations, civil society has been particularly active in the proliferation of microcredit in the Global South, although it also exists in the Global North. Grameen Bank (which is actually a government agency but operates much like an NGO and has its own board), based in Bangladesh, is one of the most prominent microcredit agencies, but there are many others of this size. Microcredit is delivered in many other shapes and sizes, including small organizations that specialize in other areas and have added microcredit as an additional service.

While civil society organizations may be the major actors in social sector initiatives, they do not always work alone or even take the lead. In many cases they partner with commercial or state organizations in order to achieve their goals (recall Fig. 1.1 in Chap. 1). For instance, in efforts to scale up the size of microcredit programs, some NGOs have increasingly looked to the private sector for capital, and in fact, some microcredit programs have become fully commercialized, such as the Compartamos Banco in Mexico. In other cases, the state helps to fund activities or might even take the lead. For instance, large state and inter-state donor agencies have funded microcredit and asset building programs around the world, and conditional cash transfer programs have often been implemented by state organizations.

Microcredit really took off in the Global South in the 1980s. The model was tried in the Global North, but it is not practiced at the same scale as in the Global South. For instance, in Canada, financial institutions and non-profit organizations offer small business loans, but this looks very different than microcredit programs in the Global South. A few EU initiatives, discussed below, will make that clearer.

Some factors that help to explain this regional difference include the different scale of existing financial institutions and the informal economy and the differences in mobility and social bonds among vulnerable people. Because the existing financial institution network in the Global North is much more extensive than countries in the Global South, there was less space for new actors to rise up. In the Global South there was, and still is, a large share of the population that is unbanked. The Global North is also characterized by a relatively small informal economy—that is, the economy based on activities that are produced by individuals, families, or very small firms with small amounts of capital and are relatively unregulated. This type of economic activity is much larger in the Global South. The Global North is characterized by a large formal economy in which production is undertaken in small, medium, and large firms that involve substantial amounts of capital and that is regulated. Finally, a key feature of microcredit has been high repayment rates that have in part been due to social collateral. Group members support and pressure their peers to repay their loans in order to maintain the credit circle and in order to get a loan themselves. This works well when people do not move around a lot and when there are strong social bonds among them. In the Global North there is more migration, and communities are often very diverse so that the bonds within communities are not as strong. In this context, it is relatively easy to move to another neighborhood or simply stop relating to the credit group. By contrast, in a village in Bangladesh, if a person does not repay a loan, he would gain a reputation, and since moving away would remove all social supports, the pressure to repay is very high.

There are many other types of finance and credit schemes. Conditional cash transfers are another intervention with social and financial dimensions. Recently they have become very popular in the Global South. But whereas cash supports[1] and microcredit have not become popular in the Global North, savings programs have, particularly in several Anglo-American countries. These programs are linked to the movement toward building assets in addition to income, associated with the asset-building movement. Like microcredit, asset building became popular because it was well aligned with a moderate neoliberal approach that sought to combine the market, human agency, and short-term subsidy. Unlike microcredit, asset building does not require group support or pressure for repayment, and so it is better suited to the characteristics of the Global North. The savings are intended for a variety of things, most importantly education and training. Here too, considering the large size of the labor market in the Global North, highlighting education and training, as compared with microcredit, is better aligned with the needs and opportunities of asset-poor people there. More recently asset-building programs have become more popular in the Global South.

Financial education has been another social sector initiative, sometimes done alone by the state and sometimes done together with civil society. Financial literacy programs have expanded rapidly in the last several years. Closely related to these are credit counselling programs, which in countries with high levels of consumer debt have grown significantly. Finally, one might identify an emerging model that integrates several of these social sector initiatives into a financial empowerment model.

Microcredit, Conditional Cash Transfers, and Asset-Building Programs

There are a number of programs coming from a social and developmental perspective that involve money and/or finances as a central means to promote human well-being. The three programs examined in this section are microcredit, conditional cash transfers, and asset-building. Each approach is quite different, based on credit, cash, and savings, respectively. And yet they have important similarities, starting with the fact that their principal goal is to assist the participant through money or finance. Another shared characteristic of these programs is that they merge development values of welfare and agency: welfare in the sense that there is generally some element of subsidy—although not with commercialized microcredit—and agency in the sense that program seeks to build the participant's agency or her capacity to achieve her own ends. The subsidy is imbedded in the program's operating costs.

As development interventions they target income- and asset-poor people, yet each approach requires some form of participant action, whether through business investment, children's school attendance, or saving for housing. Thus these approaches seek to promote values of welfare and productivity and are consistent with more progressive forms of neoliberalism associated with approaches by Tony Blair in the United Kingdom and Bill Clinton in the United States.

Microcredit

At its core microcredit is a very simple concept—a small loan—but since the 1980s it has taken on tremendous meaning for many people and many different manifestations. The reason that it has taken on such a significant meaning, arguably, is linked with the time period in which it dramatically grew, during the rise of neoliberalism and reform developmentalism. Microcredit is very distinct from the state-supported banks that arose in the 1950s in support of large-scale development projects including agricultural modernization.[2]

Beginning in the 1980s, neoliberalism increasingly came to dominate development theory and practice. A core concept within neoliberalism is the importance of private property,[3] the role of the market, and the importance of competitive firms as central actors in development. This was a shift from the state-led period when the role of the state was considered central to development thought and action. As well, neoliberalism placed more emphasis on the role of the individual than was done during the state-led approach. The particular focus was primarily on the individual as consumer—as opposed to, say, the individual as citizen. Moreover, the relative emphasis shifted from rights to responsibilities: instead of a focus on the rights of groups—labor, citizens, women, poor people, and farmers—the emphasis shifted toward their responsibilities. Individual agency and "working hard" were the prescription for many ailments associated with poverty.

Microcredit aligns well with neoliberalism as it accents work and welfare. On the one hand, microcredit provides small loans to poor people to strengthen and or build their business. Thus it supports individual agency to contribute to the economy. On the other hand, non-commercial microcredit generally involves a level of subsidization and is often combined with other social services (access to education or health care) such that there is a welfare component. But to say that microcredit is well aligned with neoliberalism is not to say that it is an ideological tool of neoliberalism. Microcredit has and can operate within other nation-centered ideologies such as state-supported capitalism and possibly even within a modest socialist approach.

Consider "reform developmentalism", an area of development thought and action, associated with the approaches of people such as Jeffrey Sachs (2011) and organizations such as the World Bank (2015). It is an approach that accepts much of the neoliberal accent on markets and individual agency and accepts that certain structural and historical inequalities exist. It sees microcredit as a means to enhance human agency and justifies the subsidy as a part of the means to righting the historical and structural inequalities. But the real chameleon quality of microcredit comes out in how closely it links with two other, more community-based ideologies, community development and post development. Community development comes in many forms, from market-oriented through reform to radical development. The first two approaches are aligned with microcredit: the former would advocate more commercially oriented microcredit, while the latter would advocate socially oriented microcredit. Radical community development would be critical of many types of microcredit, as would post development, but would arguably support a grassroots approach that is tightly linked with local savings and credit associations and that might grow into a community bank.

The Concept and History

The basic concept of microcredit is very simple: it's a small loan to a poor individual to assist her with her small business. The idea has been around for thousands of years, within and outside of familial relationships. The idea is linked to the need that people have, from time to time, to fill in income gaps or as economists say "consumption (or production) smoothing". We generally consume a regular amount of food, clothes, gasoline, and so on, and so we like regular income. But many people face irregular streams of income, with periods when that income is low. How can the income-spending gap be bridged at this point? The gap can be met by either drawing down savings (including liquidating physical assets) or by borrowing. While credit from a family member is preferable in some ways—often involving low fees or none at all fees—it is disadvantageous in other ways, for instance, it might strain important social relationships. Moneylenders are another option, but their interest charges are very high.

Microcredit, and virtually any other financial service prefaced with "micro" prefix, such as micro-insurance, micro-savings, encompasses a growing list of financial services that are linked with microcredit and now fall within the category of microfinance. Research completed during the 2000s (Rutherford 2000, 2002; Collins et al. 2009) found that poor people in a variety of settings in Bangladesh, India, and South Africa use a variety of financial services, including savings and insurance. These studies found that microcredit on its own was insufficient to meet poor people's financial service needs and in some cases poor people valued savings services so much that they were willing to pay for the service, rather than expecting interest income from it.

A key feature of modern microcredit is that it seeks to engage the clients in small groups to encourage, support, and pressure one another in investing and repaying the loan. The loan itself is provided to the individual. In this way modern microcredit is an adaptation of the village credit circle. It involves the peer support and monitoring associated with the credit circle but places it within a modern institutional structure. Perhaps this is a key component of microcredit's success: it has adapted a successful traditional institution—peer monitoring—to a modern bureaucracy.

The peer monitoring and support feature of microcredit, as compared with mainstream banking, involves shifting some of the costs and risks of lending from the creditor to the borrower. This is done by creating social collateral. Instead of a person using an asset as security for the loan, she relies on her peers. The early microcredit model in the Grameen Bank used groups made of five people, one of whom was designated as the leader. After receiving their training two members receive their loan. Once they repay the loan in full, the next two members receive their loans. Then, once these are repaid, the leader receives her loan, and once it is repaid the cycle begins again. The clients encourage and pressure their peers to repay their loans in order that they receive one. Moreover, because they are neighbors the clients are better informed than bank staff about the financial situation of any particular borrower. So the risk the lender faces is less, because there is a good chance that she hears about problems her clients are facing either from the member facing the problems or from another group member.

Another important feature of microcredit is that a principal and in some cases only target group are women. The thinking is that women are often the most vulnerable so that by directing credit to them, microcredit has the best chance to assist the poorest people. Critics complain that women are targeted because they, as compared with men, are more likely to repay their loans. This will be examined below.

As discussed above, in the Global North, producer microcredit has tended to be less successful, due to two factors. First, the smaller informal economy means that it is not seen as a viable option by vulnerable people who are more likely to see employment rather than self-employment as a life-improving step. Second, the more transient nature of local people in the Global North reduces the likelihood that peer support and monitoring are available social assets. Moreover, the commercial bank sector in the Global North is much larger than in the Global South (see Chap. 2). Conversely, NGOs in the Global South, as compared with the Global North, are very large.[4] And NGOs, as a sector, have been quick to embrace microcredit. Consumer microloans have become modestly popular in the Global North and that will be the principal focus of discussion on this topic for that region.

Size and Scope of Microcredit

Because microcredit programs vary in size and scope and are scattered around the Global South, summary data are limited and not necessarily always consistent. Estimates of the sector vary considerably. For instance, one estimate in 2008 found there were 86 million borrowers in 1395 microfinance institutions—MFIs, organizations that are solely devoted to providing microfinancial services—with a gross loan portfolio of US$45 billion (Aitken 2013). According to the latest MIX Market (Microfinance Information Exchange, Inc.) data,[5] in 2014 there were 33 million active borrowers in 1269 MFIs with a loan portfolio of US$52 billion (Table 5.1).

Bateman (2011) estimated the microfinance "penetration rate", the share of the target population that had a microcredit loan, for 22 countries in the Global South. He found that the penetration rate, at 25%, was the highest in Bangladesh, and it ranged considerably more in other countries:

- Nine countries (or states) with "medium" rates of 10 to 17%, in declining share: Andhra Pradesh, Bosnia and Herzegovina, Mongolia, Cambodia, Nicaragua, Sri Lanka, Montenegro, Vietnam, and Peru

Table 5.1 The size of the microcredit sector, by region, 2014

Region	*MFI count*	*Gross loan portfolio*	*Number of active borrowers*
Africa	308	3,082,306,018	2,857,991
East Asia and the Pacific	121	5,655,618,137	5,215,308
Eastern Europe and Central Asia	247	8,071,015,735	2,641,825
Latin America and the Caribbean	366	33,027,335,594	14,393,862
Middle East and North Africa	42	1,155,624,263	1,924,749
South Asia	185	1,474,496,141	6,508,033
Total	1269	52,466,395,888	33,541,768

Source: MIX Market, "Cross-Market Analysis", available: http://reports.mixmarket.org/crossmarket#, accessed 30 Nov. 2015

- Thirteen countries with "low" rates from 9 to 4%, in declining share: Armenia, Bolivia, Thailand, India, Paraguay, El Salvador, Burkina Faso, Kyrgyzstan, Ecuador, Guatemala, Mexico, Colombia, and Morocco (Bateman 2011, p. 4).

Females are a larger share of microcredit borrowers across most regions and overall. On average 65% of borrowers are female, and this figure ranges from as low as 35% in Eastern Europe and Central Asia to as high as 90% in South Asia (Table 5.2). High repayment, or conversely low loan loss rate, has been a hallmark of microcredit, and the MIX Market data confirms this with loan losses, on average at 1.8%, and ranging from as low as 0.1% in South Asia to as high as 6.3% in sub-Saharan Africa (Table 5.2).

The Diversity of the Model

One of the strengths of microcredit is its flexibility that allows it to be organized in many ways including traditional and modern, small and large, on its own or with other programs and services.

Regarding the traditional–modern spectrum, many economic activities we see today have some type of equivalent in a "traditional", that is, pre-corporate and pre-large state, economy.[6] Traditional credit and savings were most basically done through family and friends. At a more organized level, rotating and accumulating credit and savings schemes are found around the Global South. Here a small group commits to regular, transparent, and accountable contributions and/or distribution of a collective pot of money.[7] These traditional schemes are generally small-scale

Table 5.2 Female borrower share and loan loss rate, by region, 2014

Region	*Percent of female borrowers (weighted average (%))*	*Loan loss rate (weighted average (%))*
Africa	74.6	6.3
East Asia and the Pacific	85.2	0.2
Eastern Europe and Central Asia	35.3	0.0
Latin America and the Caribbean	42.8	2.7
Middle East and North Africa	57.7	1.3
South Asia	90.4	0.1
Sum	64.3	1.8

Source: MIX Market, "Cross-Market Analysis", available: http://reports.mixmarket.org/crossmarket#, accessed 30 Nov. 2015

and community-based. Modern microcredit organizations include NGOs, MFIs, and commercial banks. While NGOs range in size, the MFI and commercial bank tend to be a large operation. Small NGOs might concentrate on microcredit or might add it to their other programs. Other NGOs might engage in a micro-enterprise approach that assists the producer in a more holistic way through training to assist the participant to identify opportunities, create business plans, and access capital. At the other end of the informal–formal continuum are the large MFIs and commercial banks.

Large MFIs such as the Grameen Bank and others in Asia and BancoSol in Bolivia began as NGOs, or in GB's case, as a semi-autonomous government institution, almost exclusively offering microcredit. Their main aim was to identify the best practice in microcredit and then replicate it in order to increase their beneficiaries. BRAC founder Sir Fazle Abed's articulated this idea well saying that "small is beautiful"—it enables an organization to focus on poor people—"but big is necessary"; this allows it to focus on *many* poor people. Economists call this taking advantage of economies of scale. Through replication the fixed costs of the operation, for instance, head office costs, can be shared across a much larger number of clients, thereby reducing the costs per client.

Turning first to MFIs in Bangladesh, there are several that are quite large, and the total numbers of participants is over 11 million (Table 5.3). Grameen Bank was developed by the now-famous Muhammad Yunus, winner of the 2006 Nobel Peace Prize. According to data from

Table 5.3 Major microcredit programs in Bangladesh

MFI's—most recent data	*Report date*	*Loans (USD)*	*Borrowers*	*Deposits (USD)*	*Depositors*
ASA	2013	763,555,799	4,444,461	365,462,022	13,674,691
BRAC	31-03-15	1,249,807,843	1,683,735	448,563,406	5,493,867
Grameen Bank	30-06-15	1,174,434,967	7,060,000	2,185,372,443	–
RDRS	31-03-15	36,414,873	239,262	15,413,868	307,515
Total[a]		3,654,765,830	10,594,580	3,095,781,876	13,088,836

Source: Microfinance Information Exchange (Mix Market) 2015, accessed 3 Sept. 2015, available: http://mixmarket.org/; Grameen Bank 2015 Grameen at a Glance, accessed 3 Sept. 2015, available: http://www.grameen-info.org/grameen-bank-at-a-glance/

Table 5.4 Major microcredit programs in Bolivia

MFI's—most recent data	*Report date*	*Loans (USD)*	*Borrowers*	*Deposits (USD)*	*Depositors*
Banco FIE	30-06-15	1,085,220,959	236,558	954,171,757	867,851
BancoSol	30-06-15	1,109,031,271	252,442	980,957,087	697,633
CRECER	30-06-15	176,108,526	155,459	0	–
Pro Mujer—BOL	30-06-15	59,717,930	109,150	0	–
Total[a]		5,845,444,047	944,583	5,020,975,555	1,565,548

Source: Microfinance Information Exchange (Mix Market) 2015, accessed 3 Sept. 2015, available: http://mixmarket.org/

Microfinance Information Exchange, it is the second largest MFI based on loan volume, just behind the BRAC Bank, but the largest in terms of number of borrowers, at 7.1 million (Table 5.4). Yunus began as a professor and during some research noted the high interest rates poor handicraft producers paid to finance their inputs. He experimented by providing credit to individuals within a social circle and found it worked. Grameen Bank has not commercialized and continues to rely on donors' financial support in a variety of ways—soft loans, grants, bonds sold at favorable interest rates—to cover its costs (Schicks 2007).

Some MFIs have scaled up their clients and their services, for instance, BRAC Bank. Additional services include savings and insurance. Most recently they have moved very aggressively into the provision of mobile banking services. Regarding the expansion into new financial services, economists call this taking advantage of economies of scope, akin to economies of scale. But here, instead of spreading out fixed costs over a growing number of loans, the costs are spread over a growing number of services. BRAC Bank has been operating since 2001 and has 88 branches, 69 service centers or Krishi branches, 300 ATMs, and 400 SMEs (small- and medium-sized enterprises) units across the country (BRAC Bank 2015). It has 1.2 million customers and has disbursed over CAD 3.8 billion (BDT 220 billion). It has an explicit corporate social responsibility commitment and is a member of the Global Alliance for Banking on Values. BRAC Bank is engaged in lending to the SME sector, the corporate sector, the retail sector, and mobile banking.

Moving from Bangladesh to Latin America, consider BancoSol. It was transformed into a commercial bank in 1992 and is currently a major player in the Bolivian banking sector. The bank currently offers credit, savings, insurance, and local and international money transfer services (BancoSol 2015). It highlights fostering enterprise of small producers, rural and urban, male and female. BancoSol began, with support from Accion International, as the NGO PRODEM in 1986 (Schicks 2007). In 2014 it had just over 250,000 borrowers with a gross loan portfolio of US$1.1 billion. In addition it had deposits from just under 700,000 depositors for a total of just under US$1 billion (Table 5.4). In Bolivia in total, it is estimated that one million borrowers are served by MFIs in Bolivia with a total loan portfolio of just under US$6 billion with just over US$5 billion in deposits.

According to Bateman (2010) the PRODEM–BancoSol transition was the first NGO–commercial bank transformation. And it was received as an early success as the bank became both profitable and very large, in the Bolivian context. But, it is argued, competitive pressures forced BancoSol to move "upmarket", that is, to work less with the very poor and more with the less poor (Schicks 2007). Bateman notes that during the 1990s other NGOs transformed into commercialized banks, so that Bolivia became an interesting case study of the commercialization process. Proponents of this process argued that the BancoSol case demonstrates that commercialization can be a means to expanding outreach and continuing to address poverty. But Bateman points out that while indicators of success for commercialized MFIs were positive, indicators of poverty reduction and development improvement were not. Schicks (2007) notes that while it is clear that BancoSol does not work with the poorest Bolivians, it does work with a modest income group, and its financial performance is positive.

Moving to the Global North, where producer-based microcredit has not been popular, there are considerable efforts to provide consumer microloans. The impetus behind these programs is not about supporting small-scale producers. Instead, the focus here is to provide access to consumer loans in order to reduce the participant's reliance on subprime credit like payday loans. In a scan of the sector in 2009, Buckland (2009) found a relatively large number of these programs in the United States, which is not surprising considering its high population and unbanked share, and in Australia, surprising for its small population and unbanked share (Table 5.5).[8]

Table 5.5 Select microloan programs in Australia, the United States, and Canada

Organization (partner) Country Revenue	*Loan size Interest charge*	*Mode of delivery*	*Credit portfolio*	*Activities of borrowers*	*Evaluation*
Grameen America[a] United States US$18.9 million (2014)	Starts at US$1500 and increases at 15% interest	Individual recipient within group model	US$230 million in loans dispersed to 43,204 women through 18 branches in 11 cities (2014)	Producer loan: door-to-door or home-based retail, house cleaning, some storefront retailers	One study found income increased by average $2500 in six-month loan cycle
Desjardins Fédération Mutual Assistance Fund[c]	Ranges from $500 to $1500; interest varies	Individual-based	Loans come from a $500,000 "solidarity" fund through 31 locations in Québec (2009)	Consumer loans	
Good Shepard Microfinance: No interest loan scheme (NILS)[b] (National Australia Bank) Australia A$20.4 million (2014)	Average A$1200 at 0% interest	Individual-based	A$20.8 million in loans dispersed in 22 thousand loans offered in 609 locations (2012–2013)	Consumer loan: kitchen and cleaning appliances, furniture, car repair	One study found that over three-fourths of clients experienced improved economic, social, and health conditions, and almost 50% noted improved financial literacy

Sources: [a]Grameen America 2015, Dewan 2013; [b]Buckland 2009, Good Shepard Microfinance 2015; [c]Buckland 2009, Desjardins Fédération 2015

A major effort to encourage banks to engage in small consumer loans was sponsored by the US Federal Deposit Insurance Corporation's Small-Dollar Loan Pilot Project.[9] Banks made a total of 34,400 loans valued at US$40.2 million (Miller et al. 2010). Delinquency levels were a little elevated, but charge-off rates were similar to industry standards (Miller et al. 2010, p. 13). The profitability of these loan schemes was generally not well-known, and most participating banks explained that their view of the small loans was as a means to build relationships with new clients and that some of these clients would eventually use other, more lucrative financial services.[10] Some conclusions that FDIC reached from the pilot include studying the use of government loan guarantees to promote these types of funds, investigating how new technologies can advance this type of product, and, quite interesting, encouraging "broad-based" partnerships among banks, non-profits, and community groups to work together in designing and delivering small-dollar loans (Miller et al. 2010).

Grameen America is one of the few non-profit organizations in the Global North that focuses exclusively on producer microloans. Established by Muhammad Yunus it has been offering loans since 2008. The loans are made through the Grameen Bank model, via a mentoring circle, and they start at US$1500, offered at a 15% interest charge (Table 5.5). The program has grown from 500 women with US$1.1 million in loans in 2008 to 53,000 women with almost US$300 million in loans in 2015. Grameen America reported that, for 2014, it dispersed US$230 million to 43,204 women through 18 branches right across the United States in 11 cities. Typically the loans are used to support door-to-door and home-based retail businesses, house cleaning, and some store-fringe retailers. One study of the project found that average participant income rose by US$2500 within a six-month loan cycle.

One of the largest FIs in Québec, Canada, is the Desjardins Fédération, and in 2007 it set aside funds that would be directed toward "solidarity" projects that assist marginalized people. As one component of this, the federation established their Mutual Assistance Fund, a fund that would be the basis of providing small consumer loans to clients of participating *caisses populaire* (credit unions) in the federation's network in Québec. The loans range from $500 to $1000, interest charges vary by *caisse*, and in 2009 loans were offered in 31 locations. Unlike the NILS and Grameen America program, the Mutual Assistance Fund program is not growing: the number of loans declined from 705 in 2010 to 629 in 2012. The corresponding amounts in loans declined from $409 thousand to $391 thousand (Desjardins Fédération 2015).

In Australia, Good Shepherd Microfinance works with the National Australia Bank and offers a series of credit and one asset-building product. This includes the No Interest Loan Scheme (Table 5.5), the StepUp Loan, and the Adds UP Savings Plan. These loans are primarily intended as consumer loans, but the NAB offers another product, the micro-enterprise loan, valued at A$500 and A$20,000, that is intended for small businesses. Good Shephard Microfinance has been operating loan schemes since the 1980s within a social welfare model and has expanded its financial service offerings over time working with the National Australia Bank and the national and several state-level governments. Its revenue for 2014 was A$20.4 million. The Good Shepherd Microfinance loans are individually based, and financial counselling is available.

The NILS program has grown. In 2009 there were approximately 5500 loans per year, and at that time this number was projected to grow to 6500 loans in 2009 and 14,000 loans in 2012 (Buckland 2009). In fact the program grew faster than projected so that in 2012–2013, a total of A$20.8 was loaned out in 22 thousand loans offered in 609 locations across Australia. The loans were used for consumer purposes such as kitchen and cleaning appliances, furniture, and car repair. The organization has an impressive research department and collaborates with research programs such as the Centre for Social Impact at the University of New South Wales, and Good Shepherd Microfinance engages in monitoring and evaluation of its program. A recent study found that, in connection with the receiving the loans, over three-quarters of clients experienced improved economic, social, and health conditions, and 50% noted improved financial literacy.

There are many examples in the Global South of small microloan organizations. In Nepal, Vijaya Youth Club Co-operative and Credit Union (VYCCU) Savings and Credit Co-operative Limited (INAFI Nepal undated) has 9638 members and in 2012 had just over 2000 borrowers (MIX Market website). The club is registered as a cooperative with the purpose of overcoming poverty and boosting local savings. The club accepts deposits, and the most recent data find that there are Nepali rupees 318 million on deposit. Adesh, a Bangladeshi organization, operates a small microcredit program within its wide cross-section of programs that include livelihoods, education, and female empowerment. In 2013 they had just over 3200 active borrowers (MIX Market website).

The web, mobile phone apps, and information technologies in general have presented many new avenues to engage in microcredit. These technologies reduce the transactions costs for people to interact with one another for various reasons, including for lending and borrowing money or for raising funds. Peer-to-peer (P2P) lending allow the lender and borrower to find a suitable partner. For instance, Kiva, a US-based non-profit is an intermediary for this process by working with local organizations and then promoting the needs of the members of the organizations through Kiva's website (Kiva 2015). Borrowers are organized by country, type of borrower, gender, and so on. Prospective lenders can view different prospective borrowers, and if they so choose, they can sign up for membership and then examine different individual's projects to finance. There is often a crowd-sourcing component to these projects as one borrower may not finance the entire project.

Crowd-sourcing is another method that information technologies provide for microcredit. Crowd-sourcing, similar to what Kiva implicitly does for some of its projects, involves raising small amounts of capital from many people. Another example relates to a recent study in Canada regarding using crowd-funding to finance a payday loan alternative to be offered by credit unions. One claim is that Kiva fosters "connected capital", described by one author as "endowed with certain characteristics such as being patient (Kiva lenders seek long term or no returns), catalytic (Kiva lenders take big risks in order to have big impacts), accountable (Kiva lenders want feedback on their loans) and democratic (Kiva lenders number in the hundreds of thousands)" (Schwittay 2014, p. 516). But one author notes that the Kiva approach ignores structures that cause poverty and potentially creates a paternalist relationship between creditor and borrower (Schwittay 2014, p. 516).

Another component of microcredit's diversity is who offers it. Microcredit may be offered by a non-governmental organization (NGO), more commonly referred to as a non-profit organization in the Global North, or it might be offered by commercial financial institutions. While microcredit got its first impulse from the NGO sector, the last few years has seen a growing interest from commercial FIs. This is the source of a powerful tension in the microcredit movement: whether the commercialization of microcredit diminishes the capacity to achieve its stated social goals. It might be offered by one of these organizations, or it might be offered through a partnership, for example, between an NGO and a commercial FI. Microcredit in the Global South is often offered by one organization, but in the Global North there are examples of partnerships between NGOs and FIs.

Partnerships are also very important in the field of microfinance. In the Global South, partnerships are arguably the reason why microcredit has become so ubiquitous. It started with partnerships between NGOs and government donor agencies, and it now includes various market agents such as commercial banks, rating agencies, patient capital suppliers, and so on. The shift toward increasing interest in market actors will be discussed below. But for many years it was state actors that were financing most of the microcredit industry, and it was based on a partnership that saw the state as the donor and the NGO as the implementer. Each actor needed the other. The NGO needed the state's funds, and the state, given its neoliberal shift, needed a non-state actor to deliver the microcredit.

Partnerships in this area in Canada and Australia, for example, are made up FIs and non-profit organizations (Buckland 2009). The Good Shepherd organization in Australia in combination with the National Australia Bank offers two types of microcredit loans: the No interest loan and the StepUp loan. These loans are intended for consumption or educational purposes, offered at no or low interest, to people meeting certain criteria. Momentum, a Canadian non-profit organization, in conjunction with a local credit union is developing a loan product that will act as an alternative to payday loans in that it will be small-sum and short-duration product. Pawn-based loans—offered in consumer-friendly ways that include low fees and reimbursement to consumers who forgo their goods but when the goods are sold for more than the loan and fees due—are available in the United States, France, and Belgium through socially oriented pawnshops.

Analysis of Microcredit

The analysis of microcredit involves many different points and perspectives. Some central features include the simplicity of its design, the peer support and mentoring system, gender equity, poverty reach, commercialization, and economic displacement.

An important strength of microcredit is its simplicity of design: provide a loan to a borrower who repays it. This simplicity allows the organization to gain expertise in delivering a basic product to a lot of people and then maximizing the likelihood of their repaying the loan. It does not require the organization to address strategic economic issues such as assessing the limitations or expandability of key inputs or markets, because that is done by the borrower. It also does not require the organization to address other social and economic aspects of well-being such as health, education, food security, and employment. The organization only needs to focus on the delivery and repayment of its loan product.

Another key strength of microcredit is involving participants in the repayment process, related to the peer support and monitoring function of many microcredit programs. By bringing borrowers into the repayment process, higher repayment rates are the result. This builds on the borrowers' interests—by ensuring that each member repay their loan in a timely fashion, they will receive future loans. In a way one's "credit score" is dependent on the repayment rates of one's group members. This reduces the pressure and costs that the FI faces.

As we see below there are some strong critiques of larger and formal MFIs, often coming from a left-leaning perspective. However, smaller and less formal microcredit organizations are sometimes assessed quite differently. Critical analyses of microcredit are sometimes more sympathetic to small-scale projects than to large-scale ones. This is in part because it is often assumed that small-scale initiatives are more rooted in community needs and interests. Moreover, if these grassroots microcredit organizations can scale up into a cooperative bank—sometimes called a credit union—then many objections from the left are avoided. A credit union is a small- to medium-sized bank with a community-based history and tends to have products appropriate for that community. It will usually hire locally and potentially support local projects. As a coop the profits remain within the community or region. And because each member has one vote, there is embedded within it a democratic governance structure. This is in keeping with a reformed community development perspective, but it is not clear if it is aligned with a post-development perspective. This is because the large size of a coop might distance it from local control.

One of the earliest critiques of microcredit is related to its gender impact, and the critique itself has changed over time. Early on microcredit was critiqued for not having sufficient female borrowers. Grameen Bank for one addressed this critique by increasing its share of female clients. However, after this was done it was more clearly recognized that the underlying patriarchy in certain social settings biases the benefits of microcredit, regardless of who receives the loan. Studies (e.g., Goetz and Gupta 1996) found that even when women received the loans, often it was their husbands, fathers, or older brothers who decided how the loan would be used, which itself would affect who would benefit from the loan. Goetz and Gupta (1996) found that only 37% of microloans were fully controlled by women recipients. Some critics have argued that giving women credit is done to improve credit scheme performance, as women are more likely to repay the loan than are men.

The goals of microcredit to help and to foster productivity are sometimes in tension and this has meant that MFIs have struggled with the issue of poverty reach.[11] The poorer a person, generally speaking, the less able she is to use credit to boost her business. This is because depth of poverty is correlated with a number of factors that will affect her ability to utilize credit. The deeper the poverty, the more likely the person is food insecure, poorly educated, less physically healthy, and the less likely she is to be fully employed, have easy access to markets, have reasonable "power" within one's household and community, and so on. These factors create more barriers to utilizing credit effectively. Conversely, people who are "less poor", that is, who still fall within the organization's "target group" but are at the upper limit, will more likely have the assets that enable them to effectively integrate credit into their business to improve it. And subsequently, they will be better able to repay the loan. There has been a tendency within MFIs to deliver microcredit to this group, the better-off poor. Bateman observes that Grameen Bank has been deliberate about its efforts to work with the poorest people, including beggars (Bateman 2011, p. 56). But more generally, Bateman notes:

> Microfinance does, of course, reach many poor people, if not the very poorest. But the claims that it reaches the poorest of the poor and can on its own eliminate poverty contributed to what is perhaps the major problem affecting microfinance: gross exaggeration of what it can achieve. (Bateman 2011, p. 56)

An economic challenge associated with relying on many small producers in a relatively laissez-faire way is called displacement. This problem occurs when loans are made available to a group of producers who are producing goods within markets that face growth barriers. These barriers prevent the industry from expanding, so that for each microcredit recipient who enters the market, there is an existing producer who does not receive the microcredit and is forced out of the market. Of course, it doesn't work precisely like that, but that is the idea. The barriers can fall on the demand or supply side. Demand-side barriers affect the demand for the product being produced by the borrowers. A common use of microcredit in many countries is for small-scale agriculture, agro-processing, and retailing such as dairy, rice processing, and petty trading. The demand-side barrier is constraining if consumer demand is limited because incomes are stagnant, or, if incomes are rising, the good in question is "inferior" in the economic sense such that as incomes rise, quantity demand for that product declines. Supply-side barriers can also cause displacement. If the production of the good in question is contingent on certain inputs that themselves are limited, then adding credit to the industry will not enable to increase in production.

If demand- and or supply-side barriers are present, then the introduction of microcredit into a community, region, country, industry, or sector may lead to a displacement of production from former producers to the microcredit borrowers. This may help the borrowers but does not help the displaced producers. This is clearly not the goal of microcredit.

As discussed above a new pressure entered in the 1980s and 1990s, which was the commercialization of microcredit. Commercialization is attractive because of the potential pot of private capital. However, there are important risks associated with greater commercialization. Pressures on the poverty and gender reach will mount, meaning that poverty reduction and improved gender equity may be compromised. Aitken (2013) argues that commercialization places pressure on the MFI to generate profits. He argues that the MFI will off-load this risk onto the microcredit borrower. Moreover, he notes that commercial microcredit encourages debt accumulation among a disadvantaged group that "converts the poor into an asset stream". For borrowers, Aitken finds, the risks of commercialized microcredit include exposing vulnerable people to the risk associated with financial markets, expanding the distance between borrower and creditor, and leading to an increase in interest rates on loans.

MFIs are not homogeneous, and using one simple indicator (profitability) to measure performance is troublesome. MFIs must also be evaluated for their development impact which requires a holistic evaluation. This is more complex than a "bottom-line" capital market assessment and would include several dimensions including impact on poverty reduction, gender equity, and capacity building. Evaluation of MFIs should include examination of participants, as they also are not homogeneous, and in many cases they are not the poorest. Evaluation requires careful examination of goals and purpose of MFIs

Impact

One important way to assess the impact of an intervention is through evaluation. This is particularly important for microcredit considering the tremendous amount of passion around it. Passion is critical for energizing people but equally important is that people are fully informed about what they are passionate about. Only recently has a fulsome critique of microcredit emerged (e.g., Bateman 2010, 2011). Impact evaluations can assist in providing this information. Types of impact evaluations vary, and there is not entire agreement on the best approach, particularly across quantitative and qualitative approaches. On the quantitative methodological side, the generally preferred approach is the randomized controlled trial (RCT). The randomization and control features of the RCT enable the researcher to distinguish between changes caused by the intervention and changes caused by other factors. The challenge with RCTs is that they are expensive and complicated to organize, and because the control group is excluded from the benefit, present the evaluation process with an ethical challenge.

Until recently there have only been a limited number of impact evaluations of microcredit (Duvendack et al. 2011). For instance, in their systematic review of the literature, Duvendack et al. (2011) note that "rigorous quantitative evidence on the nature, magnitude and balance of microfinance impact is still scarce and inconclusive" (p. 2). The few RCTs they found did not show a strong impact of microcredit on participants. They conclude:

> We find that most of the effects assessed occur in the early stages of the causal chain (Figure 1), with both positive and negative outcomes; the bulk of estimates reported were statistically insignificant even at the beginning of the causal chain, and a significant number of estimates suggest negative outcomes throughout the causal chain. These findings are not inconsistent with at least some of the qualitative literature. (Duvendack et al. 2011, p. 74)

More recently, the *American Economic Journal* published an issue devoted to microcredit RCTs (Angelucci et al. 2015; Attanasio et al. 2015; Augsburg et al. 2015; Banerjee et al. 2015a, b; Crépon et al. 2015; Tarozzi et al. 2015). In their summary of these studies, Banerjee et al. (2015b) conclude that there is evidence that microcredit has a modest positive impact, but they find no evidence of transformative changes, reductions in poverty, or substantial improvements in living standards (p. 13). They do find that microcredit does expand business scale and sometimes profit but that this does not affect household income. They also note that the evidence does not support microcredit's harshest critics: there is little to show that microcredit harms participants (p. 14). The overall effect seems modest, but there is less evidence that it causes harm.

Cash Transfers

Microcredit has been a popular development intervention, in part because of its elasticity and the resulting variety of ways it can be implemented and how these different means of implementation align with different interests. Another reason for its popularity is that it builds on the idea of human agency: by providing the recipient with credit, she can improve her capacity and, in fact, repay the loan. Another type of monetary transaction that became popular from the 2000s involves the transfer, rather than the lending, of cash: cash transfer or conditional cash transfer programs. These programs have grown in numbers and scale throughout the Global South. Rather than a loan, they provide the recipient a stream of income, with the intent to assist vulnerable people to better meet their basic needs.

Cash transfers (CTs) allow the recipient to spend the cash however they prefer, while conditional cash transfers require her to spend it toward certain items such as education and health care for her children. Either form of cash transfer is to enable families to better support themselves through crises and make investments. In modern development, cash transfers have a close antecedent with food-for-work programs that have been used to address a crisis and build infrastructure. In some cases the transfers are done through mobile banking.

In terms of structure, conditional (CCT) and unconditional cash transfers (UCT) are delivered by the state and civil society. Also, as mentioned, these programs can be conditional or not and targeted or not. The level of conditionality of CCTs varies and in some cases is not too different from UCTs (World Bank 2015, p. 9). In some cases conditions are not monitored or enforced, in other cases they are not enforced, and in other cases they are monitored and enforced. Some cash transfer programs are targeted, while other programs are untargeted. Targeting seeks to concentrate supports toward a particular group. It means that the program clients are limited to certain groups, generally vulnerable people, based on certain criteria. CCTs are the most targeted of social programs, devoting as much as 50% of benefits to the poorest 20% (World Bank 2015, p. 3).

There are interesting similarities and differences between the microcredit and cash transfer approach. One approach uses credit the other uses a payment. The former requires repayment to ensure careful investment, while the later requires spending to follow pre-determined conditions, or, with unconditional cash transfers, it assumes the individual "knows best". The former requires an organization to deliver credit and receive repayment, whereas the latter needs to only deliver the payment. The former requires an endowment of capital and regular inflows to cover costs, whereas the latter requires a continuous flow of money to finance the payments. One important difference is that microcredit is often considered a means to boosting productivity, while cash transfers are seen as a social support. However, this is a dubious distinction, because sometimes credit supports household spending and cash transfers can sustain important household investments such as education.

While conditional and unconditional cash transfers are relatively new terms, state-supported safety nets, social welfare, or social protection have been around for many years in the Global North. As middle-income countries become wealthier, their states are in a better position to support some of their population. And some of the largest cash transfer programs are in middle-income countries. A parallel has been drawn between the growth of CCTs in the Global South and the move toward "welfare-to-work" initiatives in parts of the Global North (Fiszbein and Schady 2009). All of these programs provide supports in exchange for "desired behavior", meaning that welfare is provided to assist people to get back to work and CCTs are provided to get people to school or health care (Fiszbein and Schady 2009, p. 33).

The economic rationale for cash transfers are that they are a way to foster human capital, supporting investments that families would otherwise not engage in (Fiszbein and Schady 2009). Moreover, Fiszbein and Schady describe a political economy argument that by making social support conditional on particular spending, the program is able to attract wider social and political support. But economists are concerned that cash transfers might create disincentives by crowding out private initiative.

Current Scope and Size

Cash transfer programs began in Latin America and spread to other middle-income countries such as China, Indonesia, Turkey, and South Africa, some low-income countries such as Bangladesh, Pakistan, and Cambodia, and more recently in sub-Saharan Africa (Fiszbein and Schady 2009; World Bank 2015). The decade beginning in 1997 saw a period of rapid expansion of cash transfer schemes (Fiszbein and Schady 2009): in 1997 there were only three large-scale national schemes, but by 2008 there were over two dozen. And some programs grew rapidly. For instance, in Mexico during this period, PROGRESA grew from 300,000 beneficiaries to five million (Fiszbein and Schady 2009, p. 3). Growth continued through the early 2010. The World Bank notes that between 2010 and 2014 the number of CCTs increased from 27 in 2008 to 64 in 2014, while the number of UCTs had increased from 21 on 2010 to 40 in 2014 (World Bank 2015, p. 7). According to the World Bank, CTs, including public works, encompass 718 million people (WB 2015, p. 10). China and India each have cash transfer programs that reach between 75 and 78 million people.

The World Bank found that low-income countries, as compared with non-low-income countries, place a higher share of the social spending on targeted programs. UCT spending is considerably higher than CCT spending in all Global South regions except Latin America and the Caribbean, where it is quite even. In terms of total social protection spending, the World Bank estimates that low-, middle-, and high-income countries spend on average 1.5%, 1.6%, and 1.9% of their GDPs, respectively (World Bank 2015, p. 21). A very high share of this is spent on UCTs in Europe and Central Asia, and a declining share is spent on UCTs in East Asia/Pacific, Middle East and North Africa, South Asia, sub-Saharan Africa, and Latin America and the Caribbean (World Bank 2015, p. 24).

In some contexts, for example, Kenya, delivering cash transfers via mobile banking makes sense because of widespread adoption of mobile banking. In Columbia the government arranged for the bank, Banco Davivienda to provide mobile banking services in order to provide CCTs for close to one million participants of the program Más Familias en Acción (Marulanda Consultores 2015). The program seeks to help low-income families by providing them cash supplements to support their children's health and education. A total of 2.75 million households are participating in the program. Participants receive their transfers and are able to do other financial activities through mobile banking including withdrawals, transfers, internal remittances, and bill payments.

Impact

In their review of impact literature, Fiszbein and Schady (2009) found that CCTs have a positive effect on consumption and reducing poverty. For instance, in Mexico, where there are major CCTs, they found that the programs helped to reduce the national poverty gap.[12] One indicator of this gap, the squared poverty gap, found that CCTs reduced the poverty gap by 29% in Mexico, 13% in Jamaica, and 15% in Brazil. However, the authors concluded that there is limited evidence that CCTs create disincentives that would dampen the cash contribution (Fiszbein and Schady

2009, pp. 124–25): "Most programs, especially those making sizable transfers, have had substantial impacts on consumption and on poverty" (Fiszbein and Schady 2009, p. 125). A more recent World Bank study found that the outcomes on health, nutrition, and food security from cash transfers are positive:

> Cash transfers, both conditional and unconditional, helped increase enrollment rates of primary and secondary children by 18 percentage points in Burkina Faso compared to a control group (families not receiving a transfer) and by 8 percent in Chile ... Attendance rates, a key condition for many transfer programs, have also been improved for transfer beneficiaries, especially among secondary students. (World Bank 2015, p. 49)

This study determined that the predictability of the cash transfers is important. Where they are predictable, it was found that the impact was greatest. The authors note that predictable transfers have enabled recipients to take investments into their livelihoods, for example, agriculture. For the program to be successful, Hanlon et al. (2010) point out that it must meet two conditions: it must be perceived to be fair and assured. That is, first the broad cross-section of the population perceives the program to be fair and therefore supports it. Second, it is important that the cash transfers be seen as a certainty, allowing people to plan on them and plan with them. If there is uncertainty, then people cannot make plans with the transfers in mind.

Asset Building

The Concept and History

Asset-building programs, like microcredit and cash transfers, are another type of money-based human development program. In one common form, the matched savings scheme, it involves the participant saving money in order to invest in some personal, educational, or business asset. When the participant meets his goal, his savings are matched by the program. The asset-building literature has added to our understanding about the importance of household assets and their distinction from flows.[13] At a practical level, from the 1990s asset building has been linked with programs that seek to encourage individual savings, most notably matched savings programs. But there are many ways to encourage savings, not just through structured programs that match participant savings. Many countries in the Global North use the tax system to encourage savings through various types of tax deductions and credits.

In a sense, matched savings schemes are like the conditional cash transfer programs, but instead of requiring the person to spend the cash on certain items, the recipient is required, for a period of time, to save the money and put them in a bank account. Once the period of time elapses, she/he is required to spend the savings on some type of investment, such as education, business, or housing. Asset-building programs, like microcredit and conditional cash transfers, have antecedents, once again at the state level, involving the study and application of state investments in physical capital and infrastructure. And asset building has conceptual connections to the work in the 1950s through 1970s regarding human capital (Schultz 1959 cited in Sherraden 2005).

Michael Sherraden was a key figure behind the conceptualization of asset building as a development approach and the application of it in a practical way, through expanding matched savings schemes. He notes the asymmetry of asset policy in the United States:

> The typical American middle-class household accumulates most of its tangible and financial assets in home equity and retirement accounts, both which are subsidized through the tax system. These public policies are highly popular and have little political opposition. Most everyone agrees that asset accumulation is good for households and for the country. But the poor, for the most part, do not participate in these asset accumulation policies. Would everyone, particularly the poorest Americans benefit from asset-based policy? How can public policy promote asset accumulation for all Americans? (Sherraden 2005, p. 6)

The asset-building model aligned very closely with a progressive neoliberalism that combined welfare and productivity. It gained genuine political support in the 1990s and early 2000s from US President Clinton and UK Prime Minister Blair. Under Clinton there was talk of establishing a universal savings plan, and under Blair the plan was for universal savings for children and families (Sherraden 2005, p. 11). The subprime mortgage crisis and consequent global recession, among other things, diminished these conversations and commitments.

The Current Scope and Size

Asset-building ideas were popularized in the 1990s, and a major US-based matched savings scheme, the American Dream Demonstration project, began in the United States in 1997 (Sherraden 2005). The idea spread to other countries, particularly Anglo-American countries including Canada, the United Kingdom, and Australia. It has not been popular in continental European countries. More recently there have been efforts to promote these programs in Mexico and several countries in Asia.

Political support for asset programs declined under Bush in the United States and with the conservative government in the United Kingdom. And the Great Recession reduced the availability of funding. The United Kingdom had established the Child Trust Fund in 2005 for every British child, but with the change of government in 2010, this program discontinued support for new participants (Cramer and Williams Shanks 2014, p. 5).

After the onset of the subprime-induced recession, hopes of establishing universal programs in the United States and the United Kingdom declined. In 2014 President Obama announced the establishment of a national savings account, myRA, that is accessible to the employed, self-employed, and unemployed (King 2015). It is designed to be accessible by everyone and provide for people in retirement and protect them in a financial crisis. The concept is that the account will facilitate savings as there are no matching funds.

Analysis and Impact

Asset-building programs have garnered quite a bit of grassroots support and appear to be well aligned with the interests of vulnerable people. They have not been the target of extensive grassroots or academic critique. One interesting criticism has more to do with their absence than their operations. That is, in Global North countries have well-funded programs that assist middle-income families to accumulate assets, for example, through retirement savings programs. In these countries individual retirement savings can be used to reduce one's taxable income which acts to reduce government revenue. But these programs are not used by people who do not pay taxes, that is, those with low income and assets. These types of asset-building programs tend to be highly regressive in nature.

Impact evaluations were done on pilot projects established in the United States and Canada. The American Dream Demonstration program was a matched savings program with around 2400 participants and ran for five years to 2002 (Cramer and Williams Shanks 2014, p. 3). Evaluations found that the program had an important if mild positive impact on the participants (Stegman and Faris 2005). Similar results arose from the Canadian study (Leckie et al. 2008).

The asset-building movement has offered important conceptual insights, demonstrated that matched savings schemes can contribute to asset-poor peoples' lives, and provided insights into the financial behavior of participants. Much of this research was conducted to examine how behavior is affected by matched savings and financial literacy education. It found that both factors—financial literacy and provision of matched savings schemes—boost savings. But improved access to banking and appropriate and understandable information about one's financial options, incentives, facilitation, expectations, restrictions, and security are important institutional factors that also affect savings behavior (Cramer and Williams Shanks 2014, p. 6).

Education and Counselling on Household Finances

Education is another avenue that financialized human development programs take. Education is seen as a means to empower individuals to better manage their finances. In some cases these efforts are embedded within microcredit, cash transfers, and asset-building programs, and sometimes they are separate. Throughout the modern development period, education has been understood as an important approach to development. It has been variously seen as contributing to human capital and therefore economic growth and contributing to gender equity by ensuring active participation by girls and women. In some cases, an educated and knowledgeable population is considered one of the ultimate goals of development.

Education might be group-based or one-on-one, with the general purpose of addressing a more chronic gap by improving participants' financial literacy. Credit counselling is done one-on-one, with the purpose of assisting participants through an acute debt crisis.

The Concept and History

Financial literacy programing has rapidly expanded in the last 20 years, as evidenced by the proliferation in studies and surveys of financial literacy. The impetus has come from the identification by a growing group of policymakers, academics, and non-profit staff that there is a widening gap between the sophistication of the marketplace and the financial working knowledge of many citizens. For instance, as private retirement savings schemes move from defined-benefit to defined-cost plans, the onus shifts from employer to employee. And this shift of responsibility to the individual employee cannot be treated lightly when one considers the boom-bust cycle of the global economy, particularly the recent subprime mortgage crisis. While saving for retirement is a very middle-class activity, using a payday loan is an activity of low-income people in the Global North, and its use raises similar pressures for financial literacy.

The 2005 OECD publication *Improving Financial Literacy* is an important book for its content and is associated with a turning point, after which there was a large increase in work on financial literacy. Since the book came out, the OECD secretariat and many of the member states have been active in this field through developing indicators of financial literacy, measuring financial literacy, and building and implementing programs of financial literacy. The book *Improving Financial Literacy* is a helpful foundation for work in this area. The book was prompted by the growing number of financial products available in the marketplace, and the combination of moving from defined-benefit to defined contribution pension plans with people living longer. This means that many people will live more years in retirement but rely more on investments they alone were responsible for.

The financial marketplace is becoming more complicated, and people are more reliant for their financial well-being on their own financial choices. But this varies around the world, between rich and poor country, and from urban to rural context. While it is true that in contexts where financial products are rapidly proliferating and individuals are increasingly responsible for their financial well-being, is it true for poorer countries, remote regions, and poorer people? Here too there are needs. For instance, the proliferation of mobile banking in countries such as Kenya, the Philippines, and Bangladesh exposes a large number of people to a new level and kind of financial services that could help but risk harming them.

Financial literacy is about people's ability to manage their finances to meet their financial and life goals. The financial education literature often refers to financial literacy components: knowledge, skills, and attitude. For instance, knowledge building might be associated with understanding the risk-reward trade-off in investments; training might be necessary to develop the skill around opening and using a bank account, or awareness-raising is in relation to debt or consumerism.

Many OECD countries have implemented national surveys and are involved in delivering or supporting the delivery of financial education. The United Kingdom and the United States were two of the earliest countries active in this field, and the OECD has been an active proponent. Since the 1990s there has been a rapid growth in state support for financial education. Currently it is reported that 59 countries have a national strategy on financial literacy, and five more countries are planning one (OECD 2015, p. 11). These strategies often involve some combination of the following: developing indicators and measuring financial literacy, creating a body to oversee the implementation of the strategy, assigning explicit mandates to certain public institutions, and implementing and evaluating the strategy to ensure effective provision of financial education (OECD 2015, pp. 8–9).

There are now a variety of international surveys on financial literacy, including the World Bank's Financial Capability survey, the OECD/International Network on Financial Education (INFE) survey, and the OECD's Program for International Student Assessment (PISA) survey 2012/2015 (OECD 2015, p. 23). Indicators of financial literacy include "subjective" (self-assessments) and "objective" (numerical and problem-solving) assessments; these indicators are sometimes used individually and sometimes combined into an index. A weakness with using a standard methodology is that it assumes that identified thresholds apply to the entire population, regardless of age, gender, income level, or life goals. With regard to "basic" financial literacy, literacies around budgeting and planning for major expenses are needed by almost everyone, and this type of universal threshold makes sense. On the other hand, more "advanced" financial literacies such as understanding types of investments and their comparative risk and reward are less useful for people with low income and/or modest financial goals. It is mistaken to say that someone is illiterate because they do not understand how a sophisticated investment product works. More likely is that they have not invested to time to understand a product that has no direct bearing on their life.

As discussed in Chap. 4, behavioral economics, like financial literacy, is of great interest to policymakers and academics. And these two topics are related in important ways. A key interest in financial literacy practice is to improve people's financial knowledge, skills, and attitude so that their financial behavior becomes more aligned with their interests. A key interest in behavioral economics is to understand people's financial behavior. Behavioral economics has noted the bounded nature of human rationality, as have studies in financial literacy. In fact behavioral economics is influencing the financial literacy practice (e.g., Lusardi and Mitchell 2014). The impetus for this is probably related to the impetus driving behavioral studies, which is the evidence that at times people seem to behave in ways that do not line up with their best interests, even when they know better.

Financial Literacy Content

Curriculum material for financial literacy is generally intended to equip people to better navigate a world that is increasingly financialized. However, the content varies for different organizations and purposes. Curriculum prepared by a small non-profit organization for its members might be quite different than curriculum designed by a bank or school. Common topics include budgeting, planning, and investing. In some cases there are other features included such as a critique of capitalism and a careful consideration of what personal goals and what they mean.

The US-based Jump$tart Coalition for Personal Financial Literacy developed financial literacy curriculum for a variety of age groups for delivery within the school system and recently published the fourth edition of its *National Standards in K-12 Personal Finance Education*. The general topics it covers are spending and saving, credit and debt, employment and income, investing, risk management and insurance, and financial decision-making. The publication established benchmarks to be achieved at kindergarten, fourth grade, eighth grade, and twelfth grade. So for instance, the benchmark for "credit and debt" in kindergarten is understanding that people can borrow money and that these people are required to repay this money. By fourth grade, the student should know that credit is a financial tool, that borrowing involves interest charges, and that trustworthy borrowers can obtain credit in the future. By eighth grade, this knowledge expands to the use of credit for high-priced goods, the variety of credit sources, comparison of credit products, the cost of credit, and the powerful consequences of non-repayment. By twelfth grade the knowledge goals include leasing arrangements, cost disclosure, dealing with debt crises, credit bureaus, consumer protection regulations, collateral, debt and net worth, and credit for investment.

Related to financial literacy education, but linked with addressing over-indebted people, is credit counselling. In the Global North, particularly in Anglo-American nations, household debt has risen to record levels. There are many factors that have shaped household debt, including factors on the "demand side" such as low interest rates and consumerism and factors on the "supply side" like new financial service technologies (e.g., automated credit checks) and, for suppliers, low interest rates that compel bankers to look for new ways to bring in revenue. A certain share of consumers with debt find that it becomes unsustainable, and they have to either declare bankruptcy or engage in some sort of credit counselling program. Credit counselling assists the debtor in making arrangements with his/her creditor to streamline or consolidate the debt in order to reduce the service payments. Next, the counsellor assists the client through analysis of their debt problem and in finding solutions.

Financial literacy education is found around the world even for vulnerable people in the Global South. Take, for instance, BRAC, the previously mentioned international NGO based in Bangladesh, that offers financial literacy education reaching just over 500,000 people in Afghanistan, Bangladesh, Haiti, Tanzania, Sierra Leone, South Sudan, and Uganda (Kashfi et al. 2012). One program (Empowerment and Livelihood for Adolescents) works with girls and young women to promote female-centered supports and financial knowledge. Using a qualitative evaluation methodology of the BRAC young woman financial empowerment program, referred to above, it was found that the financial literacy component had a positive impact on the participants. The evaluation found that the participants were learning new skills, gaining confidence, and planning for the future (Kamruzzaman et al. 2012, p. 26):

> BRAC has added an innovative financial component. To navigate their way to a more prosperous future, teens from poor families require financial education, capital, livelihood skills, a sense of self-worth and an entrepreneurial mindset, all of which can be taught or encouraged. For younger girls, the emphasis is on social skills development and creating a savings mentality, but by their mid-teens—the exact age differs from country to country, and context to context—there is a demand among adolescent girls for livelihood training, financial literacy and sometimes micro-loans. (Kashfi et al. 2012, p. 1)

Analysis

As with interest in financial literacy, there has been a proliferation of financial literacy education in Western nations. Using a human capital model to theorize financial literacy education, Lusardi and Mitchell (2014) find that evaluation of financial literacy schemes is limited and note that without a clear theory of financial knowledge and its relationship to financial behavior, it is difficult to evaluate it. For instance, to evaluate a program on behavioral change such as increased savings would be inappropriate because it may not be optimal for all participants to do so (Lusardi and Mitchell 2014, p. 30). There have been few randomized controlled trials, and the few that have been done, for example, the US Jumpstart program, provide evidence that that program was not effective.

Lusardi and Mitchell discuss the controversial tension between financial literacy and financial regulation. That is, does it make more sense to direct resources to boost the financial literacy of consumers in an increasingly complicated economy or use resources to more effectively regulate the financial economy to simplify it? For instance, the state might support education about different forms of fees and interest rates for credit products, or it could require that all creditors use one uniform fee/interest rate formula, such as annual percentage rate.

One critique of financial literacy education relates to its diagnosis of ignorance or laziness of vulnerable people and thus is a variation on the "blame the victim" theme. A related criticism is that financial literacy education sometimes seeks to convert "citizens" into "consumers", meaning that programs sometimes ignore important aspects of political and social analyses necessary to understand finances and to be financially literate (Arthur 2012). Managing household finances relates to a variety of deeper social, economic, and political issues. Global recessions, inflation, financialization, and derivatives are just some things that affect our finances and that have deep structural foundations. Active citizens must understand these processes if they are to participate in an informed way in our democratic system. Passive consumers accept these forces as "natural" and cannot be changed. Their goal is to do the best they can within these limitations. Arthur (2012) examined a financial literacy curriculum in Canada and found elements of a passive consumer focus. Discussing the curriculum he observes:

> ... whenever a negative effect of globalization is mentioned, the author presents it as natural fact that offers "both challenges and opportunities for us all" ... The author additionally glosses over the negative and now "naturalized" aspects of post-Fordist capitalism by falling back on the tired narrative of the knowledge economy that will provide well-paying and enjoyable work to those who educate themselves appropriately. (Arthur 2012, p. 8)

This critique is not to say the financial literacy is not valuable. Rather, because it is *so* important, it must provide participants with a critical analysis. Without this exposure the risk is that financial literacy education promotes a passive citizen.

Financial Empowerment Programs

A more recent phenomenon has been the establishment and growth of financial empowerment models. Financial empowerment is variously defined, but central to the idea is using financial tools to overcome financial barriers to disempowerment. Microcredit, cash transfers, asset building, and financial literacy are all examples of financial empowerment programs. But the broader conception of financial empowerment programs replaces the specialized program with an approach that encompasses a number of components. In some cases the financial empowerment approach is built around a participatory process that engages asset-poor people to align the program with their needs and interests.

In Canada financial empowerment is an emerging approach associated with Asset-Building Learning Exchange, a network of organizations working on a number of areas across the country, and manifested in a number of implementing and funding organizations such as SEED Winnipeg, Momentum, and Prosper Canada. According to Prosper Canada (undated), financial empowerment involves five components:

1. Financial literacy and coaching: This involves ensuring access to high quality and unbiased financial education and counselling, including ensuring high quality training of financial educators and counsellors.
2. Access to tax filing and benefits: Some low-income people in Canada do not file their taxes and so are unable to access certain government benefits. In some cases people are unaware of the benefits and/or unable to complete their tax returns. Programs seek to inform people about their benefits and assist them in preparing their tax returns.
3. Safe financial products: This involves ensuring the provision of a series of basic banking services, including savings and credit products.
4. Savings and asset building: This involves providing savings schemes that encourage people to save and match these savings, in order to assist them to make investments into education and business.
5. Consumer protection: Education to raise awareness of fraud and dealing with personal debt crises and the regulation of fringe banks.

The financial empowerment model sounds very interesting if it can combine a level of participation of vulnerable people and communities in decision-making about their financial lives and provide them with access to a number of quality and useful financial services. It is an emerging model with considerable support from the non-profit world in Canada. However, for it to be successful, it will need to engage government and FIs for funding, programing, and/or supportive regulation. Non-profits can bring grassroots knowledge, contacts, and engagement processes, but their limited resources mean they have to rely on others.

Discussion

Civil society has been a major player in promoting everyday financialization through involvement in microcredit, cash transfers, and asset building. It is surprising that civil society has played such a critical role in this process given that, as a set of actors, and relative to the market and the state, it is likely least comfortable with everyday financialization. This involvement is partly mitigated by the way in which civil society has woven into their program ways to reduce risks to vulnerable people from everyday financialization. This is achieved in a variety of ways, from a more holistic approach to microcredit to delivering educational programs that seek to enhance vulnerable people's financial literacy.

The impact of credit and finance schemes offered by civil society generally has a positive but limited economic impact on its participants. Credit, cash, and savings schemes can help to improve a family's economic position marginally but not substantially. Given the civil society approach leads to modest benefits and seeks to control the risks of financialization, there is evidence that it makes a positive contribution toward participants' economic position, and in some cases we see evidence that it builds their sense of human well-being. More work needs to be done particularly to understand how borrowers value the economic changes that they experience.

The challenge, verbalized by those who want to commercialize microcredit, is that the organizational costs outweigh their rewards, and so they are unsustainable. However, given the discussion in Chap. 3 that finds that some commercial finance and credit schemes harm consumers, then those programs are not sustainable either. A commercial project that undermines its customers cannot thrive for long.

Notes

1. In a sense cash transfer programs are quite common in the Global North if one lumps into this category welfare and social assistance programs that provide a stream of income to people who fall below some threshold.
2. Many of these banks were criticized as being inefficient for various reasons. For instance, loans were allocated based not on the strength of the project but on the connections the borrower had with the creditor. One consequence of this was low repayment rates. Another common criticism is that they allocated subsidized credit to capital- and import-intensive projects that created few jobs and fostered dependency on external donors and markets.

3. For instance, a farmer, according to this view, will care for and invest in her land if she has ownership of the land. This is because she will benefit from these investments in the future. If she does not have individual ownership but there is some form of collective or state control, then she has less incentive to care for the land and may in fact harm the land.
4. Bangladesh, while an extreme case, has three very large NGO-styled micro-credit organizations (not to mention other NGOs)—ASA, BRAC, and Grameen Bank—and one of these, BRAC, works in several other countries and claims to be the largest NGO in the world. Many of these NGOs began through foreign funding and these foreign funds continue to finance much of their core operations. Given relative costs of living and consequent exchange rates, global South NGOs funded from the global North are sometimes very large. One American dollar will buy a lot of Bangladeshi takas, currently Taka 78 per one US dollar. Moreover, the need for NGO services in the global South has been perceived to be great, given the limited scale of government provision. NGOs in the global North are far more modest is size. BRAC, again on the extreme end of the Global South NGO continuum, spends almost US$859 million each year, which is just under one billion US dollars! Compare this to a large non-profit in Canada working in the field of financial empowerment, with a budget of $4.1 million. These are just examples, and probably extreme examples for both sides, but they provide some context to understand the relative size and shape of microcredit organizations in the Global South and Global North.
5. Since MIX Market relies on information from MFIs, not all the data are current.
6. Before the current corporate or state systems that support farmers with technical advice and access to inputs, these supports came from one's neighbor. So if a disease or pest was harming one's crop, then neighbors might have some answers. If one needed to quickly seed, transplant, weed, or harvest a crop, then neighbors were the resource to draw on.
7. The traditional economy also had mechanisms for training including mentoring in which older artisans train younger artisans—sometimes related by kinship—in a particular craft and business. Micro-enterprise programs take this model seriously by providing entrepreneurs credit and business training.
8. Since that time, the Europe 2020 Strategy was launched in 2010 and includes almost € one billion for various means to promote employment including € 200 million for microcredit organizations to enable them to provide more microloans (European Microfinance Network undated). By microloan, the European Microfinance Network means loans of up to € 25,000 for business or personal purposes. The purpose of the loans is to "Increase the availability and accessibility of microfinance for vulnerable

groups and micro-enterprises, and increase access to finance for social enterprises (EMN undated)". Clearly, given the large ceilings on these loans, even compared to Grameen America's loans, this program is dealing with a much larger scale of business and personal loan. Since the initiative is just beginning, there is nothing to say regarding impact.

9. The FDIC program began in 2008 as a pilot study with participating FIs to determine the feasibility of their offering small loans to un- and under-banked clients. In total 31 banks with 560 branches in 27 states participated (Buckland 2009). Loans were offered to individuals, and automatic savings and financial literacy programs were sometimes available. The average loan size was US$700 to US$1700 for a ten- to 16-month term, with interest rates ranging from 13 to 16%, but when the origination fee is factored in, the annual interest rate jumped to 36% (Miller et al. 2010).
10. One author noted, "Nevertheless, as a general guideline, pilot bankers indicated that costs related to launching and marketing small-dollar loan programs and originating and servicing small-dollar loans are similar to other loans. However, given the small size of SDLs [small-dollar loans] and to a lesser extent NSDLs [nearly small-dollar loans], the interest and fees generated are not always sufficient to achieve robust short-term profitability. Rather, most pilot bankers sought to generate long-term profitability through volume and by using small-dollar loans to cross-sell additional products" (Miller et al. 2010, p. 32).
11. Embedded in virtually all development programing is a fundamental tension, and that is the tension that exists between helping or supporting and self-reliance and individual agency. On the one hand, development programing seeks to help or support an individual or community to experience some type of human improvement. On the other hand, development interventions seek to build an individual's capacity to improve their own well-being. One goal is more concentrated on a particular outcome—improved nutrition, higher income, better education—and the other goal is focused more on the process—improved group capacity, strengthened individual agency, and so on. Education, health, job creation, agriculture, empowerment, and capacity building: all of these types of development programs involve a combination of outcome and process goals. Microcredit is certainly included in this list. By providing an essential input of production on better-than-market terms, microcredit is intended to assist the recipient to improve her livelihood. And microcredit is intended to stimulate productive activity on the part of the recipient, enabling her to gain access to improved inputs to enhance production. Yet as time has gone on, MFIs have faced increased pressure to become more financially self-sufficient, requiring them to place more emphasis on the productivity component of microcredit and less on the helping component.

12. For those living below the poverty line, the gap or distance between their average income and the poverty line.
13. Asset-building theory has added to our understanding of development at the theoretical and practical level (Sherraden 2005). The role of individual assets has tended to be downplayed in the economic discipline. At a theoretical level it highlights the assets that individuals hold and posits that these assets are at least as important to determine a person's well-being as are her/his income. Consider two people who face illness and job loss where one is a mortgage-free home-owner and the other a renter and have no other appreciable assets. The home-owner has more options as compared to the renter because she can sell or re-mortgage the house. The role of individual assets has tended to be downplayed in the economics discipline.

Bibliography

"Good Shepherd Microfinance | Leading the Way in Microfinance". 2015. Accessed September 1, 2015. http://goodshepherdmicrofinance.org.au/

"Grameen America". 2015. Accessed September 1, 2015. http://grameenamerica.org/

Aitken, Rob. 2013. The Financialization of Micro-Credit. *Development and Change* 44 (3): 473–499.

Angelucci, Manuela, Dean Karlan, and Jonathan Zinman. 2015. Microcredit Impacts: Evidence from a Randomized Microcredit Program Placement Experiment by Compartamos Banco. *American Economic Journal: Applied Economics* 7 (1): 151–182. https://doi.org/10.1257/app.20130537. https://search.proquest.com/docview/1642673012.

Arthur, Chris. 2012. In *Financial Literacy Education: Neoliberalism, the Consumer and the Citizen*, ed. Michael A. Peters and Chris Arthur. Rotterdam, NLD: Sense Publishers.

Attanasio, Orazio, Britta Augsburg, Ralph De Haas, Emla Fitzsimons, and Heike Harmgart. 2015. The Impacts of Microfinance: Evidence from Joint-Liability Lending in Mongolia. *American Economic Journal: Applied Economics* 7 (1): 90–122. https://doi.org/10.1257/app.20130489. https://search.proquest.com/docview/1644759584.

Augsburg, Britta, Ralph De Haas, Heike Harmgart, and Costas Meghir. 2015. The Impacts of Microcredit: Evidence from Bosnia and Herzegovina. *American Economic Journal: Applied Economics* 7 (1): 183–203. https://doi.org/10.1257/app.20130272. https://search.proquest.com/docview/1642672384.

BancoSol. 2015. Bancosol. Accessed September 2015. https://www.bancosol.com.bo/

Banerjee, Abhijit, Esther Duflo, Rachel Glennerster, and Cynthia Kinnan. 2015a. The Miracle of Microfinance? Evidence from a Randomized Evaluation. *American Economic Journal: Applied Economics* 7 (1): 22–53.

Banerjee, Abhijit, Dean Karlan, and Jonathan Zinman. 2015b. Six Randomized Evaluations of Microcredit: Introduction and Further Steps. *American Economic Journal: Applied Economics* 7 (1): 1–21.

Bateman, Milford. 2010. *Why Doesn't Microfinance Work?: The Destructive Rise of Local Neoliberalism*. New York: Zed Books.

———. 2011. *Confronting Microfinance: Undermining Sustainable Development.* Sterling, VA: Kumarian Press.

BRAC Bank Limited. Knowing BRAC Bank 'Company Profile' Shareholding Structure. Accessed May 8, 2015. http://www.bracbank.com/Shareholding-Structure.php

Buckland, Jerry. 2009. *Affordable Credit Options for Vulnerable Consumers: Identifying Alternatives to High-Cost Credit in Australia, Belgium, Canada, France, Germany, the UK, & the US.* Ottawa: Office of Consumer Affairs/ Industry Canada.

Collins, Daryl, Jonathan Morduch, Stuart Rutherford, and Orlanda Ruthven. 2009. *Portfolios of the Poor: How the World's Poor Live on $2 a Day*. Princeton and Oxford: Princeton University Press.

Cramer, Reid, and Trina R. Williams Shanks, eds. 2014. *The Assets Perspective: The Rise of Asset Building and Its Impact on Social Policy*. New York: Palgrave Macmillan.

Crépon, Bruno, Florencia Devoto, Esther Duflo, and William Parienté. 2015. Estimating the Impact of Microcredit on those Who Take it Up: Evidence from a Randomized Experiment in Morocco. *American Economic Journal: Applied Economics* 7 (1): 123–150. https://doi.org/10.1257/app.20130535. https://search.proquest.com/docview/1642672655.

Dewan, Shaila. 2013. Microcredit for Americans. *The New York Times*.

Duvendack, Maren, Richard Palmer-Jones, Jarmes G. Copestoke, Lee Hooper, Yoon Loke, and Nitya Rao. 2011. *What is the Evidence of the Impact of Microfinance on the Well-being of Poor People?* London: EPPI-Centre.

Fiszbein, Ariel, and Norbert Schady. 2009. *Conditional Cash Transfers: Reducing Present and Future Poverty*. Washington, DC: World Bank.

Goetz, Anne Marie, and Rina Sen Gupta. 1996. Who Takes the Credit? Gender, Power, and Control Over Loan use in Rural Credit Programs in Bangladesh. *World Development* 24 (1, Jan.): 45–63.

Grameen Bank. 2015. 16 Decisions of Grameen Bank | Grameen Bank– Bank for Small Business. Accessed August 31, 2015. http://www.grameen-info.org/16-decisions/

Hanlon, Joseph, Armando Barrientos, and David Hulme. 2010. *Just Give Money to the Poor: The Development Revolution from the Global South*. Sterling, VA: Kumarian Press.

Kamruzzaman, Mohamed, et al. 2012. *Social Network and Financial Literacy among Rural Adolescent Girls: Qualitative Assessment of BRAC's SoFEA Programme*. Dhaka: BRAC Research and Evaluation Division.

Kashfi, Farzana, Santhosh Ramdoss, and Scott Macmillan. 2012. *BRAC's Empowerment and Livelihood for Adolescents: Changing Mind-Sets and Going to Scale with Social and Financial Skills for Girls.* New York: UNICEF.

King, Justin. 2015. MyRA Goes National: Building A Better Savings Account. https://www.newamerica.org/asset-building/myra-goes-national/

Kiva. 2015. Kiva—About Us. Accessed November 30, 2015. http://www.kiva.org/about

Leckie, Norm, Michael Dowie, and Chad Gyorfi-Dyke. 2008. *Learning to Save, Saving to Learn: Early Impacts of the Learn$ave Individual Development Accounts Project.* Ottawa: Social Research and Demonstration Corporation.

Lusardi, Annamaria, and Olivia S. Mitchell. 2014. The Economic Importance of Financial Literacy: Theory and Evidence. *Journal of Economic Literature* 52 (1): 5–44.

Marulanda Consultores. 2015. *Going Mobile with Conditional Cash Transfers.* Washington, DC: Consultative Group to Assist the Poorest.

Miller, Rae-Ann, Susan Burhouse, Luke Reynolds, and Aileen G. Sampson. 2010. A Template for Success: The FDIC's Small-Dollar Loan Pilot Program. *FDIC Quarterly* 4: 28–41.

Organisation for Economic Co-operation and Development. 2015. *National Strategies for Financial Education: OECD/INFE Policy Handbook.* Paris: OECD.

Roy, Ananya. 2010. *Poverty Capital.* 1st Publ. ed., 1st ed. New York: Routledge.

Rutherford, Stuart. 2000. *The Poor and Their Money.* Oxford: Oxford University Press.

———. 2002. *Money Talks: Conversations with Poor Households in Bangladesh about Managing Money.* Manchester: Institute for Development Policy and Management, University of Manchester.

Sachs, Jeffrey D. 2011. *The Price of Civilization: Economics and Ethics After the Fall.* Toronto: Random House Canada.

Schicks, Jessica. 2007. Developmental Impact and Coexistence of Sustainable and Charitable Microfinance Institutions: Analysing BancoSol and Grameen Bank. *European Journal of Development Research* 19 (4, Dec.): 551–568.

Schwittay, Anke F. 2014. Making Poverty into a Financial Problem: From Global Poverty Lines to Kiva.Org. *Journal of International Development* 26 (4, May): 508–519.

Sherraden, Michael, ed. 2005. *Inclusion in the American Dream: Assets, Poverty, and Public Policy.* Oxford and New York: Oxford University Press.

Stegman, Michael, and Robert Faris. 2005. The Impacts of IDA Programs on Family Savings and Assets Holdings. In *Inclusion in the American Dream*, ed. Michael Sharraden, 216–237. Oxford: Oxford University Press.

Tarozzi, Alessandro, Jaikishan Desai, and Kristin Johnson. 2015. The Impacts of Microcredit: Evidence from Ethiopia. *American Economic Journal: Applied Economics* 7 (1): 54–89. https://doi.org/10.1257/app.20130475. https://search.proquest.com/docview/1642672571

World Bank. 2015. *World Development Report 2015: Mind, Society, and Behaviour.* Washington, DC: World Bank.

CHAPTER 6

The State: Regulating, Nudging, and Educating for Financial Inclusion

Introduction

While banks drive financialization and consumers respond to and shape it, states can and sometimes do shape the nature of these financial changes. The state regulates the financial sector, it provides services that rely on the delivery of financial services (e.g., income support), and it provides public goods such as education that are an important prospective vehicle for increasing financial literacy. In terms of financial sector regulation, Global Northern nations have a number of programs and departments responsible for this oversight. Important departments include finance, the central bank, consumer protection, and specialized bank access agencies, for instance, Canada's Access to Basic Banking Regulations and the United States' Community Reinvestment Act. In the Global South, regulations in this area are not as elaborate as in the Global North, but some developing nations such as India, China, and South Africa are quickly expanding their efforts.

At minimum, and in keeping with the objectives of neoliberalism, the state's role is to provide its citizens with safety, security, and public goods. Public goods and services are those things that the market cannot provide, as their provision is not profitable, such as public education or a clean environment (lakes, air, parks).[1] Payment systems are an important example of a mixed good with both public and private components.[2] In addition, within a neoliberal minimalist framework, states are required to operate in transparent and accountable ways; they are responsible to

J. Buckland, *Building Financial Resilience*,
https://doi.org/10.1007/978-3-319-72419-5_6

ensure that markets operate effectively and that the products of these markets are safe. Increasingly neoliberals are embracing the idea that it is also the state's responsibility to *nudge* their citizens to make better decisions.

The neoliberal view regarding poverty reduction is that economic growth will trickle down to poor people, women, and minorities. Of course there is evidence that growth can be captured by an economic elite resulting in economic inequality that itself impedes further growth (Stiglitz 2013; Osberg 2013).

This chapter examines the state's role in boosting financial inclusion through bank regulation, financial service provision, "nudging", and educating. Financial inclusion refers to an outcome in which previously marginalized people engage in the mainstream banking system voluntarily because they see how their integration will improve their financial well-being. It is assumed that financial inclusion is not an end itself but a means to improved financial and overall well-being. If financial inclusion gets in the way of improved financial and overall well-being for income- and asset-poor people, then it is not justified. For instance, if financial inclusion efforts lead to the decline of informal financial services such as group-based lending and thereby undermines a group's finances and their well-being, then this initiative mixed consequences.

Financial Sector Regulation

Regulation of the financial and insurance sector has changed considerably over the last century, including periods of de-regulation and of re-regulation. The movement toward de-regulation is associated in the United States in particular with the period preceding the 1929 stock market crash and the period preceding the 2008 subprime financial crisis. These cases were informed by market-based analysis and ideology that generally concluded that the market is the most efficient way to organize an economy and its components. For instance, the efficient market hypothesis posits that financial markets and actors encompass all salient information into asset valuation so that investors cannot systematically "beat" the market and that, by extension, markets are self-correcting. Another, opposite trend is the movement toward greater regulation. After the 1929 New York stock market crash the United States government, the leading market economy, moved to tighten regulations on the financial sector. But the neoliberal period from the 1980s led to a reversal of these trends as the United States de-regulated the sector, most notably repealing the Glass–Steagall Bill in 1999 (Van Arnum and Naples 2013). This liberalization process was pursued by other, primarily, Western countries. The 2007–2008 subprime mortgage crisis brought this process to an abrupt end.

The most recent re-regulation period has attracted considerable study. In their cross-country investigation of the relationship between banking regulations and the impact on national economies, Cihak et al. (2012) identified four key issues: "crisis" countries have looser definitions of capital and lower capital ratios; banks in crisis countries faced fewer restrictions on non-bank activities; treatment of bad loans and loan losses were less strict in crisis countries; and there were weaker incentives for the private sector to monitor banks.

As part of the response to the crisis, many states reversed direction and began to introduce greater financial sector regulation. Regulatory reform can be categorized in five areas: regulations on reserve capital, restrictions on bank activities, expansion of official supervisory power, growth of private monitoring, and establishment or expansion of deposit insurance (p. 456). The 2010 creation of the US Consumer Financial Protection Bureau is an example of the third type of change. This organization consolidates consumer protection functions in different US federal agencies and is responsible for financial education, researching financial markets, and developing and implementing consumer financial law (Waller et al. 2011, p. 11).

Cihak et al., through a quantitative analysis of a World Bank database, argue that this process has been slow: "It does not appear that the recent global financial crisis caused a major and sudden change in regulatory frameworks around the world" (Cihak et al. 2012, p. 10). These studies find that some types of regulation improve stability, but deposit insurance regulations can lead banks to take on greater risk (Hoque et al. 2015).

Barth et al. surveyed 126 countries using World Bank data to assess the impact and consequences of banking regulations. They note that although many countries have moved their regulation toward the Basel guidelines (discussed below) in areas such as boosting capital requirements and strengthening regulatory agencies, they are ambivalent about whether these changes will enhance the efficiency of the banking system (p. 24). In their multi-country study Hoque et al. (2015) are less ambivalent about the value of regulation, arguing that effective regulation will increase financial system stability and reduce risk but may dampen efficiency (p. 472), noting "Hence, policymakers should strive to find the right balance of restrictions for reducing systemic risk without decreasing efficiency" (p. 472). Several studies have called for greater market-based scrutiny of banking performance (Barth et al. 2012; Hoque et al. 2015).

Bank Soundness Regulations

The central feature of bank regulation has to do with ensuring that banks are "safe and sound". Are its assets of good quality, is its income stream sufficient, is management effective, and does it have sufficient liquid assets (easily converted to cash if needed)? Regulators monitor banks to ensure they are financially sound because bank crises, as we saw with the 2007 subprime mortgage crisis, can spill over into the rest of the economy and from one country to the rest of the world. This happens because banks provide the "fuel" for the economy in the form of credit for "real" businesses. Bank regulation can help to prevent or minimize bank crises, but regulations can also *not* prevent crises, which was the case with the neoliberal banking regulations in the United States before the subprime mortgage crisis. Challenges in banking in one country quickly affect banking (and the rest of the economy) in other countries, again evidenced by the subprime crisis. This is also seen in many other banking crises, including the 1980s international debt crisis, which saw banks from the Global North, fearing the inability of borrowers to service their debt, rapidly withdrew credit from the Global South, and thereby exacerbating a crisis initially associated with a global recession and declining commodity prices.

The Bank for International Settlements (BIS), based in Basel Switzerland, hosts the Basel process, led by the Basel Committee on Banking Supervision (Bank of International Settlements undated). As a forum for central bankers, it provides a venue for "cooperation on banking supervision … and is the global standard-setter for the prudential regulation of banks" (Bank of International Settlements undated). An important mandate of the BIS and its committee is setting global standards, done through the agreements named Basel I (1988), Basel II (2004), and, the current agreement, Basel III (Bank of International Settlements 2011). Basel III responded to concerns following the subprime mortgage crisis and associated global recession that banking regulations and Basel II were insufficient. According to BIS, Basel III seeks to address this issue by:

- Improving the banking sector's ability to absorb economic shocks
- Strengthening their risk management and governance
- Enhancing bank transparency.

According to BIS analysis, the recession that began in 2007 had deep and systemic roots in the banking system:

> One of the main reasons the economic and financial crisis, which began in 2007, became so severe was that the banking sectors of many countries had built up excessive on and off-balance sheet leverage. This was accompanied by a gradual erosion of the level and quality of the capital base. At the same time, many banks were holding insufficient liquidity buffers. The banking system therefore was not able to absorb the resulting systemic trading and credit losses nor could it cope with the reintermediation of large off-balance sheet exposures that had built up in the shadow banking system. The crisis was further amplified by a procyclical deleveraging process and by the interconnectedness of systemic institutions through an array of complex transactions. During the most severe episode of the crisis, the market lost confidence in the solvency and liquidity of many banking institutions. The weaknesses in the banking sector were rapidly transmitted to the rest of the financial system and the real economy, resulting in a massive contraction of liquidity and credit availability. Ultimately the public sector had to step in with unprecedented injections of liquidity, capital support and guarantees, exposing taxpayers to large losses. (Bank for International Settlements 2011)

Basel III establishes revised standards in several areas. First, it identifies improvements in the quality of and transparency about banks' capital assets. A bank's capital base is an important means by which it can "weather a storm" by drawing on it when loan defaults increase. But a source of vulnerability is a reduction in the quality of the capital base and inconsistent defining and reporting on it, so that Basel III sets out improved standards for capital assets. Second, it calls for improvements on how banks cover risk. Basel III finds that on- and off-balance sheet risks added to the financial crisis. To address this it establishes higher capital requirements, particularly with respect to "complex securitization exposures" (Bank for International Settlements 2011, p. 3). Next, Basel III calls for increasing banks' capital requirements (Bank for International Settlements 2011), setting a leverage ratio to determine additional capital requirements for banks that are highly leveraged. A fourth area of reform is intended to reduce how the banking system reinforces financial booms and busts and establishes a means by which banks dampen them. The BIS notes "one of the most procyclical dynamics has been the failure of risk management and capital frameworks to capture key exposures—such as complex trading activities, resecuritizations, and exposures to off-balance sheet vehicles—in advance of the crisis" (Bank for International Settlements 2011, p. 5). To address this Basel III includes forward-looking provisioning, capital conservation, and limiting excess credit growth (credit expansion that often precedes a crisis, i.e., the "bubble"). A final aspect of Basil III relates to the issue of systemic risk and interconnectedness of the financial and economic systems that compounded and dramatically expanded the financial crisis. The agreement recognizes that some banks have important international connections and so play a critical role on this point, including more controls for derivative activity and higher capital requirements for "inter-financial exposures" (BIS 2011, p. 8). Beyond improving capital requirements, Basil III is also concerned to harmonize bank liquidity standards. This will be achieved through encouraging the establishment of liquidity coverage ratio, a funding ratio, and monitoring tools.

Soundness and Income–Asset-Poor People

So far we have been talking about regulating banks as institutions, but what does bank soundness have to do with vulnerable people? On the surface it would seem not a lot, but digging more deeply we will see that there are important connections. Generally speaking it is the large borrowers and the complicated devices that are the source of greater risk for a bank's soundness. The large borrower is a threat to the bank's soundness, whereas the small borrower is of relatively little consequences. Poor people are indirectly affected through recession, rising unemployment, and declining state spending on social problems.

But sometimes poor people are directly affected by a financial crisis. For instance, the subprime mortgage crisis that started in 2007 and the international debt crisis of the early 1980s are examples where a large number of relatively poor borrowers affected banks' viability. In fact some have argued that regulations requiring banks to support financially disadvantaged communities *caused* the subprime mortgage crisis. I do not agree with that analysis, but there certainly is an important relationship between safety and soundness regulation and income-poor people. So what happened?

Placing the responsibility on poor nations regarding the international debt crisis and poor people for the subprime mortgage crisis is an important instance of blaming the victim. In both cases the system and the creditors arguably have much more responsibility for these crises than do poor people. Poor and modest-income countries and people were recipients of credit in these respective crises and no doubt had some responsibility. But both groups were relatively powerless when compared to the large banks, and they were not, generally speaking, organized (except for some leaders during the international debt crisis who called for a debtor's cartel). In the case of the international debt crisis, the commercial banks rapidly increased credit to countries in the Global South without carefully assessing their ability to repay. When a global recession hit in the early 1980s and primary commodity prices plummeted, this ability dropped sharply. Similarly, in the 2000s banks rushed in to offer subprime mortgages to low- and modest-income Americans without carefully assessing the ability of these new home-owners to repay and assuming that house prices would continue to rise. When they didn't and recession hit, many mortgage holders could not service their debt. And whereas many Global South countries and poor mortgage holders were deeply harmed by these respective crises, the same cannot be said for most banks which were protected throughout the crises, often by the state.

Today some concern has focused on the growth of small-loan products that target low-income people, associated with everyday financialization, ranging from payday loans to commercialized microcredit. Could they be the source of another financial crisis? Hard to say, but with evidence that asset- and income-poor people can be important actors in financial crises, the small-loan sector should be monitored carefully.

Bank soundness regulations can sometimes unnecessarily limit a bank. For instance, in some cases banks are disallowed from receiving loan repayments through non-bank retail outlets (Mas 2011, p. 142). This may prevent poor people who have access to a retailer with a point-of-service (POS) terminal from engaging with a bank. The POS access point might be all that is needed to attract the customer to the mainstream bank and away from a more expensive fringe bank.

Know Your Customer (KYC) requirements, to prevent money laundering, can also create a major obstacle for poor people from financial inclusion. KYC require banks to follow particular identification processes with clients. But, generally speaking, poor people with small sums of money are not money launderers. In fact, Mas (2011) argues that moving money transfers from informal channels to formal and electronic channels will better enable law enforcement. Only 17% of regulators in the Global South make exceptions to the KYC requirements for poor and unbanked people. Conversely, he notes that more than one-half of regulators in the Global South require clients to provide proof of income or employment plus proof of identity or address (Mas 2011, pp. 142–43).

But changing bank regulations must be done with care. Financial regulations were eroded from the 1980s, particularly in the United States, and the 2007 subprime mortgage crisis exploded onto the scene as a result. Studies find that better regulation reduces the likelihood of financial crises:

> In terms of returns, banks in countries with greater official power, restrictions and private monitoring performed better during the credit crisis. These results suggest that while regulatory restrictions and supervision are necessary, at the same time it is important to have better private monitoring. Hence private monitoring, which is a market mechanism to reward better banks, complements regulatory supervision. Our findings also highlight the need for regulators to access market information in regular intervals to supplement other sources of regulatory information. (Hoque et al. 2015, p. 472)

Mobile Banking Regulations

The rise of mobile banking presents another medium for banking to address financial exclusion and presents other regulatory challenges. It draws on new ICTs and therefore can be fostered through a retail network that is very modest in size and cost. Instead of expensive bank branches, it can involve simple outlets that are already engaged in complementary services. While mobile banking in the Global South has focused primarily on payments, it has grown rapidly and offers tremendous potential for growth:

> A financial revolution is in progress. It is not happening under the skyscrapers of New York or on the streets of London. It is not taking place in Beijing or Mumbai but in the slums of Nairobi and in the markets of Kisumu... It is not the micro-lending with which developing and emerging markets are

> associated but something at the other end of the financial spectrum in the traditionally least exciting part of the financial system—payments. (Klein and Mayer 2011, p. 2)

As with all regulations there are strengths and weaknesses with various options for mobile banking. One argument is that excessive regulation raises the cost of mobile banking, but it reduces the likelihood of problems such as money laundering and abusing vulnerable consumers. Balancing these and other factors are important. And given the relative newness of mobile banking systems, and discussed in chapter three, effective regulation is still emerging.

David Porteous (2006) has proposed a framework of six principles to guide regulations for mobile banking (Table 6.1). Underlying these six principles are values of openness and certainty. Openness is required to bring new providers and consumers into the market. Certainty is necessary to ensure that funds are safe and not tied with illegal activity. The principles are: e-contracting, consumer protections, interoperability, Know Your Customer, agent-based/branchless banking, and e-money legislation. E-contracting means that electronic signatures are as valid as physical ones. Consumer protection includes clear disclosure, liability falls to the provider for unauthorized transactions, and the use of simple complaint mechanisms.

Table 6.1 The Porteous regulatory index for m-banking

Principle	*Assists in certainty and/or openness*	*Group that is benefited*
E-contracting: at least make electronic signatures as good as physical signatures	Certainty	For the banked
Consumer protection: clear disclosure, liability of provider for unauthorized transactions, and simple complaint mechanism		
Interoperability: open to other account holders and businesses	Openness	
Know Your Customer: do not excessively prejudice account access by vulnerable people	Openness (primary) and certainty (secondary)	For the unbanked
Agent/branchless banking: customers can at least make withdrawals and deposits through agents outside of bank branches		
E-money legislation: ensure that e-money sufficiently capitalized and supervised	Openness	

Source: Porteous 2006; Gutierrez and Singh 2013, p. 21

Interoperability is about the ability of customers to easily switch between providers. The Know Your Customer principle relates to anti-money laundering regulation, while agent and branchless banking is about ensuring that this type of transaction is possible. The e-money principle relates to the question of if the provider can issue electronic money. Porteous notes that the first three principles focus on the already banked, while the last three principles are primarily about bringing unbanked people into the mobile banking system.

Using Porteous' principles of effective mobile banking regulation, Gutierrez and Singh (2013) examined the connection between regulation and mobile banking adoption. They found that that supportive regulation will foster mobile banking adoption (p. 16). They noted that mobile banking is of particular interest to the modest poor and financially excluded, in other words, not the poorest people in the population but those who are relatively poor and unbanked (Gutierrez and Singh 2013, p. 17). But they found an inverse relationship between the strength of consumer protection and the use of mobile banking by the poorest people:

> [A] regulatory framework that supports interoperability is associated with higher usage among the poorest. Curiously, stronger consumer protection is associated to lower usage among this segment. Increased cost of the service in the presence of strong consumer protection regulation could explain this result. Consumer protection is also found to be conducive of higher usage among people with higher education. (Gutierrez and Singh 2013, p. 17)

Regulating Fringe Banks

Fringe banks and particularly payday lenders have grown rapidly in the Global North and are spreading to the Global South, for example, South Africa. These financial service firms offer small-scale financial services that are expensive. They can be harmful for consumers who are unaware of the true costs, and they can encourage consumers to borrowing repetitively. For these reasons jurisdictions facing an influx of fringe banks have tried to regulate them. In certain jurisdictions they are disallowed, including in 14 states and the District of Columbia in the United States (Pew Charitable Trusts 2012), one of ten Canadian province (Quebec), and some countries in Europe (e.g., France and Belgium).

A common approach to payday lenders is to require them to be licensed, to present their fees in a certain way, called fair disclosure, to limit their fees to a prescribed price cap, and to disallow excessive lending. Licensing is a very basic requirement that moves fringe banks from a completely informal setting toward a semi-formalized operation. It may also allow for the collection of data by the regulator about the fringe banker. This data can be used to monitor trends in the industry and inform policymaking.

Fringe banks will often present the fees for the service in a complicated way that is difficult for the consumer to understand and make it difficult to compare the fee with other types of financial products. Requiring the fringe banker to present the fee in one simple and comparable figure improves the likelihood the consumer will understand its true cost and how it compares with the alternatives. As discussed in Chap. 3, clear information like this will lead to a reduction in uptake of payday loans.

Price caps create a ceiling above which fringe banks cannot raise their fees. This means that fringe banks must be more efficient. In other words, when faced with a price cap, fringe banks will have to cut costs and boost efficiency as much as possible. This might be done by eliminating unnecessary outlets in order to increase business volume in the remaining outlets. But it might also be done by encouraging more repeat borrowing. This is because the economics of payday lending is that the first-time loan is the most expensive to administer; it is only the second and subsequent loans that allow the payday lender to break even and begin to make a profit. That is why many jurisdictions also limit the amount of small loans available to any one person.

Loan restrictions come in a variety of forms including through limits on the size of the loan, the size of repayment limits, and limits on the number of loans available within a given time frame. These limitations are intended to prevent a consumer from getting caught in a debt cycle that leads them to insolvency and/or bankruptcy. It is a very difficult thing to regulate, however, as people can go to different outlets and different lenders. A central registry might prevent that, but it would be expensive.

There is an argument that certain fringe bank products, such as payday loans, cause harm to consumers. One response is to disallow them, as is the case in some jurisdictions, but there is also a case for nudging payday lenders to offer a less harmful loan. This was the goal of the state of Colorado in the United States, when it required payday lenders to move from a two-week one installment repayment model to a six-month term and multiple installment repayments. One study reported that the industry in

Colorado has declined in terms of outlets but that it is likely that business volume in the remaining outlets has increased. The cost to the consumer is substantially lower under the new regimen (Table 6.2). For a US $500 loan, the APR for a loan under the old two-week one repayment system was 319%, while under the new system, the APR amounted to 129%. Research found that under the new system consumers take out fewer loans (Pew Charitable Trusts 2013, p. 12).

State Support for Financial Inclusion

State support for financial inclusion in the Global North dates back a few decades. For instance, in the case of the United States, it dates back at least to the late 1970s when the Community Reinvestment Act was established. Financial inclusion became popular in other parts of the Global North in the next few decades. It has more recently gained popular support among donors and governments in the Global South. The international embrace of financial inclusion is the result of a few converging paths. First, big donors like the World Bank, the United Kingdom's Department for International Development (DfID), and the Gates Foundation in conjunction with and certain banks have seen it as an opportunity to pursue their interests. This has led to rapid growth in funds available for this initiative. Second, contemporary efforts at microcredit in the Global South date back to the early 1970s, and the work has changed over time. In the 1990s, work led by

Table 6.2 Payday loans before and after Colorado regulation changes

	Before law change (conventional payday loans)	*After law change (payday installment loans)*
Maximum loan size	$500	$500
Average annual percentage rate paid	319%	129%
Amortization (payments reduce principal over time)	No	Yes
Deferred presentment loan collateral (postdated check or authorization to debit bank account)	Yes	Yes
Amount due on next payday ($500 loan)	$575	$61
Cost to borrow $500		
For two weeks	$75	$10
For three months	$450	$125
For six months	$975	$290
For 12 months	$1950	$580

Source: Pew Charitable Trusts 2012, p. 9

David Hulme at the University of Manchester involved a method he and a group of colleagues developed called the financial diaries. This research method is a panel survey of a smaller group of people over a six- to twelve-month period in which the participants' finances are carefully tracked. The results of this work showed that poor people's finances are not simple and involve cash flow, credit, savings, and investment components. This understanding supported the notion that poor people need a number of financial services, not just credit. This was a part of the reason for the move to the term "microfinance" rather than "microcredit", as the former includes savings, insurance, and credit. More recent work by DfID has promoted and funded the expansion of mobile banking in the Global South. The work by the World Bank and funding by the Gates Foundation have been important in highlighting this agenda.

Financial Service Provision in the Global North

While commercial mainstream banks, fringe banks, and informal financial services are the principal sources of banking for vulnerable people, the state does sometimes play a role. State-owned banks or state-sponsored postal system that offers financial services are examples of this. In the early development period of the 1950s through the 1970s, state-run banks were a major focus, particularly in the Global South. This was a period when the role of the state in development was seen as critical. Many Global South states established banks, but these were not consumer but producer banks. For instance, agricultural banks were a common phenomenon at the time, with the purpose of providing credit to farmers for farm inputs. In some cases state banks were influenced by politics and this affected repayment rates and their bottom line. When the microcredit model arose in the 1970s followed by the domination of neoliberal ideology in the 1980s, support for state banks declined.

However, there are still some cases of state-sponsored banks. For instance, in the Canadian province of Alberta, the provincial government sponsors the Alberta Treasury Branches. It is a state agency—in Canadian parlance, a crown corporation. It operates much like a bank or credit union.

Access to banking is another important type of regulation affecting financial inclusion. These regulations are commonly found in the Global North, not the Global South where a large share of the population is unbanked. In the Global North there are segments of the population due to geography, poverty, history, and/or identity that are prevented from using the formal banking system so that regulations to promote access are possible. In the Global South the financial inclusion gaps are large, and mainstream banks lack basic infrastructure to provide banking to large geographic spaces and income groups.

Perhaps the best-known bank access regulation is the US's Community Reinvestment Act (CRA), enacted in 1977. The CRA identifies ways in which it expects banks to contribute to community development, which means supporting the entire community *including* asset- and income-poor portions. These ways are lending, investing, and servicing. Banks are regularly examined, and it is their responsibility to provide evidence of their contributions in these areas. The US CRA might be called an early example of the state nudging business, in that there are no specific thresholds but general principles. Carbo et al. (2005) name this approach "affirmative action", in contrast with the type of legislated approach that exists in Canada.

The CRA prohibits practices such as redlining—deliberately not delivering services to certain low-income neighborhoods—and encourages banks to provide credit to *all* residents in its working area, including people with low income and assets. Banks are regularly tested by a financial authority to determine if they are contributing to community needs. There are three kinds of tests—lending, investment, and service—which asses the bank's service provision and whether the bank has addressed the needs of poor people and communities. If banks do well in the tests, they receive good grades; these grades will lend weight to a FIs application for new deposit facilities such as a new bank branch.

For instance, the Office of the Comptroller of the Currency undertook an assessment of the Wells Fargo Bank in 2008 (Office of the Comptroller of the Currency 2008). Headquartered in Sioux Falls, South Dakota, Wells Fargo is the fifth largest holding bank in the United States with assets of US$514 billion, operating just under 3400 branches, just over 6900 ATMs, and working in 23 states (Office of the Comptroller of the Currency 2008). The assessment involved the bank's operations in a number of states for the three tests: lending, investment, and service. Wells Fargo did very well in the review, achieving the highest rating, "outstanding" on all three tests, which it also achieved in its previous review in 2004:

> We performed a lending gap analysis to determine if there were any significant clusters of census tracts or Block Numbering Areas (BNA) with low penetration of lending. We paid special attention to low- and moderate-income geographies. We also factored in the distribution of owner-occupied housing units, businesses, and farms to determine whether a low level of penetration in an area was an issue. Based on lending reports and maps detailing the volume and distribution of home mortgage and small business loans, we identified no unexplained conspicuous gaps in lending. (Office of the Comptroller of the Currency 2008, p. 13)

In the investment test, the bank was assessed as outstanding largely because of its lending to affordable housing projects—the bank provided US$125 million in "qualified CD investments", including supporting a number of affordable housing funds (Office of the Comptroller of the Currency 2008, 0.21). Its service assessment found that the bank's network is readily accessible to its clients and that branch openings and closings did not adversely affect low-income people or communities. In one region the assessors found that "[t]he bank's percentages of branches in low- and moderate-income geographies exceed the percentages of the populations residing in those geographies, reflecting excellent performance" (Office of the Comptroller of the Currency 2008, p. 22).

Wells Fargo performed well in the test for that particular iteration. This demonstrates that some US banks can perform well which is evidence that they can all do well. Given the relatively high rate of financial exclusion in the United States—9%—suggests that more could be done. And the state can play an important role in examining and publishing performance indicators and nudging banks to strengthen their financial inclusion efforts.

Canada has a lower level of financial exclusion than America, at between 3 and 5%. The Canadian approach to bank inclusion is quite different from the American one in that it relies on a narrow regulatory approach. The main regulatory components to foster inclusion include the Access to Basic Banking Regulations (2003), voluntary codes that banks participate in on issues such as adequate personal identification and annual public accountability statements produced by banks that may include discussion of their contributions to community development.

The Access to Basic Banking Regulations require that federally regulated banks open bank accounts and cash certain types of checks for anyone with adequate personal identification. In the early years of the Financial Consumer Agency of Canada (the agency assigned to monitor bank adherence to the basic banking access issue) undertook regular "mystery shopping" to measure compliance. This has not been done, or at least the results have not been made publicly available, for many years. Instead the Financial Consumer Agency of Canada (FCAC) seems to have directed much of its institutional capital toward financial education. The only way we know if banks are adhering to these regulations is if people complain to the FCAC. Sadly, there is little evidence that this is a good indicator of service quality, particularly for financially excluded people who already feel barred from society's benefits and institutions. Moreover, requiring banks to open accounts does not address a number of other barriers to inclusion such as location of branch, products provided, and staff treatment of the excluded.

The European Union is a very large grouping of diverse nations. Their diversity includes levels of financial inclusion. It is estimated that 58 million people over 15 years of age within the European Union are without a bank account and that the rate of financial exclusion ranges from below 1% in northern Europe to as high as 50% in Eastern Europe (European Commission n.d.). In 2014 the EU's Council of Ministers adopted a directive that includes making access to a basic bank account a right for all EU citizens (European Commission 2014). Once the European Parliament signs the directive, member states will have two years to implement it as national law.

Financial Inclusion in the Global South: The Alliance for Financial Inclusion

In the last few years interest in financial inclusion has really taken off in the Global South, perhaps most notably in India. From the 1970s the government of India has emphasized the importance of access to credit for households and enterprises, but it has been in the last decade that the government has highlighted the importance of access to bank accounts and transfer services (Barua et al. 2016). The efforts include a plan to provide government benefits to recipients' bank accounts. The Indian government is one of many members of an international network to promote financial inclusion. Formed in 2008, the Alliance for Financial

Inclusion (AFI) is a network of central bankers and financial regulators from 90 Global South and emerging countries. Headquartered in Kuala Lumpur, the AFI draws on evidence to promote and develop policies that will advance financial inclusion, addressing particularly the world's current unbanked. "AFI is a global network of financial policymakers from developing and emerging countries working together to increase access to appropriate financial services for the poor" (AFI undated). The work of the network is achieved through annual meetings, regional initiatives, and ongoing efforts of several working group.

The Bill and Melinda Gates Foundation is the main funder of the AFI, while the German International Cooperation provides administrative support. Other funders include the Omidyar Network (AFI undated). AFI works with Visa Inc. and Mastercard. According to a recent report, AFI consists of 125 regulatory and policymaking institutions in 96 developing and emerging countries (AFI 2015). The Maya Declaration is a 2011 agreement signed in Riviera Maya, Mexico, by members from developing and emerging countries, committed to work at financial inclusion that is rooted in the values of self-determination, peer-to-peer knowledge exchange, and fostering new forms of cooperation that involves four areas:

- Create an environment that encourages the development of new technology that will lower the costs of financial services
- Ensure that financial stability is maintained
- Promote consumer protection and financial literacy
- Monitor progress and make adjustments as needed (AFI 2015).

According to AFI, by July 2015, 54 member institutions had made "specific and measurable financial inclusion commitments" (AFI 2015). The AFI implements its mission through working groups, grants provision, and regional initiatives. Currently its six working groups are focused on "consumer empowerment, digital financial services, financial inclusion data, financial inclusion strategy, global standards, and small and medium enterprises' finances" (AFI undated).

The consumer empowerment and market conduct group seeks to promote an understanding of good practices and policies that promote the empowerment and protection of consumers. The committee includes advocating for consumer financial literacy and promoting fair disclosure with financial service through five priority areas: transparency, responsible lending, "avenues for help and redress", financial literacy, and institutional framework and supervision. The group plans to achieve its goals through surveying its members and publishing materials that encourage good policy and practice. For instance, the group is promoting the plan of the Bank Negara Malaysia, Malaysia's central bank, for consumer protection, as a case study of good practice (AFI 2011). The bank's policy was established to promote consumer empowerment and protection after the Asian financial crisis of 1997 and was extensively implemented by the global recession of 2008. The plan had six components: promote financial education, promote transparency regarding banks and their products, establish a mechanism of redress for consumers, expand the mediation bureau, introduce anti-trust regulations, and establish a deposit insurance fund (AFI 2011).

The Financial Inclusion Data Working Group seeks to promote and share measurements of financial inclusion. It is working to develop a common framework that all members will use to measure financial inclusion including indicators and methodology. This working group identifies four components of financial inclusion (AFI 2010):

- *Access*: is the component concerned with peoples' ability to use formal sector financial services. Indicators include physical proximity and affordability.
- *Quality*: is the component that considers the consumers' experience of the financial service and how it assisted her/him to meet needs and goals. Indicators include if the product characteristics are aligned with consumer needs.
- *Usage*: is a part of financial inclusion that considers the permanence and depth of use of the financial service by the household. Indicators include regularity, frequency, and length of time used.
- *Welfare*: is concerned with the impact of the financial service on the consumers' consumption, business, and overall well-being. Indicators include increases in consumption, business productivity, and improvements in self-perceived well-being.

The working group conceptualizes the data being used to analyze the nature of the financial inclusion problem and then to track changes in financial inclusion, as new inclusion policies and programs are put in place (AFI 2010). The data tracking will provide information on how effectively the new programs are working and suggest if modifications are needed. The working group plans to promote an approach that collects data on both the demand and supply side and then combine it to gain a holistic understanding of the financial inclusion equation.

Postal Banking

One way in which states have provided consumer banking services is through their postal systems. Since postal systems have branches distributed throughout a country and since they deal with delivering a particular service, there a certain amount of alignment with them and providing banking services. Interest in postal banking has ebbed and flowed over the years and is commonly seen as a means to enhance financial inclusion on the part of activists.

Postal systems have networks of outlets and through this network can provide a number of banking services, from basic transactions such as money transfers and bill payment to more extensive services such as deposit taking and investments. These networks provide the infrastructure to offer financial services and, if carefully designed, through economies of scope could reduce postal costs and in fact boost profitability. The likelihood of this outcome depends on the level of services offered by other providers, namely, banks and cooperative savings institutions. Another important aspect of postal banking is the location of its networks. In some cases these networks encompass remote, rural, and poor regions. This means that the possibility exists that the postal system can be a strategic component of a financial inclusion response. Baradaran notes:

> Most crucially, postal banking was the most successful experiment in financial inclusion in the United States. More effective than any other philanthropic or mutual effort to bank the poor, postal banking brought millions of new immigrants and rural dwellers into the U.S. banking system all at once. One of the central aims of the postal banks was also the most difficult to measure: teaching habits of thrift and saving to the poor. (Baradaran 2015, p. 207)

Baradaran (2015) attributes the US burgeoning early democracy and economy to the establishment of an extensive postal system that effectively informed the population, including those living in remote areas, and lubricated commerce. Postal banking has been around for 150 years, beginning in Britain in 1861 and spreading throughout its empire in the late nineteenth century including to Canada, New Zealand, and Australia, and then to many Western nations including Japan, but not to the United States until 1910 and Germany until 1939 (Baradaran 2015, p. 187).

In the last 30 years, postal systems have undergone dramatic changes. Once seen as a purely public institution supported by tax revenue, the postal system in many countries has moved into a public corporation or to a private corporation (Ruozi and Anderloni 2013). Traditionally postal systems were understood to be monopolies, but de-regulation and applying new ICTs to mail systems have led new private parcel delivery companies to compete with postal systems. Postal systems have moved from a collaborative system across states to more complicated systems that involve strategic alliances between public and private shippers. Important postal systems in Europe, the Netherlands, and Germany were privatized in 1998 and 2000, respectively (Ruozi and Anderloni 2013, p. 11). In the United States the postal banking service was ended in 1966, and Baradaran attributes this to several factors: the establishment of deposit insurance, which reduced private bank failures; more extensive infrastructure and more mobile transportation, enabling remotely located people to get to banks; the establishment of banking-by-mail; higher interest rates offered at private banks as compared with the postal service; and the decline in poverty, which according to Baradaran was a central source of demand for the postal banking system since its creation in 1910 (Baradaran 2015, pp. 205–06). Today there are various pressures placed on postal services. Many state-based systems have turned into separate not-for-profit corporations, and others have been completely privatized. Email and text messaging have replaced traditional physical letters, but parcel delivery has rapidly increased. Some call for the complete privatization of the post, clearly moving postal banking off the agenda. Others call for the strengthening of the public postal system—whether embedded within government or in a separate corporation—through the addition of banking services (Baradaran 2015; Anderson 2013).

The Arguments for and Against Postal Banking

There are a number of reasons why postal banking makes sense (Baradaran 2015, pp. 217–19):

- Postal systems, even relative to banks, are large and can take advantage of economies of scale. Their large networks allow them to distribute their costs over a large number of transactions keeping their fees relatively low.
- Postal systems can take advantage of economies of scope, meaning they can add services that are similar to existing ones and so build on the core capacity of the organization.

- Postal systems have existing infrastructure for processing and delivering mail that can be used for processing and delivering banking services. This includes networks, outlets, and well-trained staff. Their networks include outlets in rural communities and inner-city neighborhoods (Anderson 2013, p. 10).
- Postal systems are not-for-profit, meaning that they are not required to generate a profit and can therefore keep their fees lower than fees charged by for-profit banks. "Compared with payday lenders, the post office can use its present infrastructure and staff, thus saving money otherwise spent on advertising, marketing, personnel, and stores" (Baradaran 2015, p. 218).
- A central reason for optimism that adding banking to the postal system will work to reduce financial exclusion is that excluded people trust the postal service (Baradaran 2015; Anderson 2013). Baradaran argues that trust is an important value that has important economic consequences: it lowers costs and reduces barriers:

  > [I]n light of historical and international experience and the significant modern distrust of fringe banks, the public may view the post office as a safer and more trustworthy place to store funds. If this is the case, the post office may even decide to forego the added costs and regulatory burden of FDIC deposit insurance because the post office's position as a federal agency and its access to the Treasury's deep pockets can fulfill essentially the same function as FDIC insurance. (Baradaran 2015, p. 219)

- The rise of fringe banking in the Global North is evidence of a substantial demographic that is not being served by mainstream FIs (Anderson 2013). Anderson argues that some postal bank systems demonstrate that they are well suited to meet the financial service needs of low-income people:

  > The Kiwibank [New Zealand] and Banque Postale [France] are both excellent examples of how a postal bank can offer special services to low-income people, such as home mortgages, rent-to-buy, and even social housing loans. In the case of Kiwibank, a special mortgage program for Aboriginal peoples has been developed that could be replicated in Canada. (Anderson 2013, p. 10)

While these are strong arguments in favor of postal banking, there are also arguments against it (Baradaran 2015, pp. 217–19):

- Financial institutions such as banks and credit unions are specialized agencies that are, arguably the most efficient providers of financial services. Getting the postal system involved will reduce the FIs' market, increasing their costs, this will be done at taxpayers' expense, and it would involve them in providing services that they are not specialized in. But, Baradaran notes, "Not only are postal employees capable individuals, but providing simple financial products does not require years of skilled training. Consider the number of bank tellers, Wal-Mart, or Cash America employees who manage this very thing while earning smaller hourly wages and fewer benefits than postal employees" (Baradaran 2015, p. 221).
- Another important argument against postal banking is the view that that government is inherently inefficient and that by adding banking to a state-based postal system, inefficiencies will result. US opponents to postal banking point to the failure of Fannie Mae and Freddie Mac as examples of this. But Baradaran argues that these institutions, along with Sallie Mae (providing subsidized student loans), have pioneered services that "directly helped create the American middle class" (Baradaran 2015, p. 222).

Postal Banking in Practice

According to the latest annual report of the International Post Corporation, a Brussels-based company of 24 postal organizations and linked with 189 services around the world, revenue and profitability for the industry are steady, and the growth sectors are parcel delivery over mail and e-commerce over in-store (International Postal Corporation 2015). The study notes that financial services were a relatively higher profit segment as compared with other segments (International Postal Corporation 2015, p. 9).[3] In fact, financial services rank third after mail and parcel services in terms of contribution to revenue, sitting at 16.5% in 2015.

There are strong arguments for and against postal banking, and of course, the context matters immensely, so that a case-by-case approach is needed. Nevertheless, a strong postal system and a large unbanked population—evidenced by few bank accounts and/or a large fringe bank sector—present a scenario in which postal banking makes sense. In Canada there are growing calls for Canada Post to move into providing banking services (Box 6.1).

Box 6.1 Proposal for a postal banking system in Canada

"Canada Post already provides some financial services, such as postal money orders, domestic and international money transfers, bill payment and financial transaction and payment notices, and prepaid Visa cards. Brand new services could consist of:

- access by all banks and credit union customers to their accounts to deposit or withdraw cash, as is the case in the UK;
- savings accounts and low-fee chequing accounts;
- low-interest credit cards; and
- prepaid debit cards.

In the future, services could be extended to:

- mortgages;
- small-business loans and agricultural loans;
- insurance products;
- mutual funds and stocks; and
- special new products for low-income and Aboriginal peoples."

Source: Anderson 2013, pp. 11–12

State-Based "Nudging"

Made famous by Thaler and Sunstein's book *Nudge* (2008), nudging has become a fairly standard practice for global Anglo-American governments with regard to consumer-related financial regulations. What Thaler and Sustein, self-described libertarians, argue is that human irrationality leads people to make common mistakes that hurt their self-interest. This presents a role for the state: to step in and "nudge" its citizens to behave in ways that improve their lives. For instance, since people tend to under-save for retirement, the state should encourage higher savings contributions. Thaler and Sunstein argue this could be done in such a way as to not diminish human freedom, for instance, by establishing high default savings rates. People can freely choose lower savings rates, but the default rate is high. This is justified by the behavioral insight that, because of status quo bias, people tend to accept default rates. By establishing high savings contributions as the default, they argue, the state can, albeit in a slightly paternalistic fashion, lead citizens to achieve their own interests. Without that intervention, goes the theory (and some evidence), people will under-save and be disadvantaged in their old age.

An important point is that most of the work related to behavioral economics of finances has to do with financial consumers. But if behavioral economics is correct, then surely the bounded rationality that applies to consumers also applies to the other side of the market, the firms. Moreover, if we are all somewhat irrational when it comes to finances (and other issues), why would we assume that policymakers are rational? Bankers and policymakers can be as bounded in their thinking as consumers. What is not clear is how the individual irrationality of bankers and policymakers is filtered by their respective organizations, the bank, and the state. This is an area that behavioral economists have not yet examined. Nevertheless we will look at these issues below.

Behavioral economics has provided important insights into human behavior, and the work related to household finances is an important contribution to our understanding of financial exclusion, household financial decision-making, and individual financial mistakes. As the World Bank has demonstrated, the insights gained about consumers have a bearing on professionals such as development policymakers. They too behave, at times, in irrational ways. Overall, behavioral economics finds that people are bounded in their rationality, not entirely irrational but in certain situations and in certain ways, people behave irrationally.[4] But if every actor is bounded in their rationality, who will promote reason? Since no one group is fully rational, then all groups—consumer/civil society, business, and the state—will need to work for and hold the others accountable to rational behavior.

Much of the literature on behavioral economics assumes that the individual is permanently irrational; meanwhile, the policymaker is assumed to be permanently rational so that the solution is for the policymaker to sort out the individual's irrationality through careful policies and regulations. The trouble is that policymakers, based on the fact that they are human, are subject to the same kinds of irrationalities as individuals are. The hope is that individuals are not permanently irrational, at least not with respect to the same issue. Consider the insights from Robert Lucas and his ratio nal expectations theory, which challenges the assumption that monetary authorities can "fool" people by increasing the money supply, thereby lowering the real wage and encouraging firms to hire more workers. He argues that workers are not fooled for long and will realize they are being manipulated and begin to demand that their wages keep up with, or exceed, inflation (Lucas and Sargent 1981). This is not to say that policymakers cannot find gaps of bounded rationality and fill them but rather that policymakers face their own limitations and individuals can catch up. But it is just as important that individuals are empowered to be more rational about financial behavior.

But Are Policymakers Rational?

Behavioral economics has provided us with rich insights about actual human behavior. As the foregoing discussion has shown, we behave differently than what neoclassical economics assume. This analysis demonstrates a limitation of neoclassical economic theory. But critics of behavioral economics have pointed out the weaknesses of behavioural studies. This section will examine some of these limitations.

Behavioral economics focuses on the micro level, the level of the individual. But there are other levels that affect the social world such as communities of people, subnational regions, nations, and the global level. As Jeffrey Sachs has pointed out, placing too much emphasis on the individual level creates an unacceptable opportunity cost as it means that less attention is paid at these other, more constraining levels (Zweig 2015). For instance, we discussed structural barriers to human well-being. These are not addressed in the neoclassical model or in behavioral economics.

Beyond this critique, there are other limitations of behavioral economics. As discussed earlier in this chapter, behavioral economics relaxes the assumption about human rationality, but it does not, generally speaking, relax the neoclassical economic assumption about the frictionless world. Consistent with the neoclassical school, behavioral economics assumes that the best way to understand the world is that it is made up of individuals operating in various perfectly competitive markets. This assumption is challenged by a variety of structural theories, which will be examined below.

Without wading into the structural issue, Waldron (2014) identifies three limitations of behavioral economics that relate to its policy prescriptions. Waldron assigns three criticisms to libertarian paternalism—the approach that seeks to nudge people using "choice architecture" to make self-interested decisions. First and foremost, he argues that it insults human dignity by coercing people into certain types of decisions. He asserts that in the end nudging is paternalistic and removes from people the ability to make their own decisions.

Second, Waldron notes that since policymakers are human, they too make mistakes. Just because policymakers and behavioral economists are better educated does not guarantee they are more rational. "Of course regulators are people too. And like the rest of us, they are fallible. In the original *Nudge*, Sunstein engagingly confessed too many of the decisional foibles that Thaler exposed" (Waldron 2014). Policymakers take short-cuts to decision-making without doing comprehensive analyses. Instead they will decide using simple rules of thumb, and because they tend to be biased toward the status quo, they will follow the herd.

A final point, and related to point two, is that policymakers (for reelection) and corporate executives (for enhanced profit) sometimes seek to manipulate people.[5] They will use their knowledge of human bounded rationality in order to achieve their ends, at the expense of citizens and consumers:

> Every day we are bombarded with offers whose choice architecture is manipulated, not necessarily in our favor. The latest deal from the phone company is designed to bamboozle us, and we may well want such blandishments regulated. But it is not clear whether the regulators themselves are trustworthy. Governments don't just make mistakes; they sometimes set out deliberately to mislead us. The mendacity of elected officials is legendary and claims on our trust and credulity have often been squandered. It is against this background that we have to consider how nudging might be abused. (Waldron 2014)

In its most recent *World Development Report*, the World Bank (2015), a pre-eminent—if controversial—institution of development research assessed its staff from a behavioral economic perspective. The results reinforce what Waldron intuited: "Experts, policy makers, and development professionals are also subject to the biases, mental short-cuts (heuristics), and social and cultural influences" (World Bank 2015, p. 180). In preparation for this report, the World Bank studied headquarters and field staff to test for several types of behavioral biases. Biases were found associated in a number of areas. Interestingly many of these biases were well-known before the World Bank study. Because of the importance of this study, it will be summarized in length.

The first type of bias that was associated with World Bank professionals was using short-cuts in the face of the complexity of development (World Bank 2015, p. 181). Professionals of all sorts face complex problems with uncertain outcomes. Decision-making is influenced by the way in which the problem is *framed*. For instance, decision-making will be very different if the framing is done in a positive as compared with negative way. When a problem with identical but differently framed solutions—positive vs. negative—was presented to staff, "in the gain frame, respondents chose certainty; presented with a loss frame, they preferred to take their chances".

The second type of bias identified in World Bank staff was *confirmation bias* (World Bank 2015, p. 182). Behavioral studies have found that professionals will sometimes take short-cuts, and their decision-making, rather than being based on "hard" analysis, will be based on previous views, ideology, and worldview. Researchers tested this with World Bank professionals. They did this by presenting a sample of staff with two different types of problems: a skin cream problem without an ideological element and a minimum wage problem with an ideological element:

> Identical sets of data were presented to World Bank staff, but in different frames. In one frame, staff were asked which of two skin creams was more effective in reducing a rash. In the other, they were asked whether or not minimum wage laws reduce poverty. Even though the data were identical, World Bank respondents were significantly less accurate when considering the data for minimum wage laws than for skin cream. Views on whether minimum wage laws lower poverty tend to be related to cultural and political outlooks. Respondents supporting income equality were significantly less accurate when the data presented conflicted with their outlooks (and showed that minimum wage laws raise poverty rates) than they were when the data corresponded to their outlooks (and showed that minimum wage laws lower poverty rates). (World Bank 2015, p. 183)

This is a very important if not particularly surprising result, demonstrating that even in the face of evidence, development professionals are biased against policies that are effective in fighting poverty when the evidence is at odds with their ideological orientation. Since many World Bank professionals are either economists or influenced by neoclassical economic theory, their ideological bias is likely consistent with a neoliberal approach. Evidence that supports a contrary position tends to be discounted because of the complexity effect.

A third type of bounded rationality exhibited by WB staff was *sunk-cost bias* (World Bank 2015, p. 185). If a project is failing, financially speaking, and there is no chance of revising it to make it financially viable, then the logical response is to close it down. But behavioral studies have found that there tends to be a bias to overlook project failings if considerable expense has already been committed. In the study, World Bank staff were presented with evidence on a failing conservation program and were asked what would they do about it. The researchers found that "as the level of sunk cost increased, so did the propensity of the staff to continue [with the project]" (World Bank 2015, p. 185).

A fourth type of bias is *lack of understanding of the particular contexts* of decision-making in a developing community: middle-income urban professionals do not behave like low-income rural/slum laborers (World Bank 2015, p. 186). The study identified three ways in which World Bank staff have difficulty understanding poor people:

- The vast majority of staff have never been poor and so do not understand the decision-making process of the poor.
- Staff are trained within professions that make certain assumptions, use particular language, follow certain norms, and use particular resources that are different from those associated with local poor people. They are likely not even aware of how foreign their professional approach and worldview are to local poor people.
- World Bank staff are unfamiliar with the mental models and mindsets of poor people. This makes it difficult for them to understand the decision-making of poor people. One study compared staff's assumptions about the views of poor people with the actual views of poor people in three areas: control of their future, helplessness in dealing with life's challenges, and the safety of vaccines. The results found that "development professionals assume that poor individuals are less autonomous, less responsible, less hopeful, and less knowledgeable then they in fact are".

The *World Development Report 2015* offers important insights into the rationality of development professionals by finding that, at least at the World Bank, staff exhibit bounded rationality through how they frame problems, how they confirm their assessments, how they treat sunk costs, and how they misunderstand poor people. In each case, the analysis is followed by a prescribed solution. To deal with complexity, it is recommended that problems be broken into smaller and discrete subproblems and a consensus generated with local people about the principle problem (World Bank 2015, p. 182). Confirmation bias can be addressed by exposing people to a joint and constructive learning process with people with alternative and opposite views. Sunk-cost bias can be addressed by helping professionals realize that mistakes are made and that acknowledging them, and in some cases closing programs down, is the most sensible decision. Dealing with ignorance about poor people's context and decision-making can be addressed by having development professionals live in local communities and experience the development services or products that are being proposed. If these services are not good enough for the professional, then why would they be good enough for poor people?

The solutions posed by the report to address the bounded rationality of World Bank staff and development professionals in general are likely helpful. However, at a deeper level, the structural critique of development action is that it is often motivated by powerful interests who are driving the agenda to meet *their* goals, not the goals of poor people. In fact, the insights from this study are not unique to behavioral economic studies. There are at least two important literatures that confirm these types of biases. Post-colonial theory has critiqued modern development efforts for the way in which they construct "the other" or "the poor" and then create programs and policies that are ostensibly intended to assist them, but in fact they are a means to control them (Said 1993; Zein-Elabdin and Charusheela 2004).

The international development studies literature is also rich with critiques of professional bias, most notably in the work of Robert Chambers (2008, 1983). Chambers (1983) argues that professional academic biases toward publication, for example, leads development researchers to pursue certain types of research projects that often diverge from and possibly conflict with the interests of poor people. Chambers identified a variety of biases that prevent professionals from understanding and working with the rural poor. These include spatial, person, and analytical ones (Chambers 1983). Spatial biases keep professionals in comfortable urban settings rather than remote rural sites. These limit the professional in understanding poverty in remote rural locations. Person biases direct professionals to talk with elites, men, and non-Indigenous People. These prevent the professional from interacting and communicating with poor people. And finally, Chambers talks about analytical approaches that lead to biases. This includes a focus on quick data collection that orients professionals toward talking with the more articulate and better educated people. The academic emphasis on specialization allows the professional deep knowledge of a narrow piece of the development problem but "blinds them to what lies outside it" (Chambers 1983 p. 22). And, akin to the World Bank's confirmation bias, Chambers notes that professionals search for data that supports their own ideas: "They look for and find what fits their ideas. There is neither inclination nor time for the open-ended question or for other ways of perceiving people events and things" (Chambers 1983, p. 23).

Behavioral analysis offers important insights into human behavior. Critiques of behavioral economics are helpful in pointing to the limitations of this approach, a shortcoming associated with all approaches. Applying the approach to understanding elites, as the World Bank did with some of its staff, is a relatively new area of study. This has the potential to expand behavioral economics from being an insightful subtopic of neoclassical economics to becoming a more fulsome theoretical approach. Understanding actual elite behavior might improve our understanding of structures that reinforce poverty and inequality.

Rationality as a Process of Engaging with Marginalized People

But financial inclusion is not arranged between autonomous consumers and professionals. Individuals are involved in decision-making, but banks and the state mediate these relationships. These institutions have their own interests, and banks—like other large corporate businesses—have proved particularly adept at working with bounded rationality to promote its interests. Can businesses and the state be nudged into more socially beneficial behavior, and if so by whom? It is typically the role of the state to regulate banks. The challenge remains that as we have seen, the state's agents—policymakers—can be irrational too. Moreover, structures tend to operate in such a way as to reinforce the status quo, including the exclusion of the unbanked from financial, employment, and social resources.

In the ideal sense, the state is the representative of the people, and as such the state's role is to promote the public good. An important role of the state is to identify common consumer errors and minimize their harm through education and regulation. The state's rationale for regulating banks is to limit its negative behaviors and, possibly, encourage positive behaviors that enable it to achieve its private interests while contributing to the common good. Given the evidence presented above about policy-maker bias, what are ways to reduce that and enable them to behave more rationally, particularly when the policy relates to vulnerable people?

- *Cross-cultural training of staff*: there is a long literature on the biases of development professionals (e.g., Chambers 1983, 2005, 2008) toward urban, rich, and male. These biases give professionals at a minimum a limited understanding and in the worst case a mistaken understanding of a problem. In order to overcome this, professional staff could receive cross-cultural training.
- *Provide training on evidence-based decision-making*: the World Bank finds that development policymakers are bounded in their thinking, and one manifestation of this is a bias toward the idea that markets can work out most social and economic problems. Markets have a contribution to make to improving well-being, but they are limited, particularly with reference to people with limited income and assets who have very low demand. Policymakers should be provided training on making decisions on evidence-based, not ideological grounds.
- *Grassroots experiences*: several years ago the World Bank proposed that it establish a new wing that would have village-oriented structures akin to the Grameen Bank and require staff to live in villages to gain an understanding of the needs and interests of poor people. These experiences can be incredibly rich and provide a lifelong change in attitude and understanding toward a particular group.

Subprime mortgages, payday loans, asset-backed securities are products that have benefited some bankers more than many consumers. Advertising is a way by which businesses nudge people to purchase their goods. In the Global North markets are often dominated by a small number of large companies, and these companies may be able to control the market. They certainly control the activity that happens within their operations (e.g., intra-firm pricing). How can behavioral economic insights assist us here?

Big businesses understand bounded rationality, and that is why they spend a lot of money on advertising and marketing. Consumers are in an asymmetric relationship with business because of the size and resource differences, and so consumers are unable to counter business pressure. Consumer protection is helpful but insufficient, because of the powerful message that comes from big business. So how can banks be nudged to promote public interests rather than their own? Some banks do this more effectively than other banks, so it is not impossible.

Can the state step in to determine the factors that lead some banks to perform and some to underperform and then nudge the underperformers toward the performers? Businesses could be nudged in a variety of ways. This might be done by establishing standards (see below) that, if met, would allow banks to:

- Access funds that they automatically contribute to
- Receive special status or credits that assist them in regulatory applications (e.g., credits the United States provides to banks through its Community Reinvestment Act)

Criteria that might be included in business standards include the following:

- *Focus on needs of consumer*: Ensure that products are developed to meet consumer needs and interests, not the needs and interests of the business. Since much of the interest in microcredit and financial inclusion centers on asset- and income-poor people, it is critical that products are designed with vulnerable people's needs in mind.
- *The onus of proof*: Often new financial products are allowed onto the market with little or no evidence of their potential impact. The state might only regulate the market if there is substantial evidence of the harm the product is causing. Yet financial products can be complicated, and they can harm people. The onus of proof needs to shift so that new products must be proven to promote well-being, and not that they do not harm, which is the precautionary principle (Cartagena Protocol). Certain criteria must be met before a product is approved.
- *Evidence of harm*: Where a product is approved but there is evidence of harm being done to a substantial share of the clients, then it warrants a review. If there is evidence of harm, the product should be

disallowed or revised. An randomized control trial may be unable to conclude that the treatment sample is being harmed, but it may be able to conclude that a subgroup within the treatment sample is being harmed. Evidence should also come from mixed methodologies that include qualitative methods that amplify the voices, particularly of the vulnerable person.

- *Evidence of bad business practices*: If there is evidence that a business is manipulating the market through its market power, then the state must step in to break up the company. For instance, the payday loan market in Canada is dominated by one large foreign-owned company, National Money Mart. Its behavior should be very carefully examined by the state competition board.
- *Limit advertising and marketing*: Advertising should be kept to the minimum needed to raise consumer awareness of a given product which has already been identified to meet consumers' needs and interests.

Financial Education

The state is responsible to provide education to its population because as a public good there is no way that private agents will be able to do so at a universal level. Moreover, without checks and balances, private agents would be inclined to present education in a way that reinforces their interests, not necessarily the public interest. Increasingly it is recognized, given the prevalence of financialization, that financial education curriculum needs to be introduced or expanded in the public school system. There are different aspects and versions of this curriculum. Here we will consider two types: standard financial literacy and "constructive consumer-citizen" literacy.

The standard financial education curriculum examines attitude, skills, and knowledge regarding household finances. Issues around household finances include household budgeting, saving, investing, borrowing, buying a house, and the investment risk-reward trade-off. Skills relate to actually implementing a household budget, while knowledge relates to understanding the factors behind the risk-reward trade-off. Attitude is a critical factor, as this connects knowledge and skill on the one hand with good financial behavior on the other hand. A person might know about the risk-reward trade-off and how to compare different investment products. But choosing the right investment product depends on having an attitude to collect the needed information, to apply knowledge and skill, and then to follow through with the appropriate choice. Sometimes a distinction is made between financial literacy, where people *know* what is in their best financial interests and financial capability, where people *behave* in their best financial interests.

But much of the financial literacy curriculum is narrow in its scope. It neither critically examines the goals of financial education nor does it not critically consider the structures that define the global economy. These latter components are a part of a broader and arguably more far-reaching curriculum aimed at the constructive consumer-citizen.

The first critique of standard financial education curriculum is that it assumes that growing your household economy is the goal of household finances: maintain a budget and invest to build your future earning capacity or to finance your retirement. The curriculum typically does not ask people to critically consider their financial and certainly not their life goals. What if you want to maintain a modest living standard? Or, what if you want to reduce your ecological footprint? What if you highly value relationships and community and only weakly value your financial position? These types of questions are not addressed in the standard curriculum, and yet they are critical if people are to make informed decisions and to be motivated to succeed at them. There is a growing literature on voluntary simplicity that documents the problems associated with unconscious consumption and the benefits of deliberate living (e.g., Burch 2013).

Consumer culture is a creation of relatively recent origin, rapidly spreading around the world that shapes people's preferences and then encourages them to consume material goods in order to gain psychosocial benefits. For most of history and still much of the world, consumer culture is not the dominant process of shaping human preferences and their economies:

> Any economy must meet our basic physical needs or the economy itself will disappear because its customers will perish. The demand for goods that fill these needs is intrinsic to our human nature. But we use material goods to assist with meeting or expressing many of our psycho-social needs as well. This capacity human beings have to substitute need satisfiers is the key focus of consumer culture development. We need love and esteem. But we can

learn to perceive a diamond ring as evidence that someone loves us, and we can use diamond rings to express our love. How a psychological experience as rich, warm, complex and essential to human nature as love can become associated with a colorless hard, cold bit of stone attests to the miraculous ability we have to each ourselves to believe almost anything ... Consumer culture teaches us to want what it wants us to want by offering us substitutes for what we really want. (Burch 2013, pp. 61–62)

But the consumerist substitute is weak, and often more goods do not translate into more happiness. A growing literature on economy and happiness finds that for the Global North, there is a weak and sometimes negative relationship between rising economy and happiness (van Tuinen 2011, p. 214). Moreover, US$500 billion is spent annually on advertising, clearly limiting the autonomy of the consumer (van Tuinen 2011, p. 214).

Financial education curriculum that encourages students to work for a better life, economy, and society needs to challenge the "cookie cutter" consumer idea. It needs to encourage people to think more deeply about the good life and the means to achieve it. It is only by doing so that financial education can truly assist people to improve their well-being.

Another critical issue that most financial education misses is an examination of the underlying structure of the economy. The assumption is that the economic structure is best characterized by a market with a large number of autonomous consumers and a similar number of autonomous producers. There are no structures that need to be explained, because it is only individuals that matter. But this is not the case: there are structures beyond the market, and understanding them is critically important to understanding the economy and, by extension, one's household economy. Many industries in the Global North are dominated by large corporations, not autonomous producers. These large corporations are able to affect market outcomes through political influence and shifting consumer opinion. The work of consumer associations can sometimes influence market outcomes, but corporations are better organized to influence markets and individuals.

Once again, it is critical that an examination of the structure of the economic system is included in financial education curriculum. Individuals need to understand these structures in order to make good household financial decisions. For instance, understanding that the nature of the macro-economy is regular boom-bust cycles could have consequences on one's investment decisions.

What is the state's role in promoting a more complete financial education curriculum? For this curriculum to address the deep cultural and structural issues, it requires dramatic commitment and cannot be left to civil society. The state must play a central role. Van Tuinen identifies a number of strategies the state could pursue to reduce consumerism, including introducing more prohibitive regulations regarding advertising, taxing advertising expenditure, promoting anti-consumer advertising (e.g., Adbusters) and voluntary simplicity (discussed above), educating consumers, and establishing a fund supervised by the state to "promote non-commercial values and motives to compete with consumerism" (p. 228). However, van Tuinen is doubtful about the efficacy of this type of consumer education:

> But it may be doubted whether general campaigns for consumer literacy or empowerment will be effective in the abatement of consumerism for at least three reasons. First, behavioural economics and neuroeconomics have demonstrated that there are essential limits to consumer rationality. Second, commercial marketing systematically fans irrational behaviour, so the education efforts will permanently be on the defensive. Third, general campaigns for consumer literacy may be perceived as paternalistic, and this would undermine their effectiveness. (Van Tuinen 2011, p. 225)

Discussion

The subprime mortgage crisis in the United States in 2008 demonstrated very clearly why the state's role in bank regulation is crucial. This is the most recent global financial crisis in a long list. But the rise of everyday financialization means that the state has an additional issue to address in its regulations. Since more vulnerable people are being brought into the financial system, then the state will need to ensure that their interests are protected. The state has various tools it can use to achieve this protection including regulating, "nudging", and providing services including banking (e.g., postal banking) and education.

Nudging is a popular response today, but given the growing complexity of the financial marketplace and the bounded rationality of policymakers, this approach has limitations. For this to work it would seem that state agents need to be in dialogue (literally and figuratively) with vulnerable people in order to understand what they (vulnerable people) value.

Providing banking services through, for example, the postal system, may make sense in certain countries that already have an extensive postal network and have a limited banking network. Providing education is crucial as it is ensuring that financial literacy—in its broadest sense, that encourages students to think about the relationship between finances and the things that they value—is a component of that education.

Notes

1. The economic definition of public goods is that they are not excludable and subtractable. Neoconservatives would challenge even these limited roles for the state and argue that the market is better placed to provide these goods and services. This is driven by ideology which has challenged the definition and changed the nature of public goods. Whereas in the past education, electrical generation and supply, and policing were designed and organized as public goods, neoconservatives argue that they can be redesigned as private goods. But this is simply redesigning a system that was working, and, in fact, in many cases the performance of markets for public goods is weak.
2. A payment system is the means by which different actors pay one another and is critical for a well-functioning market economy. I am grateful to an anonymous reviewer of an earlier version of this manuscript for highlighting this point.
3. Anderson notes, "A recent study by the Conference Board of Canada, commissioned Canada Post, provided a positive analysis of the effects of financial services in post offices around the world" (Anderson 2013, p. 7).
4. Of course there are far bigger challenges to rationality, such as not responding to global climate change, not reforming the financial sector in light of the subprime mortgage crisis that prompted global recession, and not revising support for economic growth when there are loads of evidence that it is weakly linked with improving human well-being. These challenges involve many parties, strategic behavior, and complex and at times conflicting interests. They are not the subject of this discussion.
5. These insights have similarities to those of earlier rational choice theories, which found that policymakers and politicians behave in their own interests and that these interests may or may not be in concert with social interests.

Bibliography

"Bank for International Settlements". 2011. Accessed December 20, 2015. http://www.bis.org/index.htm

Alliance for Financial Inclusion. 2010. *Financial Inclusion Measurement for Regulators: Survey Design and Implementation*. Kuala Lumpur: Alliance for Financial Inclusion.

———. 2011. *Empowering and Protecting Financial Consumers: Bank Negara Malaysia's Consumer and Market Conduct Framework*. Kuala Lumpur: Alliance for Financial Inclusion.

———. 2015. *Maya Declaration: Commitments You can Bank on*. Kuala Lumpur: Alliance for Financial Inclusion.

Anderson, John. 2013. *Making the Case for Postal Banking in Canada*. Ottawa: Canadian Centre for Policy Alternatives.

Baradaran, Mehrsa. 2015. *How the Other Half Banks: Exclusion, Exploitation, and the Threat to Democracy*. Cambridge: Harvard University Press.

Barth, James R., Gerard Caprio, and Ross Levine. 2012. The Evolution and Impact of Bank Regulations.

Barua, Abheek, Rajat Kathuria, and Neha Malik. 2016. *The Status of Financial Inclusion, Regulation, and Education in India*. Tokyo: Asian Development Bank Institute.

Burch, Mark. 2013. *The Hidden Door: Mindful Sufficiency as an Alternative to Extinction*. Melbourne: The Simplicity Institute.

Carbo, Santiago, Edward P.M. Gardener, and Philip Molyneux. 2005. *Financial Exclusion*. New York: Palgrave Macmillan.

Chambers, Robert. 1983. *Rural Development: Putting the Last First*. New York: Longman Scientific & Technical.

———. 2005. *Ideas for Development*. London: Earthscan.

———. 2008. *Revolutions in Development Inquiry*. London and Sterling, VA: Earthscan Publications; Distributed by Stylus, Sterling, VA.

Cihak, Martin, Asli Demirguc-Kunt, Maria Martinez Peria, and Amin Mohensi-Cheraghlou. 2012. *Bank Regulation and Supervision Around the World: A Crisis Update*. Washington, DC: World Bank.

European Commission. 2014. *The Right to a Basic Bank Account for all European Citizens*.

———. n.d. *Access of Payment Accounts*.

Gutierrez, Eva, and Sandeep Singh. 2013. What Regulatory Frameworks are More Conducive to Mobile Banking? Empirical Evidence from Findex Data. The World Bank, Policy Research Working Paper Series: 6652.

Hoque, Hafiz, Dimitris Andriosopoulos, Kostas Andriosopoulos, and Raphael Douady. 2015. Bank Regulation, Risk and Return: Evidence from the Credit and Sovereign Debt Crises. *Journal of Banking and Finance* 50 (Jan.): 455–471.

International Post Corporation. 2015. *IPC Global Postal Industry Report*. Brussels: International Post Corporation.

Klein, Michael, and Colin Mayer. 2011. Mobile Banking and Financial Inclusion: The Regulatory Lessons. The World Bank, Policy Research Working Paper Series: 5664.

Lucas, Robert E., and Thomas J. Sargent, eds. 1981. *Rational Expectations and Econometric Practice*. Minneapolis: University of Minnesota Press.

Mas, Ignacio. 2011. Why are Banks so Scarce in Developing Countries? A Regulatory and Infrastructure Perspective. *Critical Review* 23 (1-2): 135–145.

Office of the Comptroller of the Currency. 2008. *Community Reinvestment Act Performance Evaluation*. Washington, DC: Office of the Comptroller of the Currency.

Osberg, Lars. 2013. Instability Implications of Increasing Inequality: Evidence from North America. *Economic Modelling* 35 (Sep.): 918–930.

Pew Charitable Trusts. 2012. *Who Borrows, Where They Borrow, and Why: Payday Lending in America*. Pew Center on the States.

———. 2013. *Payday Lending in America: Policy Solutions*. Pew Center on the States.

Porteous, David. 2006. *The Enabling Environment for Mobile Banking in Africa*. Boston: Commissioned by Department for International Development.

Ruozi, Roberto, and Luisa Anderloni. 2013. *Modernisation and Privatisation of Postal Systems in Europe: New Opportunities in the Area of Financial Services*. Berlin: Springer Science and Business Media.

Said, Edward W. 1993. *Culture and Imperialism*. New York: Vintage Books.

Stiglitz, Joseph E. 2013. *The Price of Inequality: How Today's Divided Society Endangers Our Future*. New York: W. W. Norton.

Thaler, Richard H., and Cass R. Sunstein. 2008. *Nudge: Improving Decisions about Health, Wealth, and Happiness*. New Haven and London: Yale University Press.

Van Arnum, Bradford M., and Michele I. Naples. 2013. Financialization and Income Inequality in the United States, 1967–2010. *American Journal of Economics and Sociology* 72 (5, Nov.): 1158–1182.

van Tuinen, Henk K. 2011. The Ignored Manipulation of the Market: Commercial Advertising and Consumerism Require New Economic Theories and Policies. *Review of Political Economy* 23 (2, Apr.): 213–231.

Waldron, Jeremy. 2014. It's all for Your Own Good by Jeremy Waldron | The New York Review of Books. Accessed November 5, 2015. http://www.nybooks.com/articles/archives/2014/oct/09/cass-sunstein-its-all-your-own-good/

Waller, Spencer W., Jillian G. Brady, R. J. Acosta, and Jennifer Fair. 2011. Consumer Protection in the United States: An Overview. Accessed April 5, 2015. http://papers.ssrn.com/sol3/papers.cfm?abstract_id=1000226

World Bank. 2015. *World Development Report 2015: Mind, Society, and Behaviour*. Washington, DC: World Bank.

Zein-Elabdin, Eiman, and S. Charusheela. 2004. *Postcolonialism Meets Economics*. Economics as Social Theory Series. London and New York: Routledge.

Zweig, Jason. 2015. The Anti-Poverty Experiment, 5 June.

CHAPTER 7

Conclusion

Credit and Finance Schemes: Helping or Harming Vulnerable People?

There is good evidence that everyday financialization is a real phenomenon and that this process is reaching around the world to affect people from all walks of life, including vulnerable people. Chapter 2 presented some evidence in support of the view that at a general level, financialization is proceeding. Common macro-level indicators include the financial sector's growing share of the economy, along with the non-bank corporate sector's revenue share from financial services. Micro-level indicators include the rising use of bank accounts, microloans, and—of particular note—the rise of certain risky financial products such as subprime mortgages and payday loans. These indicators support the notion that, at least on the supply side, financialization is on the rise in the Global South and Global North. However, there is less evidence for this than there is on the demand side. That is, are consumers actually becoming more money-oriented, as financialization scholars have argued they are?

While Sandel (2012) is strongly critical of financialization, arguing that it substitutes the care of money in place of other, more altruistic motives, Zelizer (2011) is more nuanced in her analysis. She argues that a growing role for money does not necessarily crowd out altruism, and in fact it might expand it. She argues that it depends on the context and how the rise of money and monetary motives affects people.

J. Buckland, *Building Financial Resilience*,
https://doi.org/10.1007/978-3-319-72419-5_7

This analysis has not sought to evaluate everyday financialization but a far more modest goal to assess certain credit and finance schemes that are found around the world. The data presented here find support for both Sandel's and Zelizer's arguments. For instance, in support of Zelizer's argument, microcredit and payday lending are good examples to demonstrate this point. In the case of microcredit that is carefully provided (i.e., not pressuring clients to borrow, linking credit with other supports such as business training), this type of financialization might well be liberating for certain clients. These funds can be used to improve an individual's productive capacity, which can improve her finances and can have additional benefits in terms of self-confidence, thus feeding into a virtuous circle. So in support of Zelizer's argument, there are cases where financialization can benefit a person.

On the other hand, in support of Sandel's concerns, other types of microcredit and payday lending, particularly when poorly delivered (e.g., to clients who are unable to repay, so that they must take out another loan to pay off the first), are associated with a type of financialization that is problematic. If borrowers are not clear regarding the fees, repayment deadlines, and their ability to use the funds efficiently, and/or to repay the loan, then more deeply engaging with money might harm them. If one misunderstands the true financial and non-financial costs (e.g., impact on one's credit rating) of a payday loan, then credit—a concept associated more with opportunity and productivity—might impact the person more like debt, a concept associated more with a weight that has a counterproductive impact on a person and could lead to a vicious cycle. So in this case, we can see the merits of Sandel's argument: that financialization can harm people who engage in it. But in this case the harm is not the replacement of altruism with money motives, but the encouragement of short-term borrowing that works against the long-term interests of the borrower. This result is consistent with the argument made by Zelizer, who points out that context matters and that financialization has a variable affect.

However, I believe that Zelizer's critique is not strong enough for two reasons: one, she does not focus exclusively on vulnerable people so that her analysis lumps together vulnerable and non-vulnerable people, and, two, she does not effectively link her analysis, as was done in Chap. 2, with a theory of human well-being. With this book the focus has been on vulnerable people, and it has demonstrated that their vulnerabilities mean that finance and credit schemes can help but they can also *not* help and in some cases harm. Since they cost someone something, to *not* help or to harm is counter-productive, and other, likely non-finance-based schemes, would be more useful. Moreover, if finance and credit schemes are not lending to improved esteem, sufficiency, and/or control, so Goulet's analysis goes, then they do not promote human well-being and are therefore not justifiable. Finance and credit schemes must demonstrate that they reduce vulnerability and that they enhance human well-being, otherwise, what is the point?

Consumer Behavior

The ultimate impact of credit and finance schemes on financial resilience will depend in part on how people—consumers and citizens—respond to financial programs, services, and products. Chapter 4 investigated some aspects of human behavior, including consumerism and insights about human decision-making around finances. The chapter highlighted the limits to human rationality with respect to consumption and financial decision-making. The obvious concern is that if commercially based businesses are enabled to take greater advantage of consumer short-sightedness (or another quality of our bounded rationality), then the outcome would be harmful for the consumer. The teaser rates in the subprime mortgages and the tendency for payday loans, because of their short duration, to encourage repeat borrowing are examples of financial products that do not benefit the consumer or at least some share of consumers. It seems less likely that civil society would take advantage of bounded rationality than commercial institutions do, but bounded rationality will nevertheless limit the benefit from civil society initiatives.

In the face of human irrationality, will the expansion of finance and credit schemes lead to an expansion of practices that manipulate the consumer? The possibility exists that the behavioral research has overstated the extent of human bounded rationality. This argument is built on the idea that behavioral economics involves controlled and short-term experiments that do not allow for medium- to longer-term human learning and adaptation. "You can fool some of the people some of the time but you can't fool all of the people all of the time", is an expression that comes to mind. Once forms of manipulation are uncovered and people are made aware of them, this learning can lead them to adapt their behavior to resist the manipulation. In fact, as discussed in Chap. 3, in the 1980s Robert Lucas took this argument one step further to argue that eventually people can perceive adaptive manipulation and form rational ways to resist it.

Zelizer (2011) takes the notion of human rationality in a different direction than Lucas. She agrees that rationality is not static and adds that it is not simply a matter of economic calculations. Rationality is rooted in culture, and the relationship between money and culture is two-way: culture is shaped by money, but culture can also shape the meaning of money. This leads back to the point made above about the microcredit participant who understands her holistic needs to achieve well-being and sees credit as an ingredient to that end being in a stronger position than the participant who sees credit as the only means or possibly the end in itself. The former person has applied her own meaning to money, flowing from her holistic understanding of well-being. She is less likely to be manipulated by predatory financial providers. The participant with the narrower focus on credit is more likely to rely on it and is perhaps more likely to be manipulated through questionable business practices.

Regardless of participants' views and knowledge, if they are vulnerable, then relative to large financial service firms, an asymmetric relationship will exist. The poor, individual consumer has very little power compared to the large financial service firm. So regardless of an individual's learning and adaptation capacity, he/she will face large financial service firms. These large firms may not deliberately manipulate their clients, but simply using their best practices, given their large resources, could lead to the manipulation of the client. There is a very strong risk that if left unchecked, financialization could indeed lead to greater manipulation by firms of consumers. This potential is compounded as financial firms are able to collect personal data and to use ITs to analyze, communicate, and market their services to humans, with our tendencies toward bounded rationality. This suggests the need for further state action to regulate financial institutions to ensure that the common good is protected.

It is when the interests of the vulnerable person and the finance or credit provider converge that there is the greatest chance for financial inclusion to advance human well-being. This will be discussed below.

The Supply Side of Financialization: Microcredit and Payday Lending

There are different types of banking services that deliver financial services to vulnerable people, including informal providers, fringe financial servers, and mainstream financial institutions (FIs). There is evidence that worldwide, mainstream FIs are increasing their scope. This is particularly the case if microfinancial institutions are considered as mainstream FIs. It is also clear that there continues to be large population shares in the Global South and smaller shares in the Global North that do not have access to mainstream FIs. This means that non-mainstream financial service providers are the dominant provider in these locales. In the Global South, this largely means informal financial services such as family and community-based money lending. In the Global North, fringe financial services have grown substantially and at least part of that growth has come from taking over what informal finances used to offer. It seems likely that in the future, fringe banks will continue to expand in both product offerings and countries in which they operate, including in the Global South.

In some ways it is not surprising that the commercial sector, through initiatives such as microcredit and payday lending, is exploring avenues to expand its markets. This desire to grow in size and profitability is a fairly intrinsic characteristic of capitalism, especially as incomes rise and a larger share of most countries' populations can be identified as "bankable" by commercial banks. That the non-profit sector has engaged so heavily in financially related products is a little more surprising, because of the perception that non-profits are less supportive of money as a means of development. Civil society organizations, for instance, religious organizations, have historically struggled with the role of money in development; recall the discussion of world religions and money in Chap. 1. But the fact is that parts of civil society are actively engaging with money-based programs as a means to promote human development.

This is perhaps most advanced with microcredit, where a variety of interesting things can be observed. First, most of this activity is not happening in the Global North, where finances are most advanced, but in the Global South, where finances are more informal. On the one hand, certain microcredit proponents have claimed that microcredit has qualities that align it very closely with the core values of social justice. Muhammad Yunus has been a highly articulate spokesperson for the view that a microcredit model that extends relatively small amounts of capital through a small accountability group is empowering both economically and socially. But on the other hand, commercially delivered microcredit does not look different from a purely commercial operation. It may be "dressed up" with strong development-oriented language, but in the end, it is hard to see how commercial microcredit is better aligned with the goals of social justice as compared with simple commercial banking. But as discussed in Chap. 5, microfinance is just one of variety of ways by which civil society (often with state support or, with respect to conditional cash advances, often delivered by the state) has engaged in more financialized forms of human development programing. Matched savings schemes, cash advances, and financial literacy are other common approaches. And microcredit, matched savings, and cash advances are actively using money to enhance human development, whereas financial literacy is more about *learning* to more effectively use money to build one's capacity.

The motivations behind engaging in credit and finance schemes on the part of civil society are quite different from the motivations for commercial organizations. The commercial organization is required to generate profit for its shareholders. The civil society organization is required to meet the goals that flow from its mission statement, typically rooted in social justice. Does engaging in finance and credit schemes effect civil society's ability to meet its social justice objectives? Does relying on programs that have money at their center enhance or diminish an NGO's ability to foster financial resilience? Returning to Sandel's concern, does financialization crowd out altruistic motivations, for either the program participants or the program itself? Since we undertook no comparative evaluation of money-based vs. non-money-based programs in this book, we cannot answer that question. However, based on the analysis of different types of microcredit and other products such as payday lending, the limited evidence presented here suggests that the answer to this question depends on a number of factors. A microcredit client who is pursuing a holistic change process and who sees credit as one of several "inputs"—including knowledge, skills, natural resources, and social capital—is in a stronger position to understand money as a means to the end of financial and life improvement. A person who is more fixated on finances and has fewer resources may be in a weaker position to see money as a means to an end and rather see money as an end in itself. A parallel might be applied to the microcredit provider. The provider, including the one that only works with microcredit, that understands the holistic needs of its clients and sees credit as one means to the end of improved well-being is likely in a stronger position to resist Sandel's critique of financialization causing harm. Conversely, the provider that sees credit as the only means, or possibly the end itself, is much more likely to fall into Sandel's problem.

Scale is an important issue when comparing social and commercial operations, and this issue has featured quite centrally in the microfinance literature. One argument is that socially driven microfinance is limited in its scale because the capital available to finance social operations is ultimately limited. There is only so much capital available from government and the charitable sectors, so that the scale of socially oriented microfinance is limited. And if scale is limited then efficiency is constrained, because larger-scale or larger economies bring with them lower per-unit costs. This keeps non-market microfinance in a type of vicious cycle: a small capital base keeps the scale small and per-unit costs high. High per-unit costs lead to high fees/interest rates charged to borrowers. Higher fees paid by the borrowers reduce their capacity and scale. By commercializing microfinance operations, the "economies of scale" argument continues, MFIs can tap into large private capital, raise more funds, expand their operations, and face lower-scale economies, creating a virtuous cycle again. More capital expands the lending power of the operation and lowers fees/interest rates for the borrowers, enabling them to borrow more and expand their operations. Expanded operations add to the local economy and, potentially, add further investable capital to the mix.

Neoliberal proponents argue that competitive markets are the best providers of private goods, because competition ensures the most efficient actors come to the fore. Structuralists argue that the neoliberal argument is too reductionist with respect to the impact of the loan on the client. They argue that commercial pressures force the lender to focus on a relatively well-off group and to place excessive pressure on this group to repay their loan. In a sense they are making the Sandel argument that commercialization pushes out altruism and pulls in more selfish motives. In this case the credit provider is unable to consider the interests of the borrowers because they are singularly focused on the shareholders' interests. The borrower, too, faces more pressure to repay, and this might limit the provider's operations. These are both theoretical and practical matters, and as we saw in Chap. 5, there is evidence that microcredit has failed to deliver the substantial impact that some had promised.

Bateman (2011), for one, argues for resources to be directed away from both socially oriented NGOs and purely commercial organizations and toward institutions like credit unions that can take advantage of economies of scale and are clearly driven by a social mission. He argues that these institutions can better (than either the purely commercial or social) represent local and multidimensional interests, including economic and social ones, and support small- and medium-sized enterprises. This is a strong argument. Why, with the creation of MFIs, establish an entirely new class of FIs when the existing FIs, if supported and set out a clear mission, can do the job?

An interesting question to consider is whether payday loans, if offered by a socially oriented organization rather than commercially oriented ones, would be associated with issues like unclear fees or repeat borrowing. The evidence from the United States and Canada is that when offered by a mainstream FI, such as Vancity Credit Union (Canada), the product is designed in a more transparent way that looks a lot more like a typical installment loan. Improved transparency is seen in how the fees are presented, in an interest rate than enables the consumer to compare this product with other loan products. The installment repayment enables the borrower to invest the borrowed funds, ideally increasing the borrowers' productivity and ability to repay the loan over a longer term.

One of the issues that this relates to is how the provider balances its own and its clients' short- and long-term interests. Is the provider seeking to earn a large short-term profit at the expense of its own and/or its client's long-term interests? One way to frame this issue is to ask whether certain types of financial products lend themselves to short-term interests rather than long-term interests. And if this is the case, what are the consequences for borrower and lender? Most fringe bank products, including the payday loan, are short-term and transaction-oriented products. They do not intend to address longer-term financial issues. If the borrower needs a short-term loan and can repay it within that period, then the harm is reduced. One major problem with the payday loan is when the borrower is unable to repay and must get a second and subsequent loan to pay off the first one. In this case the borrower is seeking a long-term solution by piecing together a series of short-term payday loans. And, generally speaking, this does not work well because of the issues discussed in Chap. 3.

Can the State Step Up?

Neoliberalism places fairly tight constraints on the role of the state: to engage in limited regulation of markets, for instance, ensure the soundness of the banking system, to protect consumers from egregious financial practices, and to provide some public goods like certain types of education like financial literacy. With the process of financialization underway and, indeed, with states and civil society actively promoting financial inclusion, many questions arise such as, is this relatively passive state appropriate? As financial services are directed toward increasingly vulnerable people, does the state need to play a more active role to ensure that vulnerable people are not harmed and that, to the greatest extent possible, they benefit from new financial services? How does the role as promoter of financial inclusion interact with the state's role in consumer protection? Is there a conflict of interest? Finally, what is the role of the provision of financial literacy education?

This book has made the case the credit and finance schemes offered by commercial, civil society, and the state offer opportunities and risks. The opportunities are the greatest for the least vulnerable people, and the risks are the greatest for the most vulnerable. The commercial sector is the least likely to be concerned with this fact, while that state and civil society have a greater likelihood and indeed responsibility to be more concerned with this. But civil society organizations are often small and less sophisticated than large banks, which suggests that the state play a central role in fashioning financial inclusion so that vulnerable people benefit and risks are managed. How the state does this, particularly when it is actively promoting financial inclusion, is a good question. The state, like the careful consumer/citizen and the microcredit provider, must understand the limited function of finances within the multifaceted needs of its citizens. And it must realize that commercial providers are obliged to meet the interests of their shareholders and that sometimes this is in conflict or tension with the interests of vulnerable people. Some important ways by which the state can encourage a mutually beneficial outcome include building new banking systems based on the needs of vulnerable people and implementing new schemes slowly that allow for participatory evaluations.

Financial literacy education has a role to play, when it has an impact. There is evidence that these types of programs can be delivered but that participants may not be motivated to put their learning into action. Behavioral studies suggest a more strategic approach to financial education that might involve some standardized curriculum combined with ways in which people can learn things at that moment when they are motivated to learn. Financial counselling and coaching are models that are often suggested to address the latter goal.

This book has presented evidence that credit and finance schemes affect financial resilience from the commercial, social, and state sectors. The evidence presented here is supportive of a nuanced impact on the lives of vulnerable people: in some cases these schemes appear to help vulnerable people to improve their situation, but in other cases they *do not* help or harm them. Some financial products and approaches are particularly problematic: commercially driven financial products that are aggressively marketed to vulnerable people come to mind. What appears to be critical to enhancing the likelihood that these schemes enable people is that they are understood as one means, among many, toward the goal of improving human well-being. Moreover, finance and credit schemes must take into consideration the structures and interests of vulnerable people and not assume that lender and borrower interests will converge. In many cases interests will not converge, and this may be the result of asymmetric structures or bounded rationality on the part of borrower, lender, and/or the state. Conversely, where credit and finance schemes are automatically considered a "good" and either the most important means or the end, then it is more likely that they can create risks and harm vulnerable people.

Bibliography

Bateman, Milford. 2011. *Confronting Microfinance: Undermining Sustainable Development.* Sterling, VA: Kumarian Press.

Sandel, Michael J. 2012. *What Money Can't Buy: The Moral Limits of Markets.* New York: Farrar, Straus and Giroux.

Zelizer, Viviana A. 2011. *Economic Lives: How Culture Shapes the Economy.* Princeton: Princeton University Press.

Bibliography

"Alliance for Financial Inclusion | Bringing Smart Policies to Life". 2015. Accessed December 7, 2015. http://www.afi-global.org/

"Bank for International Settlements". 2011. Accessed December 20, 2015. http://www.bis.org/index.htm

———. 2015. Accessed December 20, 2015. http://www.bis.org/index.htm

"The Big Save: How Can America Serve Better the Millions of Citizens Outside the Financial Mainstream?". 2011. *The Economist.*

"China's SMEs Head for Pawnbrokers as Credit Tightens | CER". Accessed July 8, 2015. http://www.chinaeconomicreview.com/china-sme-lending-shadow-banking-pawnshop-credit

"China's SMEs Head for Pawnbrokers as Credit Tightens | CER". 2015. Accessed August 7, 2015. http://www.chinaeconomicreview.com/china-sme-lending-shadow-banking-pawnshop-credit

"The Economist Explains: Why China is Creating a New "World Bank" for Asia | The Economist". 2015. Accessed April 27, 2015. http://www.economist.com/blogs/economist-explains/2014/11/economist-explains-6

"The Economist Explains: Why Does Kenya Lead the World in Mobile Money? | The Economist". 2016. Accessed June 7, 2016. http://www.economist.com/blogs/economist-explains/2013/05/economist-explains-18

"Global Alliance—For Banking on Values". 2015. Accessed July 29, 2015. http://www.gabv.org/

"Good Shepherd Microfinance | Leading the Way in Microfinance". 2015. Accessed September 1, 2015. http://goodshepherdmicrofinance.org.au/

"Governments Urged to Consider Legislative Response to Virtual Currencies | The Commonwealth". 2015. Accessed September 1, 2015. http://thecom-

J. Buckland, *Building Financial Resilience*,
https://doi.org/10.1007/978-3-319-72419-5

monwealth.org/media/press-release/governments-urged-consider-legislative-response-virtual-currencies
"Grameen America". 2015. Accessed September 1, 2015. http://grameenamerica.org/
"Human Development Report". c.Human Development Report.
"IMF Factsheets—IMF Conditionality; April 2015—Conditio.Pdf". 2015. Accessed April 27, 2015. https://www.imf.org/external/np/exr/facts/pdf/conditio.pdf
"The Mobile Money Revolution is Transforming Bangladesh Global Voices". 2015. Accessed August 5, 2015. http://globalvoicesonline.org/2015/01/08/the-mobile-money-revolution-is-transforming-bangladesh/
"Real-Economy-Real-Returns-GABV-Research-2014.Pdf". 2015. Accessed July 29, 2015. http://www.gabv.org/wp-content/uploads/Real-Economy-Real-Returns-GABV-Research-2014.pdf
"Sell Your Gold and Jewellery for Top Dollar at Cash Converters". 2015. Accessed August 7, 2015. http://www.cashconverters.ca/retail/sell-your-gold/
"Vijaya Youth Club Co-Operative and Credit Union (VYCCU) Savings and Credit Co-Operative Limited | INAFI Nepal". 2015. Accessed November 30, 2015. http://www.inafinepal.org.np/members/vijaya-youth-club-co-operative-and-credit-union-vyccu-savings-and-credit-co-operative
Aitken, Rob. 2007. *Performing Capital.* 1st ed. New York: Palgrave Macmillan.
———. 2013. The Financialization of Micro-Credit. *Development and Change* 44 (3): 473–499.
———. 2015. *Fringe Finance: Crossing and Contesting the Borders of Global Capital.* London: Routledge.
Alliance for Financial Inclusion. 2010. *Financial Inclusion Measurement for Regulators: Survey Design and Implementation.* Kuala Lumpur: Alliance for Financial Inclusion.
———. 2011. *Empowering and Protecting Financial Consumers: Bank Negara Malaysia's Consumer and Market Conduct Framework.* Kuala Lumpur: Alliance for Financial Inclusion.
———. 2015a. *Maya Declaration: Commitments You can Bank on.* Kuala Lumpur: Alliance for Financial Inclusion.
———. 2015b. *2015 Maya Declaration Progress Report: Commitments into Action.* Kuala Lumpur: Alliance for Financial Inclusion.
Altman, Morris. 2012. Implications of Behavioural Economics for Financial Literacy and Public Policy. *Journal of Socio-Economics* 41 (5, Oct.): 677–690.
Anderson, John. 2013. *Making the Case for Postal Banking in Canada.* Ottawa: Canadian Centre for Policy Alternatives.
Andreasen, Alan R. 1975. *The Disadvantaged Consumer.* New York: Free Press.
Angelucci, Manuela, Dean Karlan, and Jonathan Zinman. 2015. Microcredit Impacts: Evidence from a Randomized Microcredit Program Placement

Experiment by Compartamos Banco. *American Economic Journal: Applied Economics* 7 (1): 151–182. https://doi.org/10.1257/app.20130537. https://search.proquest.com/docview/1642673012.

Anson, Jose, Alexandre Berthaud, Leora Klapper, and Dorothe Singer. Financial Inclusion and the Role of the Post Office. The World Bank, Policy Research Working Paper Series: 6630.

Arthur, Chris. 2012. In *Financial Literacy Education: Neoliberalism, the Consumer and the Citizen*, ed. Michael A. Peters and Chris Arthur. Rotterdam, NLD: Sense Publishers.

Association of Development for Economic and Social Help, ADESH. 2015. Welcome to ADESH. Accessed November 30, 2015. http://www.adeshbd.org/site/common_article

Attanasio, Orazio, Britta Augsburg, Ralph De Haas, Emla Fitzsimons, and Heike Harmgart. 2015. The Impacts of Microfinance: Evidence from Joint-Liability Lending in Mongolia. *American Economic Journal: Applied Economics* 7 (1): 90–122. https://doi.org/10.1257/app.20130489. https://search.proquest.com/docview/1644759584.

Attanasio, Orazio P., Veruska Oppedisano, and Marcos Vera-Hernandez. 2015b. Should Cash Transfers be Conditional? Conditionality, Preventive Care, and Health Outcomes. *American Economic Journal: Applied Economics* 7 (2, Apr.): 35–52.

Augsburg, Britta, Ralph De Haas, Heike Harmgart, and Costas Meghir. 2015. The Impacts of Microcredit: Evidence from Bosnia and Herzegovina. *American Economic Journal: Applied Economics* 7 (1): 183–203. https://doi.org/10.1257/app.20130272. https://search.proquest.com/docview/1642672384.

Axelrod, Robert. 1984. *The Evolution of Cooperation*. New York: Basic Books.

Bajpai, Bhavna. 2010. E-Banking Management: Impact, Risks, Security. *International Journal of Research in Commerce and Management* 1 (6, Oct.): 132–136.

BancoSol. 2015. Bancosol. Accessed September 2015. https://www.bancosol.com.bo/

Banerjee, Abhijit, Esther Duflo, Rachel Glennerster, and Cynthia Kinnan. 2015a. The Miracle of Microfinance? Evidence from a Randomized Evaluation. *American Economic Journal: Applied Economics* 7 (1): 22–53.

Banerjee, Abhijit, Dean Karlan, and Jonathan Zinman. 2015b. Six Randomized Evaluations of Microcredit: Introduction and Further Steps. *American Economic Journal: Applied Economics* 7 (1): 1–21.

Bank for International Settlements. 2016. "About the Basel Committee" Bank for International Settlements. Accessed January 4, 2016. http://www.bis.org/bcbs/about.htm

Baradaran, Mehrsa. 2015. *How the Other Half Banks: Exclusion, Exploitation, and the Threat to Democracy*. Cambridge: Harvard University Press.

Barth, James, Gerard Caprio, and Ross Levine. 2012a. *Guardians of Finance: Making Regulators Work for US*. Boston: MIT Press.

Barth, James R., Gerard Caprio, and Ross Levine. 2012b. The Evolution and Impact of Bank Regulations. https://openknowledge.worldbank.org/handle/10986/12183

Barua, Abheek, Rajat Kathuria, and Neha Malik. 2016. *The Status of Financial Inclusion, Regulation, and Education in India*. Tokyo: Asian Development Bank Institute.

Basel Committee on Banking Supervision. 2011. *Basel III: A Global Regulatory Framework for More Resilient Banks and Banking Systems*. Basel: Bank for International Settlements.

Bateman, Milford. 2010. *Why Doesn't Microfinance Work?: The Destructive Rise of Local Neoliberalism*. New York: Zed Books.

———. 2011. *Confronting Microfinance: Undermining Sustainable Development*. Sterling, VA: Kumarian Press.

———. 2015a. Introduction. *Forum for Social Economics* (June/Aug.): 1–20.

———. 2015b. South Africa's Post-Apartheid Microcredit Experiment: Moving from State-Enforced to Market-Enforced Exploitation. *Forum for Social Economics*: 1–29. http://dx.doi.org/10.1080/07360932.2015.1056202

Bauer, Michal, Julie Chytilova, and Jonathan Morduch. 2012. Behavioral Foundations of Microcredit: Experimental and Survey Evidence from Rural India. *American Economic Review* 102 (2, Apr.): 39–1118.

Benartzi, Shlomo, and Richard H. Thaler. 2004. Save More Tomorrow: Using Behavioral Economics to Increase Employee Saving. *Journal of Political Economy* 112 (1, Part 2): S187.

Bendig, Mirko, Michael Unterberg, and Benjamin Sarpong. 2012. *Overview of the Microcredit Sector in the European Union*. Brussels: European Microfinance Network.

Bertrand, Marianne, and Adair Morse. 2011. Information Disclosure, Cognitive Biases, and Payday Borrowing. *Journal of Finance* 66 (6, Dec.): 1865–1893.

Bertrand, Marianne, Sendhil Mullainathan, Dean Karlan, Eldar Shafir, and Jonathan Zinman. 2009. What's Advertising Content Worth? Evidence from a Consumer Credit Marketing Field Experiment. Economic Growth Center, Yale University, Working Papers.

Bertrand, Marianne, Sendhil Mullainathan, and Eldar Shafir. 2004. A Behavioral-Economics View of Poverty. *The American Economic Review* 94 (2, May): 419–423. Papers and Proceedings of the One Hundred Sixteenth Annual Meeting of the American Economic Association San Diego, CA, January 3–5, 2004.

Better than Cash Alliance. 2015. The Journey Toward 'Cash Lite': Addressing Poverty, Saving Money and Increasing Transparency by Accelerating the Shifts to Electronic Payments: Better than Cash Alliance.

Bianchi, Nicholas, and Rob Levy. 2013. *Know Your Borrower: The Four Need Cases of Small-Dollar Credit Consumers*. Chicago: Center for Financial Services Innovation.

Biosca, Olga, and Heather Brown. 2015. Boosting Health Insurance Coverage in Developing Countries: Do Conditional Cash Transfer Programmes Matter in Mexico? *Health Policy and Planning* 30 (2, Mar.): 155–162.

bKash: Making Remittances Easier in Bangladesh | CGAP. 2015. Anonymous a.

bKash. 2015. Home | bKash. Accessed August 5, 2015. http://www.bkash.com/

Bowles, Paul, D. Ajit, Keely Dempsey, and Trevor Shaw. 2011. Urban Aboriginal use of Fringe Financial Institutions: Survey Evidence from Prince George, British Columbia. *The Journal of Socio-Economics* 40: 895–902.

Bowles, Samuel, and Herbert Gintis. 2011. *A Cooperative Species: Human Reciprocity and its Evolution*. Princeton: Princeton University.

Boyer, Robert. 2005. From Shareholder Value to CEO Power: The Paradox of the 1990s. *Competition and Change* 9 (1): 7–47. https://doi.org/10.1179/102452905X38623. http://www.ingentaconnect.com/content/maney/com/2005/00000009/00000001/art00002.

BRAC Bank Limited. Knowing BRAC Bank 'Company Profile' Shareholding Structure. Accessed May 8, 2015. http://www.bracbank.com/Shareholding-Structure.php

BRAC Bank Limited. 2015a. Knowing BRAC Bank. Accessed November 30, 2015. http://www.bracbank.com/about.php

———. 2015b. Knowing BRAC Bank » Company Profile » Shareholding Structure. Accessed August 5, 2015. http://www.bracbank.com/Shareholding-Structure.php

Bradford, William D. 2003. The Savings and Credit Management of Low-Income, Low-Wealth Black and White Families. *Economic Development Quarterly* 17 (1, Feb.): 53–74.

Brennan, Marilyn, Brian McGregor, and Jerry Buckland. 2011. The Changing Structure of Inner-City Retail Banking: Examining Bank Branch and Payday Loan Outlet Locations in Winnipeg, 1980–2009. *Canadian Journal of Urban Research* 20 (1, Summer): 1–32.

Brent, Robert J. 2013. A Cost-Benefit Framework for Evaluating Conditional Cash-Transfer Programs. *Journal of Benefit-Cost Analysis* 4 (2): 159–180.

Buckland, Jerry. 1996. The Distributional Impact of Income-Generation Programmes in Bangladesh. *Canadian Journal of Development Studies* 17 (3): 385–404.

———. 1997. Qualitative Assessment of Income-Generation Growth Linkages: A Case Study from Bangladesh. *Canadian Journal of Development Studies* 18: 673–688.

———. 2006. International Obstacles to Rural Development: How Neoliberal Policies Constrain Competitive Markets and Sustainable Agriculture. *Canadian Journal of Development Studies* 27 (1): 9–24.

———. 2009a. *Affordable Credit Options for Vulnerable Consumers: Identifying Alternatives to High-Cost Credit in Australia, Belgium, Canada, France, Germany, the UK, & the US.* Ottawa: Office of Consumer Affairs/Industry Canada.

———. 2009b. *Passing the Buck? Examining Canadian Banks Approaches to Financial Exclusion.* Winnipeg, Canada: Institute of Urban Studies, The University of Winnipeg.

———. 2011. *Money Management on a Shoestring: A Critical Literature Review of Financial Literacy and Low-Income People.* Ottawa: Task Force on Financial Literacy.

———. 2012. *Hard Choices: Financial Exclusion, Fringe Banks, and Poverty in Urban Canada.* Toronto: University of Toronto Press.

Buckland, Jerry, and Iqbal Ahmed Chowdhury. 2015. Managing Mobile Banking to Address the Needs and Protect the Vulnerability of Poor People in Bangladesh: SSRN.

Buckland, Jerry, Dion McKay, and Nolan Reimer. 2016. *Financial Inclusion and Manitoba Indigenous Peoples: Results from an Urban and a Rural Case Study.* Winnipeg: Canadian Centre for Policy Alternatives.

Burch, Mark. 2013. *The Hidden Door: Mindful Sufficiency as an Alternative to Extinction.* Melbourne: The Simplicity Institute.

Buvinic, Mayra, and Rebecca Furst-Nichols. 2014. Promoting Women's Economic Empowerment: What Works? The World Bank, Policy Research Working Paper Series: 7087.

Canadian Bankers Association. 2015. Banks and Financial Literacy. Accessed August 18, 2015. http://www.cba.ca/en/component/content/category/79-banks-and-financial-literacy

Caplovitz, David. 1967. *The Poor Pay More: Consumer Practices of Low-Income Families.* New York: The Free Press.

Carbo, Santiago, Edward P.M. Gardener, and Philip Molyneux. 2005. *Financial Exclusion.* New York: Palgrave Macmillan.

Carroll, Toby, and Darryl S.L. Jarvis. 2015. The New Politics of Development: Citizens, Civil Society, and the Evolution of Neoliberal Development Policy. *Globalizations* 12 (3, Apr./May): 281–304.

Cartwright, Peter. 2004. *Banks, Consumers and Regulation.* Hart Pub.

Casey, Michael J. 2012. *The Unfair Trade: How Our Broken Global Financial System Destroys the Middle Class.* New York: Crown Business.

Cash America International. 2015. *Form 10-K.*

Cashco Financial. Welcome to Cashco Financial. https://cashcofinancial.com/

Caskey, John P. 1994. *Fringe Banking: Check-Cashing Outlets, Pawnshops, and the Poor.* New York: Russell Sage Foundation.

CGAP. 2015. Credit Reporting at the Base of the Pyramid. Accessed August 28, 2015. http://www.cgap.org/publications/credit-reporting-base-pyramid

Chambers, Robert. 1983. *Rural Development: Putting the Last First*. New York: Longman Scientific & Technical.

———. 2005. *Ideas for Development*. London: Earthscan.

———. 2008. *Revolutions in Development Inquiry*. London and Sterling, VA: Earthscan Publications; Distributed by Stylus, Sterling, VA.

Chan, Selina Ching, and David T. Owyong. 2010. Pawnshops in Singapore: Traditional Microfinance in a Modern Society. In *Routledge Studies in the Growth Economies of Asia*, ed. Aditya Goenka and David Henley, 84–94. London and New York: Taylor and Francis; Routledge.

Chandran, Nyshka. 2015. Can Bitcoin Help the World's Unbanked? Accessed July 8, 2015. http://www.cnbc.com/id/102720768

Chen, Greg. 2014. bKash Bangladesh: What Explains its Fast Start? | CGAP. Accessed July 7, 2015. http://www.cgap.org/blog/bkash-bangladesh-what-explains-its-fast-start

———. 2015. BKash Bangladesh: What Explains Its Fast Start? | CGAP. Accessed July 21, 2015. http://www.cgap.org/blog/bkash-bangladesh-what-explains-its-fast-start

Chowdhry, Bhagwan. 2015. Show Me the (New) Money. *Zocalo Public Square + » Show Me the (New) Money*, Mon, 29 June.

Cihak, Martin, Asli Demirguc-Kunt, Maria Martinez Peria, and Amin Mohensi-Cheraghlou. 2012. *Bank Regulation and Supervision Around the World: A Crisis Update*. Washington, DC: World Bank.

Coggan, Philip. 2012. *Paper Promises: Money, Debt and the New World Order*. London: Allen Lane; Penguin Books.

Cohen, Robert, Luigi Di Paola, Renee Sheehy, and Vincenzo Visco Comandini. 2008. The Distribution of Post Offices in Italy and the United States. *Review of Network Economics* 7 (2, June): 325–336.

Coleman, James S. 1988. Social Capital in the Creation of Human Capital. *American Journal of Sociology* 94 (Supplement): 95–120.

Collins, Daryl, Jonathan Morduch, Stuart Rutherford, and Orlanda Ruthven. 2009. *Portfolios of the Poor: How the World's Poor Live on $2 a Day*. Princeton and Oxford: Princeton University Press.

Collin, Dominique. 2011. Aboriginal Financial Literacy in Canada: Issues and Directions. Canadian Task Force on Financial Literacy. Accessed May 18, 2015. http://www.financialliteracyincanada.com/documents/consultation-2/Collin-09-02-2011-eng.pdf

Corr, Caroline. 2007. *Alternative Financial Credit Providers in Europe*. Brussels: Directorate-General for Employment, Social Affairs and Equal Opportunity, European Commission.

Cramer, Reid, and Trina R. Williams Shanks, eds. 2014. *The Assets Perspective: The Rise of Asset Building and Its Impact on Social Policy*. New York: Palgrave Macmillan.

Crépon, Bruno, Florencia Devoto, Esther Duflo, and William Parienté. 2015. Estimating the Impact of Microcredit on those Who Take it Up: Evidence from a Randomized Experiment in Morocco. *American Economic Journal: Applied Economics* 7 (1): 123–150. https://doi.org/10.1257/app.20130535. https://search.proquest.com/docview/1642672655.

Cross, Philip. 2015a. A Longer-Term Perspective on Canada's Household Debt—Longer-Term-Perspective-on-Canadas-Household-Debt.Pdf. Fraser Institute. Accessed May 20, 2015. http://www.fraserinstitute.org/uploadedFiles/fraser-ca/Content/research-news/research/publications/longer-term-perspective-on-canadas-household-debt.pdf

Cross, Hannah. 2015b. Finance, Development, and Remittances: Extending the Scale of Accumulation in Migrant Labour Regimes. *Globalizations* 12 (3, Apr./May): 305–321.

d'Alcantara, G., and A. Gautier. 2013. The Postal Sector as a Vector of Financial Inclusion. *Annals of Public and Cooperative Economics* 84 (2, June): 119–137.

Daly, Herman E. 2008. *A Steady-State Economy.* London, UK: Sustainable Development Commission.

Daly, Herman, and John B. Cobb. 1989. *For the Common Good: Redirecting the Economy Toward Community, the Environment, and a Sustainable Future.* Boston: Beacon Press.

Danubrata, Eveline, and Khettiya Jittapong. 2013. Pawnshops Hit Paydirt as Southeast Asians Sweat before Pay Day | Reuters. Accessed July 8, 2015. http://www.reuters.com/article/2013/09/10/us-asia-pawnshopsidUSBRE98908520130910

———. 2015. Pawnshops Hit Paydirt as Southeast Asians Sweat before Pay Day | Reuters. Accessed August 7, 2015. http://www.reuters.com/article/2013/09/10/us-asia-pawnshops-idUSBRE98908520130910

———. 2016. Pawnshops Hit Paydirt as Southeast Asians Sweat before Pay Day | South China Morning Post. Accessed January 3, 2016. http://www.scmp.com/business/economy/article/1307509/pawnshops-hit-paydirt-southeast-asians-sweat-pay-day

Datta, Saugato, and Sendhil Mullainathan. 2014. Behavioral Design: A New Approach to Development Policy. *Review of Income and Wealth* 60 (1): 7–35. https://doi.org/10.1111/roiw.12093. http://onlinelibrary.wiley.com/doi/10.1111/roiw.12093/abstract.

Dawson, William Harbutt. 1913. Municipal Pawnshops. *The Economic Journal* 13 (50): 248–251.

Desjardins Federation. Solidarity-Based Finance. Accessed September 2, 2015. https://www.desjardins.com/ca/about-us/social-responsibility-cooperation/socially-responsible-financial-products-services/solidarity based-finance/#

Dewan, Shaila. 2013. Microcredit for Americans. *The New York Times.*

DFC Global Corporation. 2008. *Form 10-K.* Berwyn, IL: DFC Global Corporation.

———. 2013. Form 10-K.

———. 2014. *Form 10-K.* Berwyn: DFC Global Corp.

Duncombe, Richard. 2012. An Evidence-Based Framework for Assessing the Potential of Mobile Finance in Sub-Saharan Africa. *The Journal of Modern African Studies* 50 (3, Sep.): 369–395.

Duvendack, Maren, Richard Palmer-Jones, Jarmes G. Copestoke, Lee Hooper, Yoon Loke, and Nitya Rao. 2011. *What is the Evidence of the Impact of Microfinance on the Well-being of Poor People?* London: EPPI-Centre.

Easyhome. 2014. *Annual Report.* Mississauga: Easyhome.

Ellison, Anna, Tony Dignan, Rob Forster, and Claire Whyley. 2010. *Interim Evaluation of the National Illegal Money Lending Projects.* London: Policis.

Epstein, Gerald A., ed. 2005. *Financialization and the World Economy.* Cheltenham, UK: Edward Elgar.

Estevan, Fernanda. 2013. The Impact of Conditional Cash Transfers on Public Education Expenditures: A Political Economy Approach. *European Journal of Political Economy* 32 (Dec.): 268–284.

European Commission. 2014. *The Right to a Basic Bank Account for all European Citizens.*

———. n.d. *Access of Payment Accounts.*

European Microfinance Network. 2015a. Introduction. Accessed November 30, 2015. http://www.european-microfinance.org/index.php?rub=microfinance-in-europe&pg=introduction

———. 2015b. Microfinance and EU. Accessed November 30, 2015. http://www.european-microfinance.org/index.php?rub=microfinance-in-europe&pg=microfinance-and-eu

Feiner, Susan F., and Bruce B. Roberts. 1999. Hidden by the Invisible Hand: Neoclassical Economic Theory and the Textbook Treatment of Race and Gender. In, ed. April Laskey Aerni and KimMarie McGoldrick, 43–65. Ann Arbor: University of Michigan Press.

Ferguson, Niall. 2008. *The Ascent of Money: A Financial History of the World.* New York: Penguin.

Fiszbein, Ariel, and Norbert Schady. 2009. *Conditional Cash Transfers: Reducing Present and Future Poverty.* Washington, DC: World Bank.

Foster, John Bellamy. 2007. The Financialization of Capitalism. *Monthly Review* 58 (11, Apr.): 1–12.

Frank, Robert. 1999. *Luxury Fever: Why Money Fails to Satisfy in an Era of Excess.* Princeton: Princeton University Press.

Fullbrook, Edward. 2000. *A Guide to What's Wrong with Economics.* London: Wimbledon Publishing Company.

Galbraith, John Kenneth. 1992. *The Culture of Contentment.* Boston: Houghton Mifflin Co.

Garcia, Gillian G.H. 2009. Sovereignty Versus Soundness: Cross-Border/Interstate Banking in the European Union and in the United States: Similarities,

Differences and Policy Issues. *Contemporary Economic Policy* 27 (1, Jan.): 109–129.

Garon, Thea, and John Thompson. 2015. *Short-Term Gain, Long-Term Pain: Examining the Growing Payday Loan Industry in B.C.* Vancouver: Vancity Credit Union.

Gathergood, John. 2012. Self-Control, Financial Literacy and Consumer Over-Indebtedness. *Journal of Economic Psychology* 33 (3): 590–602.

Gitter, Seth R., James Manley, and Bradford L. Barham. 2013. Early-Childhood Nutrition and Educational Conditional Cash Transfer Programmes. *Journal of Development Studies* 49 (10, Oct.): 1397–1411.

Godinho, Vinita. 2014. Money, Financial Capability and Well-being in Indigenous Australia. RMIT University.

Goenka, Aditya, and David Henley, eds. 2010. *Southeast Asia's Credit Revolution: From Moneylenders to Microfinance.* Routledge Studies in the Growth Economies of Asia. London and New York: Taylor and Francis; Routledge.

Goetz, Anne Marie, and Rina Sen Gupta. 1996. Who Takes the Credit? Gender, Power, and Control Over Loan use in Rural Credit Programs in Bangladesh. *World Development* 24 (1, Jan.): 45–63.

Goulet, Denis. 1995. *Development Ethics.* 1st Publ. ed. New York: Apex Press.

Graeber, David. 2014. *Debt: The First 5,000 Years.* New York: Melville House Publishing.

Graham, Carol, and Milena Nikolova. 2013. Does Access to Information Technology Make People Happier? Insights from Well-being Surveys from Around the World. *Journal of Socio-Economics* 44 (June): 126–139.

Grameen Bank. 2015. 16 Decisions of Grameen Bank | Grameen Bank—Bank for Small Business. Accessed August 31, 2015. http://www.grameen-info.org/16-decisions/

Grant, Tavia, and Janet McFarland. 2015. Payday Loans: Predatory Loan Sharks Or Crucial Fix in a Pinch?—The Globe and Mail. Accessed July 27, 2015. http://www.theglobeandmail.com/report-on-business/payday-loans-predatory-loan-sharks-or-crucial-fix-in-a-pinch/article24463029/

Graves, Steven M. 2003. Landscapes of Predation, Landscapes of Neglect: A Location Analysis of Payday Lenders and Banks. *The Professional Geographer* 55 (3): 303–317.

Gutierrez, Eva, and Sandeep Singh. 2013. What Regulatory Frameworks are More Conducive to Mobile Banking? Empirical Evidence from Findex Data. The World Bank, Policy Research Working Paper Series: 6652.

Hagendorff, Jens, and Maria J. Nieto. 2015. The Safety and Soundness Effects of Bank M&A in the EU: Does Prudential Regulation have any Impact? *European Financial Management* 21 (3, June): 462–490.

Hagendorff, Jens, Maria J. Nieto, and Larry D. Wall. 2013. The Safety and Soundness Effects of Bank M&As in the EU: Does Prudential Regulation Have Any Impact? Banco de Espana, Banco de Espana Working Papers: 1236.

Hall, Sarah, and Andrew Leyshon. 2013. Editorial: Financialization, Space and Place. *Regional Studies* 47 (6, June): 831–833.

Hanlon, Joseph, Armando Barrientos, and David Hulme. 2010. *Just Give Money to the Poor: The Development Revolution from the Global South*. Sterling, VA: Kumarian Press.

Harriss, John. 2002. The Case for Cross-Disciplinary Approaches in International Development. *World Development* 30 (3, Mar.): 487–496.

Hembruff, Jesse, and Susanne Soederberg. 2015. Debtfarism and the Violence of Financial Inclusion: The Case of the Payday Lending Industry. *Forum for Social Economics* (July/Aug.): 1–20.

Hewitson, Gillian. 2013. Economics and the Family: A Postcolonial Perspective. *Cambridge Journal of Economics* 37 (1, Jan.): 91–111.

Higgins, Benjamin. 1968 [1959]. *Economic Development: Principles, Problems, and Policies*. New York: WW Norton Inc.

Hoque, Hafiz, Dimitris Andriosopoulos, Kostas Andriosopoulos, and Raphael Douady. 2015. Bank Regulation, Risk and Return: Evidence from the Credit and Sovereign Debt Crises. *Journal of Banking and Finance* 50 (Jan.): 455–474.

Hudson, David. 2015. *Global Finance and Development*. 1st Publ. ed. London: Routledge.

Hulme, David, and Paul Mosley. *Finance Against Poverty*. Vol. 1. Routledge.

INAFI Nepal. 2015. Vijaya Youth Club Co-Operative and Credit Union (VYCCU) Savings and Credit Co-Operative Limited. Accessed November 30, 2015. http://www.inafinepal.org.np/members/vijaya-youth-club-co-operative-and-credit-union-vyccu-savings-and-credit-co-operative

International Monetary Fund. 2012. *World Economic Outlook*. Washington, DC: IMF.

International Post Corporation. 2015. *IPC Global Postal Industry Report*. Brussels: International Post Corporation.

Jagtiani, Julapa, Ian Kotliar, and Ramain Quinn Maingi. The Evolution of U.S. Community Banks and Its Impact on Small Business Lending. Federal Reserve Bank of Philadelphia, Working Papers: 14–16.

Jantti, Markus, Ravi Kanbur, and Jukka Pirttila. 2014. Poverty, Development, and Behavioral Economics. *Review of Income and Wealth* 60 (1): 1–6.

Jerold, V.A. 2008. Financial Inclusion and Literacy in India—A Critical Study. *Indian Journal of Finance* 2 (3, July): 25–33.

Johnson, Simon, and James Kwak. 2010. *13 Bankers: The Wall Street Takeover and the Next Financial Meltdown*. New York: Pantheon Books.

Jump$tart Coalition for Personal Financial Literacy. 2015. JumpStart.Org | National Standards. Accessed November 27, 2015. http://www.jumpstart.org/national-standards.html

Kamruzzaman, Mohamed, et al. 2012. *Social Network and Financial Literacy among Rural Adolescent Girls: Qualitative Assessment of BRAC's SoFEA Programme*. Dhaka: BRAC Research and Evaluation Division.

Kanbur, Ravi. 2002. Economics, Social Science and Development. *World Development* 30 (3, Mar.): 477–486.

Kaneko, Yuko, and Masahiko Metoki. 2008. Postal Savings for National Development—The Experience of Japan and Future Perspective in a Globalized World. *Public Organization Review* 8 (3, Sep.): 233–252.

Kartashova, Katya, and Ben Tomlin. 2013. House Prices, Consumption and the Role of Non-Mortgage Debt. Bank of Canada, Working Papers.

Kashfi, Farzana, Santhosh Ramdoss, and Scott Macmillan. 2012. *BRAC's Empowerment and Livelihood for Adolescents: Changing Mind-Sets and Going to Scale with Social and Financial Skills for Girls.* New York: UNICEF.

Kempson, Elaine, and Adele Atkinson. 2009. *Measuring Levels of Financial Literacy at an International Level.* Paris: Organization for Economic Cooperation and Development.

Kelly, Sonja E., and Elisabeth Rhyne. 2015. *By the Numbers: Benchmarking Progress Toward Financial Inclusion.* Washington, DC: Center for Financial Inclusion.

Kessler, Oliver, and Benjamin Wilhelm. 2013. Financialization and the Three Utopias of Shadow Banking. *Competition and Change* 17 (3): 248–264.

Khir, Mohamed Fairooz Abdul. 2011. Revisiting the Fiqh Characterisations of the Rahn-Based Islamic Microcredit Product. *ISRA International Journal of Islamic Finance* 3 (2, Dec.): 151–157.

King, Justin. 2015. MyRA Goes National: Building A Better Savings Account. https://www.newamerica.org/asset-building/myra-goes-national/

Kiva. 2015. Kiva—About Us. Accessed November 30, 2015. http://www.kiva.org/about

Klein, Michael, and Colin Mayer. 2011. Mobile Banking and Financial Inclusion: The Regulatory Lessons. The World Bank, Policy Research Working Paper Series: 5664.

Klontz, Bradley T., Sonya L. Britt, and Kristy L. Archuleta, eds. 2015. *Financial Therapy: Theory, Research, and Practice.* Heidelberg: Springer International Publishing.

Krippner, Greta R. 2005. The Financialization of the American Economy. *Socio-Economic Review* 3 (2): 173–208.

Kroll, Christian. 2015. Global Development and Happiness: How can Data on Subjective Well-being Inform Development Theory and Practice? *Oxford Development Studies* 43 (3, Sep.): 281–309.

Kus, Basak. 2012. Financialisation and Income Inequality in OECD Nations: 1995–2007. *Economic and Social Review* 43 (4, Winter): 477–495.

Lapavitsas, Costas. 2009. Financialised Capitalism: Crisis and Financial Expropriation. *Historical Materialism* 17 (2): 114–148. https://doi.org/10.1163/156920609X436153. http://booksandjournals.brillonline.com/content/journals/10.1163/156920609x436153.

———. 2013. *Profiting Without Producing: How Finance Exploits Us All.* London: Verso.

Lapavitsas, Costas, and Jeff Powell. 2013. Financialisation Varied: A Comparative Analysis of Advanced Economies. *Cambridge Journal of Regions, Economy and Society* 6 (3, Nov.): 359–379.

Leckie, Norm, Michael Dowie, and Chad Gyorfi-Dyke. 2008. *Learning to Save, Saving to Learn: Early Impacts of the Learn$ave Individual Development Accounts Project.* Ottawa: Social Research and Demonstration Corporation.

Lee, Jean. 2014. Bangladesh's bKash Adoption Puzzle | Financial Access Initiative. Accessed August 5, 2015. http://www.financialaccess.org/blog/2014/04/bangladesh's-bkash-adoption-puzzle

Levy, Rob, and Joshua Sledge. 2012. *A Complex Portrait: An Examination of Small-Dollar Credit Consumers.* Chicago: Center for Financial Services Innovation.

Leyshon, Andrew, Shaun French, and Paola Signoretta. 2008. Financial Exclusion and the Geography of Bank and Building Society Branch Closure in Britain. *Transactions of the Institute of British Geographers* 33 (4): 447–465.

Leyshon, A., and N. Thrift. 1996. Financial Exclusion and the Shifting Boundaries of the Financial System. *Environment and Planning A* 28 (7, July): 1150–1156.

Leyshon, Andrew, and Nigel Thrift. 1997. *Money/Space: Geographies of Monetary Transformation.* New York and London: Routledge.

Lipton, Michael. 2007. Plant Breeding and Poverty: Can Transgenic Seeds Replicate the 'Green Revolution' as a Source of Gains for the Poor? *Journal of Development Studies* 43 (1, Jan.): 31–62.

Livesey, Bruce. 2012. *Thieves of Bay Street.* Toronto: Random House.

Loureiro, Andre Oliveira Ferreira, and Marcos Costa Holanda. 2013. The Impact on Consumption of More Cash in Conditional Cash Transfer Programs. *Economia Aplicada/Brazilian Journal of Applied Economics* 17 (4, Oct.): 557–577.

Loxley, John, ed. 2007. *Transforming Or Reforming Capitalism: Towards a Theory of Community Economic Development.* Winnipeg: Fernwood Publishing.

Lucas, Robert E., and Thomas J. Sargent, eds. 1981. *Rational Expectations and Econometric Practice.* Minneapolis: University of Minnesota Press.

Luong, May. 2011. The Wealth and Finances of Employed Low-Income Families. *Perspectives on Labour and Income* 23 (3, Fall): 3–13.

Lusardi, Annamaria. 2008. Household Saving Behavior: The Role of Financial Literacy, Information, and Financial Education Programs. National Bureau of Economic Research, Inc., NBER Working Papers: 13824.

Lusardi, Annamaria, and Olivia S. Mitchell. 2014. The Economic Importance of Financial Literacy: Theory and Evidence. *Journal of Economic Literature* 52 (1): 5–44.

Mader, Philip. 2015. *The Political Economy of Microfinance: Financializing Poverty*. New York: Palgrave Macmillan.

Mader, Philip, and Sophia Sabrow. 2015. All Myth and Ceremony? Examining the Causes and Logic of the Mission Shift in Microfinance from Microenterprise Credit to Financial Inclusion. *Forum for Social Economics*. 1–27. https://openknowledge.worldbank.org/handle/10986/12183

Martin Christopher, Catherine. 2015. Mobile Banking: The Answer for the Unbanked in America? *Catholic University Law Review* 65: 221–252.

Martin, Thibault, Amelia Curran, and Judith Lapierre. 2006. Banking in Winnipeg's Aboriginal and Impoverished Neighbourhood. *The Canadian Journal of Native Studies* XXVI: 331–359.

Marulanda Consultores. 2015. *Going Mobile with Conditional Cash Transfers*. Washington, DC: Consultative Group to Assist the Poorest.

Mas, Ignacio. 2011. Why are Banks so Scarce in Developing Countries? A Regulatory and Infrastructure Perspective. *Critical Review* 23 (1–2): 135–145.

Mayer, Robert. 2003. Payday Loans and Exploitation. *Public Affairs Quarterly* 17 (3): 197–217.

Mbiti, Isaac, and David N. Weil. 2011. Mobile Banking: The Impact of M-Pesa in Kenya. National Bureau of Economic Research, Inc., NBER Working Papers: 17129.

McKee, Katherine, Michelle Kaffenberger, and Jamie M. Zimmerman. 2015. *Doing Digital Finance Right*. Washington, DC: Consultative Group to Assist the Poorest.

Melzer, Brian T. Spillovers from Costly Credit. Center for Economic Studies, U.S. Census Bureau, Working Papers.

Migone, Andrea. 2007. Hedonistic Consumerism: Patterns of Consumption in Contemporary Capitalism. *Review of Radical Political Economics* 39 (2, Spring): 173–200.

Miller, Rae-Ann, Susan Burhouse, Luke Reynolds, and Aileen G. Sampson. 2010. A Template for Success: The FDIC's Small-Dollar Loan Pilot Program. *FDIC Quarterly* 4: 28–41.

MIX Market. n.d. *Cross Market Analysis*. Washington, DC: Microfinance Information Exchange, Inc.

Money Max. 2015. Money Max Home Page. https://moneymax.com.sg/

Montgomerie, Johnna. 2006. The Financialization of the American Credit Card Industry. *Competition and Change* 10 (3): 301–319.

———. 2007. Giving Credit Where It's Due: Public Policy and Household Debt in the United States, the United Kingdom and Canada. *Politics and Society* 25 (3): 109–142.

———. 2009. The Pursuit of (Past) Happiness? Middle-Class Indebtedness and American Financialisation. *New Political Economy* 14 (1, Mar.): 1–24.

Moore, Holly. 2014. Rent-to-Own Practices in Canada would be Illegal in Parts of U.S.—Manitoba—CBC News. Accessed June 8, 2015. http://www.cbc.ca/

news/canada/manitoba/rent-to-own-practices-in-canada-would-be-illegalin-parts-of-u-s-1.2850023
———. 2015. Rent-to-Own Practices in Canada Would Be Illegal in Parts of U.S.—Manitoba—CBC News. Accessed August 6, 2015. http://www.cbc.ca/news/canada/manitoba/rent-to-own-practices-in-canada-would-be-illegal-in-parts-of-u-s-1.2850023

Mullainathan, Sendhil, and Eldar Shafir. 2009. Savings Policy and Decisionmaking in Low-Income Households. In *National Poverty Center Series on Poverty and Public Policy*, ed. Rebecca M. Blank and Michael S. Barr, 121–145. New York: Russell Sage Foundation.

———. 2013. *Scarcity: Why having Too Little Means so Much*. New York: Henry Holt; Times Books.

National Australia Bank. 2015. AddsUP Savings Plan. Accessed September 2, 2015. http://cr.nab.com.au/what-we-do/adds-up-savings-plan

Norberg-Hodge, Helena. 1991. *Ancient Futures: Lessons from Ladakh for a Globalizing World*. San Francisco: Sierra Club Books.

Nussbaum, Martha C. 2006. *Frontiers of Justice: Disability, Nationality, Species Membership*. Boston: Harvard University Press.

Office of the Comptroller of the Currency. 2008. *Community Reinvestment Act Performance Evaluation*. Washington, DC: Office of the Comptroller of the Currency.

Okholm, Henrik B., and Anna Moller. 2013. Vulnerable Users in Times of Declining Demand: The Case of Basic Bank Services in Norway and Sweden. In *Advances in Regulatory Economics*, ed. Michael A. Crew and Paul R. Kleindorfer, 148–162. Cheltenham, UK and Northampton, MA: Elgar.

Organisation for Economic Co-operation and Development. 2005. *Improving Financial Literacy: Analysis of Issues and Policies*. Paris and Washington, DC: Author.

———. 2015. *National Strategies for Financial Education: OECD/INFE Policy Handbook*. Paris: OECD.

Osberg, Lars. 2013. Instability Implications of Increasing Inequality: Evidence from North America. *Economic Modelling* 35 (Sep.): 918–930.

Ostrom, Elinor. 1990. *Governing the Commons: The Evolution of Institutions for Collective Action*. Cambridge: Cambridge University Press.

Packman, Carl. 2014. *Payday Lending: Global Growth of the High Cost Credit Market*. Palgrave Pivot 1st ed., 2014 ed. New York: Palgrave.

Packman, Carl, ed. 2012. *A Short History of Payday Lending*. Vol. 81. http://www.historyworkshop.org.uk/a-short-history-of-payday-lending/.

Pahl, Jan. 2008. Family Finances, Individualisation, Spending Patterns and Access to Credit. *Journal of Socio-Economics* 37 (2, Apr.): 577–591.

Parada, Marcia, and Great Bull. 2014. *In the Fast Lane: Innovations in Digital Finance*. Toronto: The Mastercard Foundation.

Parthasarathi, Prasannan. 1997. *Religion and Consumption*. United Nations Development Report.

Pearlman, Sarah. 2012. Too Vulnerable for Microfinance? Risk and Vulnerability as Determinants of Microfinance Selection in Lima. *Journal of Development Studies* 48 (9, Sep.): 1342–1359.

Pew Charitable Trusts. 2012. *Who Borrows, Where They Borrow, and Why: Payday Lending in America*. Pew Center on the States.

———. 2013. *Payday Lending in America: Policy Solutions*. Pew Center on the States.

Pierce, Nancy. 2008. *Payday Lending: The Credit Union Way*. Madison: CUNA Lending Council.

Polanyi Levitt, Kari. 2013. *From the Great Transformation to the Great Financialization: On Karl Polanyi and Other Essays*. Winnipeg: Fernwood Publishing.

Porteous, David. 2006. *The Enabling Environment for Mobile Banking in Africa*. Boston: Commissioned by Department for International Development.

Prahalad, C.K. 2010. *Fortune at the Bottom of the Pyramid: Eradicating Poverty with Profits*. Upper Saddle Hall: Pearson Education Inc.

Prosper Canada. 2015. Overview—Prosper Canada. Accessed November 30, 2015. http://prospercanada.org/Financial-Empowerment/Overview.aspx

Putnam, Robert. 1993. *Making Democracy Work: Civic Traditions in Modern Italy*. Princeton: Princeton University Press.

Real World Economics. 2015. A Brief History of the Post-Autistic Economics Movement. Accessed June 22, 2015. http://www.paecon.net/HistoryPAE.htm

Richardson, Thomas, Peter Elliott, and Ronald Roberts. 2013. The Relationship between Personal Unsecured Debt and Mental and Physical Health: A Systematic Review and Meta-Analysis. *Clinical Psychology Review* 33 (8): 1148–1162. https://doi.org/10.1016/j.cpr.2013.08.009. http://www.ncbi.nlm.nih.gov/pubmed/24121465.

Ritholtz, Barry. 2009. *Bailout Nation: How Greed and Easy Money Corrupted Wall Stree and Shook the World Economy*. Hoboken: John Wiley and Sons, Inc.

Roodman, David, and Jonathan Morduch. 2014. The Impact of Microcredit on the Poor in Bangladesh: Revisiting the Evidence. *Journal of Development Studies* 50 (4, Apr.): 583–604.

Roy, Ananya. 2010. *Poverty Capital*. 1st Publ. ed., 1st ed. New York: Routledge.

Ruozi, Roberto, and Luisa Anderloni. 2013. *Modernisation and Privatisation of Postal Systems in Europe: New Opportunities in the Area of Financial Services*. Berlin: Springer Science and Business Media.

Rutherford, Stuart. 2000. *The Poor and Their Money*. Oxford: Oxford University Press.

———. 2002. *Money Talks: Conversations with Poor Households in Bangladesh about Managing Money*. Manchester: Institute for Development Policy and Management, University of Manchester.

Ryoo, Soon, and Yun K. Kim. 2014. Income Distribution, Consumer Debt and Keeping Up with the Joneses. *Metroeconomica* 65 (4, Nov.): 585–618.

Sachs, Jeffrey D. 2011. *The Price of Civilization: Economics and Ethics After the Fall.* Toronto: Random House Canada.

Said, Edward W. 1993. *Culture and Imperialism.* New York: Vintage Books.

Sandel, Michael J. 2012. *What Money Can't Buy: The Moral Limits of Markets.* New York: Farrar, Straus and Giroux.

Sawada, Michiru. 2013. Measuring the Effect of Postal Saving Privatization on the Japanese Banking Industry: Evidence from the 2005 General Election. *Pacific-Basin Finance Journal* 21 (1, Jan.): 967–983.

Sayid, Osman, Abdelghani Echchabi, and Hassanuddeen A. Aziz. 2012. Investigating Mobile Money Acceptance in Somalia: An Empirical Study. *Pakistan Journal of Commerce and Social Sciences* 6 (2): 269–281.

Scharwatt, Claire, Arunjay Katakam, Jennifer Frydrych, Alix Murphy, and Nika Naghavi. 2014. *2014 State of the Industry: Mobile Financial Services for the Unbanked.* London: Groupe Speciale Mobile Association, GSMA.

Schicks, Jessica. 2007. Developmental Impact and Coexistence of Sustainable and Charitable Microfinance Institutions: Analysing BancoSol and Grameen Bank. *European Journal of Development Research* 19 (4, Dec.): 551–568.

Schmid, Greg. 2002. Postal Banks in the Digital Age: Creating a New Role. In, ed. Roberto Ruozi and Luisa Anderloni, 253–269. Heidelberg and New York: Springer.

Schumacher, E.F. 1973. *Small is Beautiful: Economics as if People Mattered.* New York: Harper and Row Publishers.

Schwittay, Anke F. 2014. Making Poverty into a Financial Problem: From Global Poverty Lines to Kiva.Org. *Journal of International Development* 26 (4, May): 508–519.

Sen, Amartya. 1999. *Development as Freedom.* New York: Alfred A. Knopf Inc.

Sexsmith, Kathleen. 2006. *Aboriginal Employment in the Banking Sector in Manitoba.* Edited by Kathleen Sexsmith. Canadian Centre for Policy Alternatives.

Shefrin, Hersh M., and Richard H. Thaler. 1993. The Behavioral Life-Cycle Hypothesis. In *Economics and Psychology*, ed. Shlomo Maital and Sharone L. Maital, 166–200. Cheltenham, UK: Edward Elgar.

Sherraden, Michael, ed. 2005. *Inclusion in the American Dream: Assets, Poverty, and Public Policy.* Oxford and New York: Oxford University Press.

Siklos, Pierre L. 2004. *Money, Banking, and Financial Institution: Canada and the Global Environment.* 4th ed. Toronto: McGraw-Hill Ryerson.

Simpson, Wayne, and Dana Bazarkulova. 2013. *Payday Loans Consumer Profile Based on the 2009 Canada Financial Capabilities Survey.* Winnipeg: University of Manitoba.

Simpson, Wayne, and Jerry Buckland. 2016. The Dynamics of Financial Institution Location in Toronto: Who is Serving the Inner City? *Economic Development Quarterly*: 1–29. (forthcoming).

Slavova, Milanka. 2014. Consumerism as a Source for Innovation and Product Development. *Economic Alternatives* (2): 5–19.

Soros, George. 2009. *The Crash of 2008 and What It Means: The New Paradigm for Financial Markets.* New York: Public Affairs.

Spechler, Martin C. 1990. *Perspectives in Economic Thought.* New York: McGraw-Hill Publishing Company.

Stanford, Jim. 2015. *Economics for Everyone: A Short Guide to the Economics of Capitalism.* 2nd ed. Ottawa: Pluto Press.

Stegman, Michael, and Robert Faris. 2005. The Impacts of IDA Programs on Family Savings and Assets Holdings. In *Inclusion in the American Dream*, ed. Michael Sharraden, 216–237. Oxford: Oxford University Press.

Stiglitz, Joseph E. 2013. *The Price of Inequality: How Today's Divided Society Endangers Our Future.* New York: W. W. Norton.

Stockhammer, Engelbert. 2012. Financialization, Income Distribution and the Crisis. *Investigacion Economica* 71 (279, Jan.): 39–70.

Stuart, Guy, and Monique Cohen. 2011. *Cash in, Cash Out Kenya: The Role of M-PESA in the Lives of Low-Income People.* Washington, DC: Microfinance Opportunities.

Sugiyama, Natasha Borges. 2011. The Diffusion of Conditional Cash Transfer Programs in the Americas. *Global Social Policy* 11 (2–3, Dec.): 250–278.

Sulaiman, Nor Surilawana Hj, Siti Fatimah Kassim, Ibrahim Alzoubi, Khaled Ashaboul, and Mashitah Zainol Abidin. 2014. The Comparison between Ar-Rahnu and Conventional Pawn Broking. *Global Business and Economics Research Journal* 3 (5): 57–65.

Sweet, Elizabeth, Arijit Nandi, Emma Adam, and Thomas McDade. 2013. The High Price of Debt: Household Debt and its Impact on Mental and Physical Health. *Social Science and Medicine* 91: 94–100.

Tarozzi, Alessandro, Jaikishan Desai, and Kristin Johnson. 2015. The Impacts of Microcredit: Evidence from Ethiopia. *American Economic Journal: Applied Economics* 7 (1): 54–89. https://doi.org/10.1257/app.20130475. https://search.proquest.com/docview/1642672571

Tercelli, Ilaria. 2013. The Most Effective Means of Social Protection? An Evaluation of the Impact of Conditional Cash Transfers on Schooling and Child Labour in Peru. *Basic Income Studies* 8 (2, Dec.): 173–202.

Thaler, Richard H., and Cass R. Sunstein. 2008. *Nudge: Improving Decisions about Health, Wealth, and Happiness.* New Haven and London: Yale University Press.

Thaler, Richard H., and Shlomo Benartzi. 2007. Save More Tomorrow: Using Behavioral Economics to Increase Employee Saving. In *Recent Developments in Behavioral Economics*, ed. Shlomo Maital, 131–154: Elgar Reference Collection. International Library of Critical Writings in Economics, vol. 204. Cheltenham, UK and Northampton, MA: Elgar.

Tobbin, Peter. 2012. The Adoption of 'Transformational Mobile Banking' by the Unbanked: An Exploratory Field Study. *Communications and Strategies* 86: 103–120.

Todaro, Michael P., and Stephen C. Smith. 2015. *Economic Development*. 12th ed. Boston: Pearson.

United Nations Development Program. 1998. *Human Development Report 1998*. New York: UNDP.

———. 2015. *Human Development Report*. New York: UNDP.

Uppal, R.K. 2012. M-Banking Services—A Milestone for Customers. *International Journal of Business Economics and Management Research* 3 (11, Nov.): 19–31.

Vaithilingam, Santha, Mahendhiran Nair, and Balachandher Krishnan Guru. 2013. Do Trust and Security Matter for the Development of M-Banking? Evidence from a Developing Country. *Journal of Asia-Pacific Business* 14 (1): 4–24.

Van Arnum, Bradford M., and Michele I. Naples. 2013. Financialization and Income Inequality in the United States, 1967–2010. *American Journal of Economics and Sociology* 72 (5, Nov.): 1158–1182.

van der Zwan, Natascha. 2014. Making Sense of Financialization. *Socio-Economic Review* 12 (1): 99–129.

van Tuinen, Henk K. 2011. The Ignored Manipulation of the Market: Commercial Advertising and Consumerism Require New Economic Theories and Policies. *Review of Political Economy* 23 (2, Apr.): 213–231.

Villasenor, John, and Darrell West. 2015. The 2015 Brookings Financial and Digital Inclusion Project Report. Brookings Institution Reports. https://search.proquest.com/docview/1787813332

Vollmer, Uwe, Diemo Dietrich, and Ralf Bebenroth. 'Behold the 'Behemoth'. The Privatization of Japan Post Bank. Research Institute for Economics and Business Administration, Kobe University, Discussion Paper Series: 236.

Waldron, Jeremy. 2014. It's all for Your Own Good by Jeremy Waldron | The New York Review of Books. Accessed November 5, 2015. http://www.nybooks.com/articles/archives/2014/oct/09/cass-sunstein-its-all-your-own-good/

———. 2015. It's All for Your Own Good by Jeremy Waldron | The New York Review of Books. Accessed May 11, 2015. http://www.nybooks.com/articles/archives/2014/oct/09/cass-sunstein-its-all-your-own-good/

Waller, Spencer W., Jillian G. Brady, R. J. Acosta, and Jennifer Fair. 2011. Consumer Protection in the United States: An Overview. Accessed April 5, 2015. http://papers.ssrn.com/sol3/papers.cfm?abstract_id=1000226

———. 2015. Consumer Protection in the United States: An Overview. Accessed May 4, 2015. http://papers.ssrn.com/sol3/papers.cfm?abstract_id=1000226

Weber, Beat. 2016. Bitcoin and the Legitimacy Crisis of Money. *Cambridge Journal of Economics* 40 (1, Jan.): 17–41.

White, Lawrence J. 2009. Wal-Mart and Banks: Should the Twain Meet? A Principles-Based Approach to the Issues of the Separation of Banking and Commerce. *Contemporary Economic Policy* 27 (4, Oct.): 440–449.

Woolcock, Michael, and Deepa Narayan. 2003. Social Capital: Implications for Development Theory, Research and Policy. In *Elgar Reference Collection. Critical Studies in Economic Institutions*, ed. Elinor Ostrom and T.K. Ahn, vol. 2, 416–440. Cheltenham, UK and Northampton, MA: Elgar; Distributed by American International Distribution Corporation, Williston, VT.

World Bank. 2014a. *Global Financial Development Report 2014: Financial Inclusion.* Washington, DC: International Bank for Reconstruction and Development.

———. 2014b. *The Little Data Book on Financial Development 2014.* Washington, DC: The International Bank of Reconstruction and Development.

———. 2015a. From Billions to Trillions: Transforming Development Finance Post-2015 Financing for Development: Multilateral Development Finance. Accessed April 27, 2015. http://siteresources.worldbank.org/DEVCOMMINT/Documentation/23659446/DC2015-0002(E)FinancingforDevelopment.pdf

———. 2015b. *Global Financial Development Report 2015/2016: Long-Term Finance.* Washington, DC: World Bank.

———. 2015c. *World Development Report 2015: Mind, Society, and Behaviour.* Washington, DC: World Bank.

———. 2015d. Poland—Second Finance Development Policy Loan. Accessed April 27, 2015. http://www.worldbank.org/en/news/loans-credits/2013/06/18/poland-second-finance-development-policy-loan

———. 2015e. *The State of Social Safety Nets 2015.* Washington, DC: World Bank.

Yang, Ann Shawing. 2009. Exploring Adoption Difficulties in Mobile Banking Services. *Revue Canadienne Des Sciences De l'Administration/Canadian Journal of Administrative Sciences* 26 (2, June): 136–149.

Yelowitz, Aaron, and Matthew Wilson. 2015. Characteristics of Bitcoin Users: An Analysis of Google Search Data. *Applied Economics Letters* 22 (13–15): 1030–1036.

Zein-Elabdin, Eiman, and S. Charusheela. 2004. *Postcolonialism Meets Economics.* Economics as Social Theory Series. London and New York: Routledge.

Zelizer, Viviana A. 2011. *Economic Lives: How Culture Shapes the Economy.* Princeton: Princeton University Press.

Zurlo, K.A., W. Yoon, and H. Kim. 2014. Insecured Consumer Debt and Mental Health Outcomes in Middle-Aged and Older Americans. *Journal of Gerontology, Series B: Psychological Sciences and Social Sciences* 69 (3): 461–469.

Zweig, Jason. 2015. The Anti-Poverty Experiment, 5 June.

Index[1]

[1] Note: Page numbers followed by 'n' refer to notes.

J. Buckland, *Building Financial Resilience*,
https://doi.org/10.1007/978-3-319-72419-5

The manufacturer's authorised representative in the EU is Springer Nature Customer Service Centre GmbH, Europaplatz 3, 69115 Heidelberg, Germany. If you have any concerns regarding our products, please contact ProductSafety@springernature.com

Printed and bound by CPI Group (UK) Ltd, Croydon, CR0 4YY
25/09/2026
02222859-0005